MEMORY AND MOURNING

MEMORY AND MOURNING
STUDIES ON ROMAN DEATH

edited by

Valerie M. Hope

and

Janet Huskinson

OXBOW BOOKS
Oxford and Oakville

First published in the United Kingdom in 2011. Reprinted in 2017 by
OXBOW BOOKS
The Old Music Hall, 106–108 Cowley Road, Oxford OX4 1JE

and in the United States by
OXBOW BOOKS
1950 Lawrence Road, Havertown, PA 19083

Paperback Edition: ISBN 978-1-84217-990-1
Digital Edition: ISBN 978-1-8421-754-9 (epub)

A CIP record for this book is available from the British Library

Library of Congress Cataloging-in-Publication Data

Memory and mourning : studies on Roman death / edited by Valerie M. Hope and Janet Huskinson.
p. cm.
Includes bibliographical references and index.
ISBN 978-1-84217-990-1 (pbk.)
1. Death--Social aspects--Rome--History. 2. Memory--Social aspects--Rome--History. 3. Mourning customs--Rome--History. 4. Funeral rites and ceremonies--Rome--History. 5. Death in literature. 6. Latin literature--History and criticism. 7. Death in art. 8. Architecture and society--Rome--History. 9. Rome--Social life and customs. 10. Rome--Antiquities. I. Hope, Valerie M., 1968- II. Huskinson, Janet. III. Title.

HQ1073.5.R66M46 2011
393'.90937--dc22

2010054111

For a complete list of Oxbow titles, please contact:

UNITED KINGDOM
Oxbow Books
Telephone (01865) 241249, Fax (01865) 794449
Email: oxbow@oxbowbooks.com
www.oxbowbooks.com

UNITED STATES OF AMERICA
Oxbow Books
Telephone (800) 791-9354, Fax (610) 853-9146
Email: queries@casemateacademic.com
www.casemateacademic.com/oxbow

Oxbow Books is part of the Casemate Group

Cover image:
Marble sarcophagi with lid, Roman, depicting a young girl on her deathbed, surrounded by mourners.

For

Milly and Thomas

Contents

Acknowledgements

In November 2007 and February 2008 the Department of Classical Studies of the Open University hosted two one day conferences entitled 'Memory and Mourning: Death in Ancient Rome', and this volume is a result of those events. We would like to thank the staff at the Birmingham regional centre and Walton Hall, Milton Keynes for their help in organising these conferences, especially Trevor Fear and Bronwen Sharp; and the Arts Faculty of the Open University for financial support. Thanks are also due to all the speakers and participants who made these days stimulating and thought-provoking. For the process of turning conference into publication we are grateful to all the contributors, and the staff at Oxbow, for their patience and efficiency. Trevor Fear, Emma-Jayne Graham, Jessica Hughes, Paula James and Phil Perkins have offered advice and support in various ways which has been much appreciated. Finally we acknowledge our families for their never-ending support and give special thanks for the births in 2009 of a daughter (for VH) and a grandson (for JH) – the perfect antidotes to all that 'death'.

Abbreviations

AE	*L'Année Épigraphique*
CIL	*Corpus Inscriptionum Latinarum*
CLE	*Carmina Latina Epigraphica*
ILGN	*Inscriptions Latines de la Gaule Narbonnaise*
ILS	*Inscriptiones Latinae Selectae*
LIMC	*Lexicon Iconographicum Mythologiae Classicae*

Introduction

Valerie M. Hope

> 'Death is a very badly kept secret; such an unmentionable topic that there are over 650 books now in print asserting that we are ignoring the subject' (Walter 1991, 294).

In the 1960s Gorer argued that death was a modern taboo; a subject to be avoided rather than confronted, one that caused embarrassment and social awkwardness (Gorer 1965). In modern British society, and elsewhere in the western world, it can be asserted that the living are isolated from the dying and the dead. Death is medicalised; death is the preserve of doctors and death specialists, such as undertakers; death happens in hospitals, hospices and care homes; and death is a characteristic of the elderly, who are often socially dead before their physical death. However, death as a subject for sociologists, anthropologists, historians and archaeologists is very much alive and kicking. Death, of the self and others, may still be a cause of social anxiety, but scholarship's engagement with death, including the outing and challenging of the taboo, has placed new emphasis on how people die, how dead bodies are treated and how the dead are remembered (see *e.g.* Walter 1994; Howarth 2007).

In the Roman world death was not a taboo. Mortality rates were, in all probability, high and death was something which had to be confronted rather than shunned. Yet it is only recently that death as a subject has been embraced by Roman historians. This is not to say that death has been ignored, but often the approach has been a fragmented one. The evidence for dying, death, mortuary rituals and bereavement – such as cemeteries, epitaphs, monuments and consolation literature – has been extensively explored. The richness of this varied evidence is acknowledged (see Hope 2007, for the range of evidence), as is its ability to provide valuable insights into the Roman world, including how, in the face of death, societal norms could be constructed, challenged, and even transgressed. Recent work has greatly enhanced our understanding of many aspects of the rituals and processes surrounding death, such as wills, deathbeds, undertakers, funerals, and the *imagines*; funerary monuments their design and use by different social groups; epitaphs and how they present and reflect society; the cemetery, its organisation and role in structuring identities of communities and individuals; and the literary presentation and narratives of death scenes, suicides and mourning.[1] Many of these studies are, however, defined and confined by the choice of material evidence and or literary genre; the interactions, tensions and dynamics between different bodies of evidence are rarely united. Even recent books that have put 'death' or 'Roman death' in the title (Edwards 2007; Erasmo 2008; *cf.* Toynbee 1971; Hopkins 1983; Hinard 1987; 1995; Morris 1992) can fall short of expectations in terms of these titles, since these books are not about death per se, but the presentation of some aspects of death and dying in a limited range of sources. Without doubt it is essential to focus, or specialise, on certain aspects, or rituals or types of evidence related to Roman death practices in order to obtain a relevant level of detail and analysis, yet in doing this there is a danger of isolating the evidence from the very fact of death itself, and all that was, and is, encompassed in the process of death and dying.

The papers in this volume follow the tradition of engaging with evidence in detail: how literary authors presented death and funerals (Brooke; Houghton; Hulls; Schultze); how stonemasons and commemorators represented the dead (Carroll; Huskinson); how the rituals of the deathbed and funerals reflected society's concerns and anxieties (Graham; Hope; Noy; Šterbenc Erker). The volume is unusual, however, in uniting a range of evidence and approaches, such as different literary genres (poetry, oratory, history) and placing these literary texts alongside material, monumental, epigraphic and archaeological evidence. Cumulatively the chapters map the process of dying and bereavement from the deathbed (Noy) through the preparation of the corpse (Graham; Šterbenc Erker), the funeral (Šterbenc Erker), and the literary representation of speeches, funerals and the dead (Brooke; Houghton; Schultze), moving then to the commemoration of the dead and the comforting of the bereaved, through memorials (Carroll; Huskinson), portraits (Hope; Huskinson), literature (Hulls) and mementos (Hope). The chapters range across evidence and genres – poetry, oratory, history, epitaphs, funerary monuments and portraiture – seeking to contextualise this evidence in terms of the attitudes and expectations which surrounded death, commemoration and bereavement. The authors relate their case studies to the process of death and dying and what this reveals about Roman society. To this end two themes are focused upon: memory and mourning. These are key themes in the study of Roman death, which place emphasis on the main protagonists: the dead and how they should be remembered and the bereaved and how they should mourn. These inter-related themes bring to the fore a variety of evidence, approaches and theories, all of which highlight the significance of studying Roman death.[2]

Memory is often a contentious issue. Not only do individuals dispute how, what and who should be remembered, but scholars also disagree as to how memory is to be defined and the relevance of the term in academic study. Debates about appropriate memories and memorials became particularly prevalent during the twentieth century, against a backdrop of changing means of communication, the impact of world wars, oppressive totalitarian regimes and the birth of the heritage industry (Connerton 2006, 316–18). It was, and has continued to be, a boom time for memory, 'memory has become a best-seller in a consumer society' (Le Goff 1992, 95), even if accompanied by un-resolvable disputes. In the aftermath of the First World War, for example, there was much discussion as to the role in society of public events and monuments, such as Armistice Day and war memorials (Gregory 1994; Winter 1995). Were these to commemorate the war or the victory; to celebrate conflict or peace; for the dead or the bereaved; for the survivors or the victims? What was being remembered could be disputed, but also adapted or privatised according to individual experiences or preferences. In more recent times the public interest in how Diana, Princess of Wales should be memorialised, has also caused tension and dispute, as traditional decorum has competed with memories of the 'people's princess' (Walter 1999). In academic research and scholarship memory has also become a 'buzz word' or key term, and a cross over point between disciplines, although in itself a far from coherent topic or theme. How memory is to be defined, identified and studied, and the relationship between memory and history in particular has been much debated. Terms such as individual memory, social memory, collective memory, cultural memory, public memory and memory-work have been coined to shape the debate and delineate separate but related processes. However, the very definition of these terms has in itself become contentious (see *e.g.* Connerton 1989; Fentress and Wickham 1992; Cubitt 2007, 13–14).

It is the very looseness and flexibility in its definition that, in part, has given memory its appeal. Admittedly for some this has also rendered it a near valueless concept (Cubitt 2007, 5–6). Memory means different things to different people, or at least evokes different processes and methods of analysis. Memory is the mental sensation of remembering; or it is the accurate recall of data and information; or it is a 'story' of past experiences. Memory can be defined as innately personal and individual – no one's memories can be exactly the same as another's –; or memory can be defined as social, collective and shared – an act prompted by common frameworks such as landscape, environment, monuments and memorials. But can individual memory co-exist with social or collective memory? Should 'memories' prompted by reminders of people, places, things and events, not personally experienced by the individual be classed as memories at all? It is this balance between individual memory and social or collective memory that has framed discussions since the 1980s (see *e.g.* Lowenthal 1985; Nora 1996; Connerton 1989). Cubitt has recently argued that, 'what we need are not immutable definitions, but ways of bringing different understandings of memory into contact with each other, of exploring their frictions and intersections, of comparing their different purposes and assumptions' (Cubitt 2007, 7).

Memory involves a relationship to the past that is based on human awareness. As a cognitive process memory may be individual or personal, but the term is also readily attached not just to people but also to objects, events and acts which promote memory. As scholars and researchers we cannot access the mental process of the memory of individuals, but only how memory is expressed through texts, objects, words and so forth. Memory is also culturally defined; how people construct a narrative of memory or express memory is conditioned by their experience of the world around, the societal, religious or cultural context, and also its performative and sensory components (see *e.g.* Hallam and Hockey 2001, 24; Williams 2006; Jones 2007; Graham, this volume). Memory is a process centred initially on the individual, but which can be shared, and thus contribute to a sense of the past, a social memory, which builds a communal or collective identity (Cubitt 2007, 14–15).

In the Roman world memory was regarded as both individual and social, it was acknowledged that memory was a personal mental process, but that memory could also be a social or unifying act. Pliny the Elder described memory as 'the boon most necessary for life' (*HN* 7.24). The ability to remember was wondered at and admired by the ancients. Some sought to understand how human memory functioned, while others marvelled at this capacity viewing it as divine gift (Aristotle, *Mem*; *De an.* 2 and 3; Quintilian 11, 2.7). The physical or mental workings of human memory may have been ill understood, but it was known that memory in its natural state could be augmented. Memory was a skill (Yates 1966; Coleman 1992). Pliny the Elder noted individuals who were famed for impressive feats of memory, such as being able to list the contents of all the volumes in a library (*HN* 7.24). Such memory tricks were often the specialism of orators. Mnemonic techniques helped people to remember the words, content and topics of speeches (Cicero, *De or.* 2; *Ad Herennium* 4). Cicero described sight as one of the keenest of the senses (*De or.* 2, 357); appeals to the eye could stimulate memory. Indeed memory was often seen as a visual process and thus that which was striking and novel stayed in the mind the longest (*Ad Herrenium* 3.22). Orators were taught to imagine themselves walking through a building looking at images and objects that would trigger memories of the topics of their speech or the memory could be viewed as a storehouse (Augustine, *Conf.* 10.8.12). But the human capacity to remember was not just an oratorical trait since this shared ability both preserved and created awareness in a common past. For Cicero the essential role of an orator was to recall the past, to preserve collective memories of great peoples and deeds (*De or.* 2.36). Orators made the best historians, and oratory and history both needed to promote what was deemed worthy of remembrance.

In the Roman world memory could be an area for competition and debate. Deciding who or what would be remembered was an aspect of power, authority and prestige. Memory was about controlling the past, defining the present and planning for the future. Recent studies have explored how Rome's rulers entwined its present and its past through media such as literature, buildings, sculpture and coinage (for example Zanker 1988; Edwards 1996; Favro 1996; Cooley 2000; Gowing 2005). One of the most powerful illustrations of the importance of memory, how it could be constructed, edited and ultimately destroyed is *damnatio memoriae* – the range of penalties, designed at obliterating memory – which could be used against the condemned (Varner 2001; 2004; Flower 2006). The art of forgetting illustrates the art of remembering. Such widespread or public examples of 'memory work' can perhaps be defined as the creation of a shared, collective or social memory, but this was a memory that was largely centred on the preferences and needs of the ruling minority which was then projected onto society overall. Part of the inherited thought world of this group was a desire to be remembered as successful public figures, to leave a suitable legacy, something which *damnatio memoriae* sought to prevent or at least compromise. Reputation (*fama*) both in life and after death was important. Pliny the Younger said, 'my idea of the truly happy man is of one who enjoys the anticipation of a good and lasting reputation, and, confident in the verdict of posterity, lives in the knowledge of the fame to come' (Pliny, *Ep.* 9.3; *cf.* Polybius 6.53; Sallust, *Iug.* 4.53; Cicero, *Fam.* 5.12). Self presentation was crucial. It was important to create an image of the present for the future (*cf.* Foxhall 1995, 133). The ideal was to achieve this through a successful public career, but there were other practical options that focused on memorialising the name of the individual. For Cicero, when writing to his friend Lucceius, text was all important and the best way of achieving immortality is a history outlining Cicero's achievements to be written by Lucceius. A well composed work will be a lasting memorial that will achieve more than 'all the portraits and statues under the sun' (*Fam.* 5.12; *cf.* Tacitus, *Agr.* 46; Pliny, *Ep* 3.12), in the meantime Cicero hoped to enjoy his little bit of fame while still alive. The longevity of literary texts was a much vaunted theme (for examples see Hope 2007, 73–4), but there were other ways of promoting memory – such as statues, portraits, foundations, buildings – strategies which embraced texts, monuments and rituals (*cf.* Connerton 1989 on inscribing and incorporating practices; and Hope 2003, 116–20). Remembering was a sensory experience; sight and hearing may have been promoted, and to some degree prioritised, through texts and oratory (see above), but smell, touch, taste and habitual actions made memories and aided recall.

Recent work has highlighted the significance of memory in Roman society, how it was promoted, prompted, contested and even destroyed (*e.g.* Gowing 2005; Flower 2006; Larmour and Spencer 2007). Much of this work has focused on what can loosely be described as public, social or collective memory, and memory objects and texts which sought to build a communal or shared identity. A good deal of this memory promotion was centred, in its origins at least, on the wealthy, predominantly male elite, although the intended audience was much wider. As individuals most people were not to be remembered for their reputation, or by a statue, inscription, literary text or grand monument. However, they still participated in or were affected by the common or shared language and frameworks of memory that defined the lived Roman environment. Moreover the rituals, customs and expectations surrounding death suggest that memory, individual and personal, as well as collective, did matter to many people; it was not just the great and the good who competed for the privilege of being remembered. Modest monuments and epitaphs gave the dead a voice, recording people's names, relationships and careers, giving public acknowledgement to a life and marking a grave. We can question how long these memories lasted, how many years a grave was tended, or an epitaph read, but people were active in the desire to be remembered as individuals. Remembering the dead was a duty which involved textual and physical memorials, and also ritual and habitual actions (Hope 2003, 116–17). Graves were visited, offerings made and the dead had their place in the annual calendar of festivals (Graham 2005). The dead were individuals, but also a collective and continuing presence.

The papers in this volume explore different facets of memory promotion, and how this manifested itself in material, textual and habitual forms such as funerary monuments, portraits, jewellery, wills, oratory, history writing, and personal rituals, dress and appearance. Houghton touches on the distortion of the usual memory procedures, such as the funeral and *laudatio,* by poets whose poetic 'deaths' were composed to reflect the 'life of love'. The importance of public memory, especially of the reputations of the famous and infamous, is highlighted in the papers by Schultze and Brooke both of whom explore texts which to some degree promoted and or manipulated the reputations and memories of the dead. As Schultze notes a prime function of an ancient author, especially an historian, was to transmit memory, and to shape judgements of that memory. For Dionysius of Halicarnassus the deaths and funerary rites of important individuals could provide an opportunity to have the last word on someone's life and actions. Brooke, in looking at Cicero's *Pro Rabirio*, explores how events, actions and reputations could be re-written in the Roman courtroom to suit political objectives; how the dead were called forth almost as witnesses in rival narratives which sought to justify the present by appealing to the past. The promotion of the memory of individuals of more modest means and reputations is explored by Huskinson and Carroll who both evaluate funerary monuments. For freed slaves, without ancestors and often little family, self presentation in the funerary medium had a certain attraction for creating memories (Carroll). The close reading of individual memorials can also demonstrate how memory was constructed and attitudes toward death itself given voice (Huskinson). Concerns for memory could shape deathbed behaviour, as explored by Noy; the deathbed was a place to create or control memories (*e.g.* through the will or death-mask), but the actual death, especially if the dying person was abroad or absent from loved-ones, could affect the final requests and also shape how the bereaved remembered the final moments of their loved-one. This shaping of individual memories is also explored by Graham who considers the rituals that surrounded the dead, and in particular how the corpse itself impacted upon memories of the funeral and pre-funeral rituals for the bereaved and undertakers. This emphasises the sensory aspects of memory, and its habitual or embodied nature, themes also noted by Hope in considering how material memories of the dead were preserved not just through funerary monuments and at the cemetery, but also by personal portraits, jewellery and other keepsakes. The chapters highlight how memories of the dead were shared and public, and could be contested and manipulated, but also the active role that the bereaved (or living survivors) played in choosing how to remember the dead, the actual death and the ensuing sense of loss.

Connerton has observed, 'few aspects of memory have received more sustained attention than has the work of mourning' (Connerton 2006, 318). Connerton is speaking specifically of the relationship between collective mourning and memory following mass death events such as the holocaust, world wars and genocide, but his comment highlights the clear link between memory and mourning. A central aspect to mourning is finding a public and private place for the dead, thereby constructing an acceptable memory. Yet as with memory, mourning can become contentious. How one should mourn, as how one should remember (especially the dead) – whether an intimate acquaintance, a public figure or the victims of mass horrors – is not always easily or readily resolved. A tension exists between grief, which is perceived as private, and mourning, the public expression of that grief. In the twentieth century, with death shunned, grief came to be viewed as an illness from which people needed to recover, preferably as quickly as possible, emotionally detaching themselves from the dead, and turning the latter into a memory (Worden 1991; Walter 1996; Stroebe 1997; Howarth 2007, 23). The definition of grief as an illness and the clinical division of grief into a 'grieving process' with recognised phases such as 'anger' and 'denial' has been challenged (Walter 1996; Silverman and Klass 1996; Small 2001). The bereaved can and do continue to interact with the dead and retain a sense of continuity with them. Not everyone wants or can be simply 'cured' of their grief. Equally how people grieve is culturally and socially conditioned (Charmaz, Howarth and Kellehear 1997; Parkes, Laungani and Young 1997). It is debatable whether grief, or any emotion, is universal (Tarlow 2000; Konstan 2006), but where it is experienced and expressed the emotion of grief is not necessarily the same. Such differences can be even more apparent in rituals of mourning. The distinction between grief and mourning, as private and public acts, may not be absolute, but acceptable mourning practices are framed by social, cultural and religious expectations.

In the ancient world there was an awareness that how people reacted to a death could and did differ. How one expressed grief was thought to be conditioned by gender, education, status and culture. Seneca the Younger wrote: 'Despite suffering the same bereavement women are wounded more deeply than men, barbarians more than the civilised and the uneducated more than the learned' (*ad Marc.* 7.3) For elite, mainly philosophical writers, it was important to mourn with the dignity and control of a Greco-Roman gentleman. It can be difficult to escape the stereotypes created by these authors, of, for example, women weeping hysterically and 'stiff upper lipped' men. But other genres, especially poetry, did give space for tears, and acknowledged that the expression of grief was a necessary human reaction and not a failing. It is then possible to explore how people were expected to mourn, to give public expression to loss, but less easy to relate the available evidence to the individual's emotional reality.

The study of mourning, mourning rituals and the expression of grief in the Roman world is an emerging topic and one that to date has been shaped largely by issues of gender and genre. Women's prominent role in mourning ritual (laying out the body, calling out the name of the deceased, beating their breasts, singing laments and so forth) could be seen to both elevate and demean them (Richlin 2001; Mustakallio 2005; Corbeill 2004, 67–106); and how an individual mourned was often evaluated in terms of gender, with weak men behaving like women and strong women behaving like men (Wilcox 2006). These gender contrasts underpinned many literary descriptions of mourning. Tacitus' father-in-law Agricola, for example, apparently got the balance just right at the death of his infant son reacting, 'without the showy bravery of many a man or collapsing into tears and grief like a woman' (Tacitus, *Agr.* 29.1). However gender distinctions were not the only factor which shaped mourning and aspects such as relative status (Šterbenc Erker, this volume) and chronological period require further exploration. Discussions of literary descriptions of mourning also tend to be confined by genre, focused mainly on philosophical consolations or poetic consolations, with little exploration of how genres interacted or possible changes in attitudes across time (Erskine 1997; Wilson 1997; Markus 2004; Wilcox 2005a; 2005b; 2006; Hope 2009, 121–149). Further, beyond literature, there has been little investigation of how mourning impacted upon and shaped other evidence such as epitaphs, funerary monuments and material culture.

The study of mourning in the Roman world, as with the study of mourning in many other historical and also pre-historical periods, remains in its infancy due to understandable apprehensions about engaging with the emotions. On the one hand there is something a little unsettling to the modern eye that issues other than grief may have primarily shaped responses to death (*cf.* Hockey 1996, 7), on the other hand it is often apparent that the surviving evidence either constructs or conceals emotion, making it more appropriate to investigate conventions, social codes and social structures. Indeed the public side of mourning fits neatly into such studies, while mourning's overlap with the raw emotion of grief does not. The gap between individual experience (and the impact of death) and societal conventions, however, may not be so un-bridgeable. Recent work on sarcophagi has re-emphasised the funerary context of these items, including the context of mourning (Zanker and Ewald 2004) and this highlights the need for further evaluation of attitudes toward death, bereavement and emotion, and how these may have shaped the surviving evidence (*cf.* Sourvinou-Inwood 1995; Tarlow 1999; 2000; Konstan 2006 also Morris 1989, 296–320).

In this volume several chapters address Roman mourning customs and the presentation of grief and mourning. Observing rituals, including handling the corpse, helped the bereaved to accept their grief and understand their new place in their familial and social world (Graham). Doing things properly could be important: an appropriate display of mourning and mourners, especially for freed slaves, was significant (Carroll) and, as Noy explores, the non-observance of the usual deathbed rituals could have a negative impact upon the bereaved; final farewells, privately at the deathbed or publicly at the funeral, facilitated proper mourning. However, the mismatch or tension between private emotion and public demeanour is often apparent. Šterbenc Erker examines the public behaviour of mourners and the inversion of the usual norms in terms of dress, demeanour and actions. How one mourned, or was expected to mourn, was dictated not just by gender but also by status, especially one's own standing in relation to the status of the deceased. Mourning was about display, and as such could be used for personal and political ends. Brooke notes the exploitation of the emotion of grief in the courtroom and how this could be classified as excessive or wrongful by opponents. Literary descriptions often distorted the reality of funerary and mourning rituals (Houghton) and even consolation literature, as Hulls notes in investigating Statius' consolation to Claudius Etruscus, ostensibly designed to comfort the bereaved, could explore and promote political themes. Funerary monuments could also express the tension between private and public (Huskinson; Carroll; Hope). Often on display to all, monuments could construct public identities and memories (see above) while also expressing an acute sense of loss and grief (Huskinson). Varied memorials including funerary monuments, portraits, jewellery and poetic consolations were all symbols of loss and served to commemorate not just the dead, but also the grief of the bereaved (Huskinson; Hulls; Hope). The bereaved, whatever the dictates of decorum, could choose to carry and display symbols of their grief (Hope). The memory of the dead (as they were alive) could become entwined with the memory of the death and the memory of the subsequent mourning.

Death is a life crisis, a time of change, transformation and transition, for the dead and the bereaved. Thus how dying, death and death rituals are used, described, presented and interpreted is fundamental to any society. The intentions of this volume are to highlight how death was interwoven with Roman life, to emphasise the diverse evidence and approaches current in scholarship and to challenge boundaries between traditional academic disciplines. In many ways the volume provides a 'taster' of the evidence and what can be achieved, in what is still an expanding field of study. There are many gaps which remain to be filled; for example, work on mourning hitherto has been driven largely by literary genres and or gender (see above); Roman views and beliefs concerning the afterlife have been little scrutinised of late; and investigations into how the act of dying, the very moment of death, was both faced and then presented is a subject of growing interest (see Van Hooff 2004; Edwards 2007). The chapters here are wide ranging, but individually and collectively they highlight the significance of studying the evidence for Roman death and death rituals, and how concerns for memory and mourning both shaped and were reflected in that evidence.

Notes

1 Wills, deathbeds, undertakers, funerals, and the *imagines*: *e.g.* Champlin 1991; Flower 1996; Bodel 1999; 2000; Noy 2000a; 2000b; Bodel 2004; van Hooff 2004. Funerary monuments: *e.g.* Zanker 1975; Kleiner 1977, 1987; Kockel 1993; Huskinson 1996; Koortbojian 1996; Davies 2000; Hope 2001; Mouritsen 2005; Hackworth Petersen 2006. Epitaphs: *e.g.* Hopkins 1966; MacMullen 1982; Saller and Shaw 1984; Hopkins 1987; Meyer 1990; Joshel 1992; Woolf 1996; Hope 1998; 2000; Handley 2003; Carroll 2006. The cemetery: *e.g.* von Hesberg and Zanker 1987; von Hesberg 1992; Pearce *et al.* 2000; Hope 2001; Cormack 2004. Literary presentation and narratives: *e.g.* Van Hooff 1990; 2003; Hill 2004; Wilcox 2005a; 2005b; 2006; Edwards 2007; Dufallo 2007; Erasmo 2008; Ker 2009.

2 Note that the following volumes were published too late to be read and cited by the majority of contributors to this volume: Erasmo 2008; Fögen 2009; Hope 2009; Ker 2009.

Bibliography

Bodel, J. (1999) Death on display: looking at Roman funerals. In B. Bergmann and C. Kondoleon (eds), *The Art of Ancient Spectacle*, 259–81. New Haven and London, Yale University Press.

Bodel, J. (2000) Dealing with the dead. Undertakers, executioners and potter's fields in ancient Rome. In V. Hope and E. Marshall (eds), *Death and Disease in the Ancient City*, 128–51. London, Routledge.

Bodel, J. (2004) The organisation of the funerary trade at Puteoli and Cumae. In S. Panciera (ed.), *Libitina e Dintorni: Atti dell' XI Rencontre franco-italienne sur l'épigraphie (Libitina, 3)*, 149–70. Rome, Quasar.

Carroll, M. (2006) *Spirits of the Dead. Roman Funerary Commemoration in Western Europe.* Oxford, Oxford University Press.

Champlin, E. (1991) *Final Judgments. Duty and Emotion in Roman Wills, 200 BC–AD 250.* Berkeley, University of California Press.

Charmaz, K., Howarth, G. and Kellehear, A. (eds) (1997) *The Unknown Country: Death in Australia, Britain and the USA.* Basingstoke, MacMillan.

Coleman, J. (1992) *Ancient and Medieval Memories. Studies in the Reconstruction of the Past.* Cambridge, Cambridge University Press.

Connerton, P. (1989) *How Societies Remember.* Cambridge, Cambridge University Press.

Connerton, P. (2006) Cultural Memory. In C. Tilley *et al. Handbook of Material Culture*, 315–324. London, Sage.

Cooley, A. (2000) Inscribing history at Rome. In A. Cooley (ed.), *The Afterlife of Inscriptions. Reusing, Rediscovering, Reinventing and Revitalizing Ancient Inscriptions*, 7–20. London, Institute of Classical Studies.

Corbeill, A. (2004) *Nature Embodied: Gesture in Ancient Rome.* Princeton, Princeton University Press.

Cormack, S. (2004) *The Space of Death in Roman Asia Minor.* Vienna, Phoibos.

Cubitt, G. (2007) *History and Memory.* Manchester, Manchester University Press.

Davies, P. (2000) *Death and the Emperor. Roman Imperial Funerary Monuments from Augustus to Marcus Aurelius.* Austin and Cambridge, University of Texas Press.

Dufallo, B. (2007), *The Ghosts of the Past. Latin Literature, the Dead and Rome's Transition to a Principate.* Columbus, Ohio State University Press.

Edwards, C. (1996) *Writing Rome. Textual Approaches to the City.* Cambridge, Cambridge University Press.

Edwards, C. (2007) *Death in Ancient Rome.* New Haven and London, Yale University Press.

Erasmo, M. (2008) *Reading Death in Ancient Rome.* Columbus, Ohio State University Press.

Erskine, A. (1997) Cicero and the expression of grief. In S. Morton Braund and C. Gill (eds), *The Passions in Roman Thought and Literature*, 36–47. Cambridge, Cambridge University Press.

Favro, D. (1996) *The Urban Image of Augustan Rome.* Cambridge, Cambridge University Press.

Fentress, J. and Wickham, C. (1992) *Social Memory.* Oxford, Blackwell.

Flower, H. I. (1996) *Ancestor Masks and Aristocratic Power in Roman Culture.* Oxford, Clarendon Press.

Flower, H. I. (2006) *The Art of Forgetting: Disgrace and Oblivion in Roman Political Culture.* Chapel Hill, University of North Carolina Press.

Fögen, T. (ed.) (2009) *Tears in the Graeco-Roman World.* Berlin, de Gruyter.

Foxhall, L. (1995) Monumental ambitions. The significance of posterity in Greece. In N. Spencer (ed.), *Time, Tradition and Society in Greek Archaeology. Bridging the 'Great Divide'*, 132–49. London, Routledge.

Gorer, G. (1965) *Death, Grief and Mourning in Contemporary Britain*. London, Cresset Press.

Gowing, A. (2005) *Empire and Memory: the Representation of the Roman Republic in Imperial Culture*. Cambridge, Cambridge University Press.

Graham, E. -J. (2005) The quick and the dead in the extra-urban landscape: the Roman cemetery at Ostia/Portus as a lived environment. In J. Bruhn, B. Croxford and D. Grigoropoulos (eds), *TRAC 2004. Proceedings of the Fourteenth Roman Archaeology Conference, Durham 2004*, 133–43. Oxford, Oxbow Books.

Gregory, A. (1994) *The Silence of Memory: Armistice Day 1919–1946*. Oxford and Providence, RI, Berg.

Hackworth Petersen, L. (2006) *The Freedman in Roman Art and Art History*. Cambridge and New York, Cambridge University Press.

Hallam, E. and Hockey, J. (2001) *Death, Memory and Material Culture*. Oxford, Berg.

Handley, M. (2003) *Death, Society and Culture: Inscriptions and Epitaphs in Gaul and Spain, AD 300–750*. British Archaeological Reports, International Series 1135. Oxford, Archaeopress.

von Hesberg, H. and Zanker, P. (1987) *Römische Gräbertrassen: Selbstdarstellung, Status, Standard*. Munich, C. H. Beck.

von Hesberg, H. (1992) *Römische Grabbauten*. Darmstadt, Wissenschaftliche Buchgesellschaft.

Hill, T. D. (2004) *Ambitiosa Mors. Suicide and Self in Roman Thought and Literature*. New York and London, Routledge.

Hinard, F. (1987) *La Mort au Quotidien dans le Monde Romain*. Paris, De Boccard.

Hinard, F. (1995) *La Mort, les Morts et l'au-delà dans le monde Romain*. Caen, University of Caen Press.

Hockey, J. (1996) The view from the west: reading the anthropology of non-western death ritual. In G. Howarth and P. Jupp (eds), *Contemporary Issues in the Sociology of Death, Dying and Disposal*, 3–16. Basingstoke, MacMillan.

Hope, V. M. (1998) Negotiating identity and status: the gladiators of Roman Nîmes. In J. Berry and R. Laurence (eds), *Cultural Identity in the Roman Empire*, 179–95. London, Routledge.

Hope, V. M. (2000) Fighting for identity: the funerary commemoration of Italian gladiators. In A. Cooley (ed.), *The Epigraphic Landscape of Roman Italy*, 93–114. London, *Bulletin of the Institute of Classical Studies* 73.

Hope, V. M. (2001) *Constructing Identity: the Roman Funerary Monuments of Aquileia, Mainz and Nimes*, British Archaeological Reports, International Series 960. Oxford, Archaeopress.

Hope, V. M. (2003) Remembering Rome. Memory, funerary monuments and the Roman soldier. In H. Williams (ed.), *Archaeologies of Remembrance. Death and Memory in Past Societies*, 113–40. New York, Boston, Dordrecht, London, Moscow, Kluwer/Plenum.

Hope, V. M. (2007) *Death in Ancient Rome. A Sourcebook*. London and New York, Routledge.

Hope, V. M. (2009), *Roman Death. The Dying and the Dead in Ancient Rome*. London and New York, Continuum.

Hopkins, K. (1966) On the probable age structure of the Roman population. *Population Studies* 20, 245–64.

Hopkins, K. (1987) Graveyards for historians. In F. Hinard (ed.), *La Mort, les Morts et l'au-delà dans le Monde Romain*, 113–126. Caen, University of Caen Press.
Hopkins, K. (1983) *Death and Renewal*. Cambridge, Cambridge University Press.
Howarth, G. (2007) The rebirth of death: continuing relationships with the dead. In M. Mitchell (ed.), *Remember Me. Constructing Immortality*, 19–34. New York and London, Routledge.
Huskinson, J. (1996), *Roman Children's Sarcophagi: their Decoration and its Social Significance*. Oxford, Oxford University Press.
Jones, A. (2007) *Memory and Material Culture*. Cambridge, Cambridge University Press.
Joshel, S. (1992) *Work, Identity and Legal Status at Rome. A Study of the Occupational Inscriptions*. Norman and London, University of Oklahoma Press.
Ker, J. (2009), *The Deaths of Seneca*. Oxford, Oxford University Press.
Kleiner, D. E. E. (1977) *Roman Group Portraiture: the Funerary Reliefs of the late Republic and Early Empire*. New York, Garland.
Kleiner, D. E. E. (1987) *Roman Imperial Funerary Altars with Portraits*. Rome, G.Bretschneider.
Kockel, V. (1993) *Porträtreliefs Stadtrömischer Grabbauten*. Mainz, Zabern.
Konstan, D. (2006) *The Emotions of the Ancient Greeks: Studies in Aristotle and Classical Literature*. Toronto, Toronto University Press.
Koortbojian, M. (1996) In *commemorationem mortuorum*: text and image along the 'street of tombs'. In J. Elsner (ed.), *Art and Text in Roman Culture*, 210–33. Cambridge, Cambridge University Press.
Larmour, D. and Spencer D. (eds) (2007) *The Sites of Rome. Time, Space, Memory*. Oxford, Oxford University Press.
Le Goff, J. (1992) *History and Memory*. New York, Columbia University Press.
Lowenthal, D. (1985) *The Past is a Foreign Country*. Cambridge, Cambridge University Press.
MacMullen, R. (1982) The epigraphic habit in the Roman empire. *American Journal of Philology* 103, 234–46.
Markus, D. D. (2004) Grim pleasures: Statius's poetic consolationes. *Arethusa* 37.1, 105–36.
Meyer, E. (1990) Explaining the epigraphic habit in the Roman Empire: the evidence of epitaphs. *Journal of Roman Studies* 80, 74–96.
Morris, I. (1989) Attitudes toward death in Archaic Greece. *Classical Antiquity* 8, 296–320.
Morris, I. (1992) *Death-Ritual and Social Structure in Classical Antiquity*. Cambridge, Cambridge University Press.
Mouritsen, H. (2005) Freedmen and Decurions: epitaphs and social history in Imperial Italy. *Journal of Roman Studies* 95, 38–63.
Mustakallio, K. (2005) Roman funerals: identity, gender and participation. In K. Mustakallio, J. Hansks, H-L. Sanio, V. Vuolanto (eds), *Hoping for Continuity. Childhood, Education and Death in Antiquity and the Middle Ages*. Rome, *Acti Instituti Romani Findlandiae* 33, 179–190.
Nora, P. (1996) *Realms of Memory: the Construction of the French Past* I, *Conflicts and Divisions*. Trans A. Goldhammer. New York, Columbia Press.
Noy, D. (2000a) Building a Roman funeral pyre. *Antichthon* 34, 30–45.
Noy, D. (2000b) Half-burnt on an emergency pyre: Roman cremations which went wrong. *Greece and Rome* 47, 186–196.
Parkes, C. M., Laungani, P. and Young, B. (eds) (1997) *Death and Bereavement Across Cultures*. New York, Routledge.

Pearce, J., Millet, M. and Struck, M. (2000) *Burial, Society and Context in the Roman World.* Oxford, Oxbow.

Richlin, A. (2001) Emotional work: lamenting the Roman dead. In E. Tywalsky and C. Weiss (eds), *Essays in Honor of Gordon Williams. Twenty-five years at Yale,* 229–48. Schwab, New Haven.

Saller, R. and Shaw, B. (1984) Tombstones and Roman family relations in the Principate: civilians, soldiers and slaves. *Journal of Roman Studies* 74, 124–56.

Silverman, P. R. and Klass, D. (1996) Introduction: What's the problem? In D. Klass, P. R. Silverman and S. L. Nickman (eds) *Continuing Bonds: New Understandings of Grief,* 3–27. Washington DC, Taylor and Francis.

Small, N. (2001) Theories of grief: a critical review. In J. Hockey, J. Katz and N. Small (eds), *Grief, Mourning and Death Ritual,* 19–48. Buckingham and Philadelphia, Open University Press.

Sourvinou-Inwood, C. (1995), *'Reading' Greek Death. To the End of the Classical Period.* Oxford, Clarendon Press.

Stroebe, M. (1997) From mourning to melancholia to bereavement and biography: an assessment of Walter's new model of grief. *Mortality* 2, 255–63.

Tarlow, S. (1999) *Bereavement and Commemoration. An Archaeology of Mortality.* Oxford, Blackwells.

Tarlow, S. (2000) Emotion in archaeology. *Current Anthropology* 41.5, 713–46.

Toynbee, J. M. C. (1971) *Death and Burial in the Roman World.* London, Thames & Hudson.

Van Hooff, A. J. L. (1990) *From Autothanasia to Suicide. Self-killing in Classical Antiquity.* London and New York, Routledge.

Van Hooff, A. J. L. (2003) The imperial art of dying. In L. de Blois *et al.* (eds), *The Representation and Perception of Roman Imperial Power,* 99–116. Amsterdam, Gieben.

Van Hooff, A. J. L. (2004) Ancient Euthanasia: 'good death' and the doctor in the Graeco-Roman world. *Social Science and Medicine* 58.5, 975–85.

Varner, E. R. (2001) Portriats, plots and politics: *damnatio memoriae* and the images of Imperial women. *Memoirs of the American Academy at Rome* 46, 41–93.

Varner, E. R. (2004), *Mutilation and Transformation. Damnatio Memoriae and Roman Imperial Portraiture.* Leiden, Boston and Cologne, Brill.

Walter, T. (1991) Modern death: taboo or not taboo? *Sociology* 25 (2), 293–310.

Walter, T. (1994) *The Revival of Death.* London, Routledge.

Walter, T. (1996) A new model of grief. *Mortality* 1, 7–27.

Walter, T. (ed.) (1999) *The Mourning for Diana.* Oxford and New York, Berg.

Wilcox, A. (2005a) Sympathetic rivals: consolation in Cicero's letters. *American Journal of Philology* 126.2, 237–55.

Wilcox, A. (2005b) Paternal grief and the public eye: Cicero *ad Familiares* 4.6. *Phoenix* 59.3–4, 267–87.

Wilcox, A. (2006) Exemplary grief: gender and virtue in Seneca's consolations to women. *Helios* 33.1, 73–100.

Williams, H. (2006), *Death and Memory in Early Medieval Britain.* Cambridge, Cambridge University Press.

Wilson, M. (1997) The subjugation of grief in Seneca's *Epistles.* In S. Morton Braund and C. Gill (eds), *The Passions in Roman Thought and Literature,* 48–67. Cambridge, Cambridge University Press.

Winter, J. (1995) *Sites of Memory, Sites of Mourning: the Great War in European Cultural History.* Cambridge, Cambridge University Press.

Woolf, G. (1996) Monumental writing and the expansion of Roman society in the early Roman Empire. *Journal of Roman Studies* 86, 22–39.
Worden, J. W. (1991) *Grief Counselling and Grief Therapy: A Handbook for the Mental Health Practioner*. Second edition. New York, Springer.
Yates, F. (1966) *The Art of Memory*. London, Routledge and Kegan Paul.
Zanker, P. (1975) Grabreliefs römischer Freigelassener. *Jahrbuch des Deutschen Archäologischen Instituts* 90, 267–315.
Zanker, P. (1988) *The Power of Images in the Age of Augustus*. Translated by A. Shapiro. University of Michigan Press.
Zanker, P. and Ewald, B. (2004) *Mit Mythen leben,. Die Bilderwelt der romischen Sarkophage*. Munich, Hirmer.

1

'Goodbye Livia': Dying in the Roman Home

David Noy

The classic 'good death' in Roman literature is that of the emperor Augustus as described by Suetonius (*Aug.* 99). Augustus was dying at the family home in Nola, in the same room as his father, at an advanced age. He was surrounded by friends and family. He was fully conscious and in command of proceedings, able to worry about his appearance and to come up with some appropriate last words. For the large number of people who were present near the deathbed he recited the end of a Menander play, which simultaneously showed education, mental lucidity and wit (since it asked the audience for applause). He had some personal words for his wife: 'Livia, live on, mindful of our marriage. Goodbye!' (one might ask how such a private remark came into the public domain). The ritual of catching the last breath was performed: Suetonius describes it in a slightly unusual way, as dying 'in Livia's kisses' (*in osculis Liviae*). The death was peaceful and painless, and the sort of death Augustus himself had wished for: Suetonius says that he regularly used the Greek term *euthanasia* in its original sense of 'good death', as something to be hoped for (*cf.* van Hooff 2004, 976, 981). This was the opposite of the view taken by Julius Caesar who, according to Suetonius (*Iul.* 87) 'scorned such a slow sort of death [referring to Cyrus' last illness as described by Xenophon] and wished for a sudden and quick one for himself'. Caesar's death fits into the pattern of violent and dramatic ends which receive much attention in Roman literature (discussed in depth by Edwards 2007), but Augustus' was a more attainable and satisfactory model for people who were not regularly faced with violence. It was also a model which emperors who died peacefully tried to follow (van Hooff 2003, 112–13).

Scenes of peaceful death are not common in Roman art, but they can be found on a number of sarcophagi, and in a few other examples of funerary art, offering a visual equivalent of Suetonius' literary description. They can represent a mythological death (the favourite being that of Meleager: see LIMC *s.v.* Meleager; a different sort of allusion to Meleager can be found in one of the monuments discussed by Huskinson in this volume) or a real-life one (usually on a life-cycle sarcophagus; see Huskinson 1996). The dying or deceased person is always young, often a child, and to that extent the art departs from the ideal which Augustus represents. In other respects, the scene emphasises the peaceful and painless death (see also Huskinson, this volume). One such scene is shown in Fig. 1.1. The deceased is shown in a pose which without the

Fig. 1.1. Child's deathbed scene on a sarcophagus (British Museum, GR 1805.7–3.144). Photograph ©The Trustees of the British Museum.

context would be hard to distinguish from sleep. The domestic setting is indicated by various artistic details: the bed on which the deceased lies; the slippers and pet dog under the bed. The seated figures in mourning poses at either end of the bed represent the parents, while other female figures make more extravagant gestures of mourning, leading the scene to be labelled a *conclamatio* (the ritual calling out of the deceased's name) by Huskinson (1996, 21). The scene is a generic one, found in many slightly different versions, and it emphasises the pathos of the situation as well as the parents' emotional attachment and the household's status (Huskinson 2005, 96), but it has a message of consolation too. If a child must die, these are the best circumstances for it to happen in: peacefully, at home and surrounded by family members. With Meleager, where all surviving versions probably derive from one artistic prototype, the death of a hero in his prime can also be read as containing a visual version of the idea sometimes expressed in Roman epitaphs: 'even Hercules died'. Meleager scenes, although not the deathbed, were sometimes shown with child protagonists, increasing the pathos further (Huskinson 1996, 108–9; 2005, 97). The sarcophagi come from a later period than the literary texts cited so far, primarily the mid-second to early-third centuries AD, but Christian descriptions of idealised death scenes show that many aspects of the 'good death' remained unchanged for several centuries, particularly the 'death as sleep' motif and the importance of dying at home and/or among family and friends: there are lengthy examples in descriptions of the deaths of Monica (Augustine, *Conf.* 9.11–12) and Paula (Jerome, *Ep.* 108.28–30).

The domestic setting of these idealised deaths will be the focus of this paper. The way in which someone died was important to how they were remembered, which is why imperial biographies tend to give emperors 'appropriate' deaths. It was also important to the mourners, whose capacity to perform their role in full was greatly enhanced if the death took place at home with due preparation, and with appropriate ceremony afterwards. Nowadays, dying in familiar surroundings is usually presented as the opposite of a lonely death in hospital. For a Roman, the alternative to dying at home was often envisaged, especially in poetry, as a lonely death abroad, perhaps in exile. Fear of such a death is expressed in literature of all genres, as either a theoretical possibility or, as it was for Ovid, a real issue (*Tr.* 3.3.37–51, tr. P. Green):

> ..... Far off, then, my imminent dissolution,
> on an unknown shore, a fate made desolate
> by its very setting. I'll languish on no familiar deathbed,
> have none to weep for me in the grave; no tears
> dropped on my face by my lady who will bring my spirit
> a brief reprieve. I'll have no last words [*nec mandata dabo*], there'll be
> no loving hand to close my fluttering eyelids,
> no final lamentation [*clamore supremo*]. I shall lie
> sans funeral rites, sans tomb, unmourned, unhonoured,
> in a barbarian land. When you hear this

surely your heart will be stirred to its depths, and surely
  you'll strike your loyal breast with timid hand?
Surely you'll throw out your arms in furious frustration
  towards this place, clamour [*clamabis*] your wretched man's
name in the void? Yet don't rip your cheeks, don't tear your hair out…

As with much Latin poetry concerning death and mourning (on which, see Houghton, this volume), this is effectively a description of what normally happened, at least (as Houghton shows) within the elegists' somewhat unrealistic world, written in terms of what the poet does *not* expect for himself. Ovid lists many deathbed rites which are familiar from literature or art: the closest relative being at the bedside and closing the eyes; the *conclamatio* around the corpse; dramatic female mourning gestures after the death (the same details are described by Lucan, *B.C.* 2.21–6; see Šterbenc Erker, this volume, on such rites). His point is to emphasise the distress caused to him by the fear that he will not receive such care and consolation. Failure to be present at the death would be seen as an additional grief for the bereaved too. Ovid imagines his wife performing a long-distance *conclamatio* as she will be unable to carry out the normal one by the laid-out body. Dying 'on an unknown shore' was a frightening prospect and in this case an exacerbation of Ovid's already severe punishment.

Apart from psychological considerations, there were also practical reasons why an ideal Roman death involved being at home with friends and family. Ovid's fear of lacking a funeral and tomb expresses part of this, and other things were also expected to happen before or after death which required the right setting and the right people. Three aspects of this will be discussed here, as illustrations of the usually unspoken reasons why death at home was so important to the Romans: final requests by the dying person; the making of the death-mask; the correct disposal of the body. The first two of these have not received much attention in English-language scholarship. All three, when studied in detail and in conjunction with each other, with the anecdotal literary evidence and scattered archaeological finds placed in context, can offer insight into a variety of ways in which the Roman dead were remembered and mourned.

Final requests

The so-called Testamentum Relief in the Capitoline Museum (Fig. 1.2), which is studied in detail by d'Ambra (1995), depicts an imaginative death scene, full of symbolism rather than the apparent realism of some of the sarcophagi (see also Huskinson, this volume; Hope, this volume). Its original context is unknown and there is no accompanying inscription, but it was probably displayed on the façade of a tomb (Koortbojian 2005, 291). It can be dated by the hairstyles to the time of Trajan, making it earlier than the sarcophagi mentioned above.

The central figure is a young man shown in a heroic semi-nude pose. He is not represented as dying in the normal way, as if sleeping, but the context makes it fairly

Fig. 1.2. The Testamentum Relief (Capitoline Museum, Rome). Altmann 1905, fig. 161.

clear that he is the deceased in the tomb, shown in his home surroundings. D'Ambra thinks that the bed on which he reclines alludes to the bier on which the corpse would be carried in the funeral procession, but it could also be seen as the about-to-be deathbed. It symbolises peaceful and domestic death as on the sarcophagi, alluding to the 'death as sleep' motif which could not be depicted here because of the activities which are shown as taking place.

In his right hand he holds something which has been restored as a purse, although it is unclear if that is what was originally there. In his left hand he has a partly unrolled scroll. This has usually been interpreted as his will (hence the name by which the relief is known), but d'Ambra notes that wills are normally envisaged as tablets rather than scrolls, and suggests that it could be more generally symbolic of literacy or the authority of written documents. To the right is a seated female figure with a veiled head, whose pose is suggestive of mourning since it is similar to the mothers' on the deathbed sarcophagi, although at the same time she has a hand on the young man's shoulder as a gesture of consolation. D'Ambra identifies her as the mother, and this seems much more likely than a wife, especially as a mother at the end of the bed became conventional in deathbed scenes on sarcophagi. Showing the dying man on a bed, with personal possessions in his hands and with his mother beside him, provides visual cues for the viewer to imagine the death as taking place at home.

Behind the bed, a man is represented as an *imago clipeata*, showing that he is already dead, and he can safely be taken as the father (the young man would not normally be able to make a will if his father was still alive). The *imago* perhaps suggests the commemoration of the ancestors in the atrium of an aristocratic home (Polybius 6.53); according to the Elder Pliny (*HN* 35.2.6) *imagines clipeatae* displayed high on the wall had replaced the traditional ancestor-masks by his time (discussed below; *cf.* Flower 1996, 41–2). It also shows continued links between the living and the dead, with the deceased father literally watching over his family (Koortbojian 2005, 291–3; Hope, this volume). D'Ambra suggests that the family were ex-slaves and so had no more images to display. Artistic practicalities may also have been a consideration: the sculptor could hardly depict cupboards full of ancestral images as described by Pliny. In either case, there is a clear implication that the events are taking place in the family home under the posthumously watchful gaze of at least one ancestor.

The other figure is a small slave holding an abacus. This must be another allusion to wealth, and to being in control of one's affairs at the last, as a dying person was expected to be in a good death. The document is not shown rolled up as a scroll normally would be, but loosely folded to indicate that it has recently been opened, before the young man hands it over to his mother. The abacus and the document together suggest that suitable arrangements were being made for his estate before his death.

Romans normally made their wills well before death, but the deathbed codicil was common, and in some cases the whole will might be remade (Champlin 1991, 69). Appian (*B Civ.* 1.105) has an anecdote about how Sulla dreamed his death was imminent, made his will the next day and died that evening. Sulla can hardly have been without a will previously, so this must be a case of remaking it. Appian notes it as something exceptional that the will-making was completed in one day, and clearly the will of a wealthy Roman was not normally dealt with in a hurry. Apart from anything else, seven witnesses had to be invited, and various references suggest that it could turn into a social occasion, although not an event of great solemnity since remaking the will was so common (Champlin 1991, 76). The dying person could also give a specific verbal instruction, such as this one described by Cicero (*Fin.* 2.58) which must be a way round the Lex Voconia which prevented the richest people from nominating women as their heirs:

> If a dying friend asked you to give back his estate to his daughter, but did not write it down anywhere as Fadius wrote it, nor mention it to anyone else, what will you do? Of course you will give it back. Epicurus himself would perhaps have given it back, as did Sex. Peducaeus… Although no-one knew that he had been asked to do so by C. Plotius, a distinguished *eques* from Nursium, he came of his own accord to the woman, explained the man's instruction to her although she knew nothing, and gave back the estate.

This seems to assume intimate deathbed conversations with close friends, a role given to Livia in the description of Augustus' death. Plotius had a specific reason for making verbal instructions – he wanted to do something which was illegal in a written will – but the principle of last-minute changes was a common enough one, and there are many legal texts discussing complications which might arise. Reading the will before the funeral (*e.g.* Dio 56.32–3 on Augustus' will) was necessary because arrangements about the funeral might be specified, and in particular slaves might be manumitted precisely to give them a role in the funeral (see Carroll, this volume).

Other arrangements which did not involve altering the will could be made, and these are occasionally recorded in epitaphs. P. Manlius Syrus appears to have given deathbed instructions to his heirs for an annual rose-scattering and feast at the tomb of himself and his wife (*AE* 1991, 805). M. Ulpius Philotas, an imperial freedman, gave instructions about his tomb which his wife duly carried out (*CIL* VI 8553). Both men are described as dying (*moriens*) when they made these arrangements. Someone with dependants might commend them to the protection of friends or relatives (e.g. Propertius 4.11.73; Cicero, *Verr.* 2.1.152), or of the army if it was an emperor dying (Dio, *Ep.* 72.34.1; Lactantius, *De mort. pers.* 24). The Younger Pliny (*Ep.* 2.20.5) mentions how the dying Verania cursed the wickedness of Regulus for swearing a false oath to her – the opposite of the more usual *commendatio*. Such statements, as well as more usual last words like those attributed to Augustus, obviously assumed that someone was going to be there to hear them and write them down or act upon them. The Testamentum Relief indicates in various ways that deathbed arrangements are being made, even if the exact nature of the arrangements is unclear.

Seneca advises that you should finish your life like a *fabula*: '*tantum bonam clausulam impone*' (*Ep.* 77.20). Connors (1994, 228) shows that a *clausula* in this context could be the end of an extended text (such as a play or a poem), often with a witty or memorable twist, or the final syllables in an artfully constructed sentence. In either case, the instruction could be translated as 'just round it off with some good last words'. Augustus pre-empted Seneca's advice, but for most people the last words were more likely to have a practical than a literary content. In either case, the words would show that the dying person remained in full control of their faculties and could be remembered accordingly – imperial biographies suggest that last words were one of the things most likely to be remembered. When Ovid laments '*nec mandata dabo*', which Green translates as 'I'll have no last words' but might be better rendered 'I'll give no last instructions', arrangements about business, property or burial are what he has in mind. If he dies alone in exile, there will be no-one to carry out his *mandata*, and no-one to remember that he was still lucid.

Death-masks

Between the moment of death and the beginning of the funeral, it was expected that the deceased would be treated with due respect by mourners: the eyes would be closed; the corpse washed and anointed; mourning rituals such as the *conclamatio* performed around it while it was laid out, in the atrium of the home if the family was wealthy.

Persius (3.103–5) describes the corpse arranged on a high bed (*alto compositus lecto*), heavily anointed and with its feet towards the door (Hope 2007, 97–9, provides some other sources; see also Graham, this volume, Šterbenc Erker, this volume). The laid-out corpse was probably dressed in its best clothes, as Trimalchio wished to be (Petronius, *Sat.* 78; Martorelli 2000 gives some archaeological examples from early Christian inhumations), another reason for the process being performed most satisfactorily at home. A less discussed ritual, which must also have been dependent on dying at home (assuming that home was Rome itself or another large city where specialist undertakers were available), was the preparation of a death-mask.

It is debatable how common death-masks were, and Toynbee (1971, 47) notes that neither Polybius nor the Elder Pliny refers to them in contexts where they might be expected to. The only clear reference in Latin literature is where Quintilian (6.1.40) describes a woman trying to win sympathy in court by displaying an *imago* of her husband but producing undesired hilarity through its ugliness as it was 'wax cast from an old man's corpse' (*senis cadaveri cera erat infusa*). There is some similarity to the language used by the Elder Pliny (*HN* 35.44.153), who states that Lysistratus of Sicyon, brother of Lysippus (fourth century BC), invented the process of pouring (*infusa*) wax into a gypsum mould taken from the face (*e facie ipsa*) to form an *imago*, but does not say if it was done during life (as Pollini 2007, 250 assumes) or after death. Drerup (1980, 106) takes Quintilian's description as referring to this process.

Since other practical details about how the body was prepared after death are missing in literature as well, presumably because the process was left to professionals (the *pollinctores*) and the people who wrote about it had no need to describe it in full, it is not surprising that there is almost no clear reference to death-masks. They were something different from *imagines* in the sense of the wax ancestor-masks commemorating holders of magisterial office which were kept in individual cupboards in the atria of elite family homes and displayed at funerals. When the disgraced D. Junius Silanus killed himself in 140 BC (see Flower 2006, 64, with a full list of sources), his father T. Manlius Torquatus not only refused to attend the funeral but spent the time receiving clients in his atrium under the *imago* of his distinguished ancestor Torquatus (d. 203 BC). The rejection of Silanus by his family is emphasised by the fact that the atrium of the family home is where his body would normally have been laid out, with the ancestral *imagines* symbolically involved in the mourning.

Ancestor-masks are described by the Elder Pliny (*HN* 35.2.6) as *expressi cera vultus*, 'faces pressed out in wax', which Jackson (1987, 35) understands as 'a form most typical of a cast from a mould taken on the features – in this case of the deceased'. Aristocratic Romans often commissioned portraits of themselves, and this would be an obvious point at which to create the ancestor-mask too. Flower states (1996, 2) that 'there is no evidence to suggest any connection between *imagines* and death masks', but she also lists (1996, 36 n.24) a large number of scholars such as Jackson who have claimed that there was such a relationship. Flower thinks (1996, 2 n.4) that the *S.C. de Cn. Pisone patre* 'suggests that the *imago* was made during a man's lifetime', presumably on the grounds that the S.C. enjoins the Calpurnii not to let Piso's *imago* be displayed in the home or used in a funeral procession with other family *imagines*, and that (she does not make this argument explicit) an *imago* of Piso would not have been created in the circumstances of his death. In fact, none of the 109 literary testimonia to *imagines* collected by Flower gives any clear information about how or when they were made. It could also be the case that the creation of an *imago* after death was so normal that the S.C. assumes it happened *even* in the case of Piso, who was presumably given some of the normal rites accorded to a corpse since his death was suicide not execution. Pollini (2007, 238) points out that although it may have been normal to prepare a wax *imago* from a life-mask, there must have been occasions when someone died before this had been done and a death-mask had to be used as a model instead.

The main evidence for death-masks comes from a small number of surviving examples and from the influence which they had on portraits. There is a very full study by Drerup (1980), which argues strongly for their importance, and most studies since then have accepted their significance (*e.g.* Carroll 2006, 38–9; her fig. 13 shows a death-mask from a tomb at Lyon). Drerup's catalogue contains 20 examples. These are not the wax masks of Quintilian's description except in one case from Naples Museum (Drerup 1980, 93–4) where a wax mask has glass eyes inset and traces of real hair. The others are gypsum moulds or casts; plaster would clearly have a much better chance of surviving than wax. The process followed in the Renaissance and later (Drerup 1980, 95–6), which is likely to have been what the Romans did too since it is consistent with the description of Lysistratus' invention, was to pack gypsum plaster, usually plaster of Paris, over the face of the corpse and remove it when hard to form a 'negative' mould which could then be oiled and filled with more plaster (or wax) to make a 'positive' cast of the original. There is no literary evidence to explain the circumstances in which the Romans did it or who it was done by. Flower (1996, 37–8) suggests similarities between wax ancestor-masks and theatrical masks, both of which had to be worn by actors. Dio (63.9.5) says that Nero wore theatrical masks, sometimes resembling himself, 'but the women's masks were all fashioned after the features of Poppaea, in order that, though dead, she might still take part in the spectacle' (*cf.* Flower 2006, 204). However, the technique of preparing a death-mask would have been somewhat different, as it did not involve distorting 'reality' in the same way and the mask did not need to be worn, so it may have been a speciality of the *pollinctor*.

The tomb of C. Valerius Herma and his family in the Vatican Necropolis (Tomb K18 = Mausoleum H, built *c.*AD 160; it has recently been restored and reopened to visitors) contained three death-masks (Drerup 1980, nos. T34–6; Mielsch and von Hesberg 1986, 196–8, Abb. 246–50), or more precisely two masks and one mould. One is of a bearded man, probably Herma himself, and two of very young children, one of whom is likely to be the son Olympianus mentioned in the main epitaph (Feraudi-Gruénais 2001, 53):

> C. Valerius Herma made (the tomb) also
> for Flavia T. f. Olympias his spouse and
> Valeria Maxima his daughter and C. Valerius
> Olympianus his son and their freedmen
> and freedwomen and their descendants.

Another epitaph shows that Olympianus was aged four when he died, which fits the age attributed to the mask. Maxima was aged twelve according to the reconstruction of a fragmentary epitaph, so the third mask cannot be hers. There was also an *alumnus* aged three named Valerius Asiaticus, to whom this mask might belong (Wallace-Hadrill 2005, 19–20). One child's death-mask could have been the model for a stucco head of a boy (no. 6 in Mielsch and von Hesberg 1986, 196), and there are similarities between the mask of the bearded man and one of the portraits of C. Valerius Herma found in the tomb, but in the latter case the death-mask is unlikely to have been the model for the portrait, which was probably made when Herma commissioned the tomb.

The tomb has niches for cremation urns and arcosolia for inhumations (Feraudi-Gruénais 2001, 51; Mielsch and von Hesberg 1986, 152–9), as often occurs in the period when cremation was gradually replaced by inhumation. Herma himself was buried in a sarcophagus, as were other members of his extended family of ex-slaves. There is no obvious reason why death-masks were preserved in this tomb, although it was lavishly decorated. Mielsch and von Hesberg (1986, 198) simply attribute it to 'Pietätsgründen' but that does not explain why this family should have felt it important to place the masks in the tomb when most others apparently did not. Perhaps there is a connection to the presence of various portraits of the family members. The life-size heads of a bearded man and a woman, assumed to be Herma and Olympias, probably come from figures placed in an aedicula (Mielsch and von Hesberg 1986, 151). Full-length stucco figures in niches are thought to represent Herma (twice), Olympias and Maxima (*ibid.*, 166–71, 203–4). There were also marble heads of a bearded man and veiled woman, assumed to be Herma and Olympias (*ibid.*, 186–92, Abb. 230–3). Stucco portrait busts depict Olympias, Maxima, and a boy whose hairstyle is probably too late for him to be Olympianus (*ibid.*, 192–6, Abb. 235–42). Herma was evidently proud of his name's divine associations, in view of the depiction of (probably) Hermes and numerous stucco herms in the tomb, and of his education: scrolls and writing instruments are depicted above his portrait, and there are also figures of two philosophers who could be his teachers. A striking concentration of portraiture was displayed within the tomb, as well as dionysiac figures and various other gods.

Perhaps the masks, having served their purpose as models, were considered worth preserving because of Herma and his family's interest in the use of different media for portraiture. Whatever the reason, the preservation of these death-masks shows that they were made for children as well as for adults, and were therefore not just for the creation of ancestral *imagines* which by definition could only represent mature males who had earned them (Bettini 2005, 200). Herma has usually been thought to be a freedman (since his wife has a filiation in the epitaph but he does not), so the practice of making death-masks was not limited to the senatorial elite. There are of course no references to the preparation of a death-mask for Augustus, or to any of the other activities of the *pollinctores* on his body, and it might be supposed that there was no need to make one when his image was already so widely disseminated in various media. Children who died unexpectedly were presumably unlikely to have had portraits made while they were alive, increasing the importance of the death-mask, but Herma's death-mask was preserved even though there were already lifetime portraits of him, so the mask was not exclusively a substitute for lifetime portraiture.

The relationship between death-masks and Roman portraiture has been much debated (*e.g.* Crawford 1977, 53 n.17; Drerup 1980, 124–9; a more negative view is taken by Smith 1981, 31). Some sculptured portraits contain physical features which seem to derive from death-masks, either elements of physiognomy which suggest the features after death, or details derived from the casting process. Some examples are discussed by Jackson (1987, 35–42), who points out that unflattering features such as hollow eyes and sunken cheeks are more likely to come from minimal adaptation of a death-mask than from a lifetime portrait. Jenkins and Williams (1987, 13–14) study a bronze head of a woman wearing a sprang hairnet, which was produced by casting, and endorse a suggestion that it was cast from a death-mask, although the whole head is portrayed with the hairnet visible at the back so there must have been additions to the usual front-only mask.

For most purposes (such as the creation of portraits), a direct copy of the death-mask would be unsatisfactory, as Quintilian's anecdote illustrates. One important consideration is that the deceased's eyes would be closed in the death-mask (as can be seen in Drerup's photographs) whereas Roman portraiture needed open eyes. Even the portraits which seem most clearly to show death-mask features have their eyes open. Jitta (1932, 48) notes: 'The mask was not exactly copied but was worked up in such a way that at least the features most typical of death had disappeared.' It would also be necessary to show the deceased in a better state than he/she was likely to be on the deathbed, although the examples from the tomb of Valerius Herma show that the *pollinctor* might do a good job arranging the face before the mask was made. Fig. 1.3 shows a terracotta portrait bust of a man dated to *c.*50 BC. Trapp (1977, 94) describes it as 'in effect, a reworked death mask. The artist has … merely "assisted" nature in opening the eyes and adding a few other cosmetic touches …'. While this may overstate the case, there are clearly some of the features which have been thought to derive from the death-mask, notably the downturned mouth and smoothing out of most wrinkles. Normally the death-mask's function would only be to provide a model for conversion into a more permanent and aesthetically pleasing form, particularly but not exclusively in the case of someone who had not had a portrait made before death (see Hope, this volume). It was not important in itself like the *imago*, but only as a means to an end – another reason for the lack of reference to it in literature, since Polybius and the Elder

Fig. 1.3. Terracotta bust of a man, late Republican period, about 50 BC, 35.7 × 18 cm (Museum of Fine Arts, Boston). Museum purchase with funds donated by contribution, 01.8008. Photograph © 2010 Museum of Fine Arts, Boston.

Pliny only describe what was visible to all. This might also explain why the provenanced death-masks all come from tombs. Once the death-mask had been used as a model, it was no longer required as the family would have a better way of remembering the deceased (although high quality portraits could also be buried with the deceased, as Herma's tomb shows). The death-mask may have been placed in the tomb at the time of burial or, perhaps more probably, been added later after it had been used.

Ovid's list of things to be feared about death in exile quoted above goes from the moment of death (closing his eyelids) through mourning around the laid-out body (*clamore, i.e. conclamatio*) to funeral rites (*sine funeribus*). He does not need to go into detail about the correct preparation of the body for the funeral but the implication is probably that *sine funeribus* includes not just the funeral itself but the treatment of the body beforehand: anointment, dressing in best clothes, using a chinstrap to stop the jaw dropping open, and perhaps preparing a death-mask. Presumably in Tomi there would be no-one who knew how to do it, and no-one who wanted to keep a death-mask of Ovid anyway, since he cannot have expected his portrait to be displayed or his memory preserved there.

Correct disposal of the body

The dying person wanted to be sure that his/her body would be cared for properly, from the closing of the eyes to its final disposal in a tomb, as Ovid shows clearly. Some of the processes involved, such as the provision of a death-mask, required the specialised services of professionals, but most were dependent on friends or relatives to carry them out, or at least to arrange them (see Graham, this volume). Thus, dying at home normally offered an assurance of correct physical treatment afterwards. It is unclear how far this was thought to affect prospects in the afterlife, and concern seems rather to have been for respect and memory. However, much Roman writing about the treatment of the corpse implies a vague idea, not really expressed or thought through, that the deceased would somehow be aware of what happened to the corpse. This is the implication of Trimalchio's statement (Petronius, *Sat.* 71): 'It's a very bad idea to have nice homes while alive and not care about the ones where we'll have to live for longer.' The idea is derided by Lucian (*Luct.* 14–19), along with many other beliefs and practices concerning death.

At home, it could be assumed that the relatives of the deceased would perform the rituals, and it would be particularly scandalous if they did not. Undue haste in the proceedings was considered disrespectful if not downright suspicious, as in the case of Britannicus, who was cremated on the night of his death with modest funerary provisions which had been prepared in advance (Tacitus, *Ann.* 13.17). While it was acceptable for someone to plan their own funeral, like Trimalchio, it was not normal to plan too much for someone else's funeral. The treatment of Britannicus was justified by

Nero as 'ancestral tradition', meaning presumably that children were normally buried with little ceremony (although most references such as Plutarch, *Cons. ad Ux.* 11–13 are to the burial of infants, not teenagers like Britannicus) but someone of importance could normally expect to be laid out while preparations were made for the funeral and rituals of lamentation were performed around the body. If the corpse was in the home at this stage, there would be more people to do this, and in due course more people to attend the funeral. Servius (*ad Aen.* 5.64) says that the laying-out lasted for seven days but other sources suggest that this was not the norm, and he was perhaps thinking of the seven days for which wax images of Severan emperors lay in state (Herodian 4.2.3). Suetonius (*Tib.* 51) comments that, when Livia died, there was a delay of several days (*complurium dierum*) while Tiberius' arrival for the funeral was awaited, and the body began to grow corrupt; the implication appears to be that 'several days' was an unusually long delay even for someone as important as Livia, and that the ability to postpone the decay of the body was fairly limited. However, the story may simply be exaggerated to show Tiberius in a bad light.

What happened to those who did not die at home? Lack of technology for preserving a corpse limited the options. The corpse of Aristobulus II of Judaea was embalmed in honey and kept by the Romans 'for a long time' after he was poisoned by the Pompeians in 49 BC and before Antony could arrange for its burial in the royal tomb (Josephus, *BJ* 1.184), but that was not a normal Jewish burial rite, as is also shown by a garbled rabbinic story that Herod preserved his wife Mariamne's body in honey for seven years (Bab. Talmud, *Baba Bathra* 3b). The evidence naturally refers to people who, although they did not die at home, still had someone interested in carrying out proper rituals, *i.e.* the opposite of the anonymous corpses collected at Rome and placed on common pyres or in burial pits (Hope 2007, 132–3; Carroll 2006, 69–78; Graham 2006, 77–84). Fear of ending up as an unidentified corpse can be found in many places in literature, for instance as a feature of descriptions of plague (*e.g.* Livy 41.21). The regulations for the contracting undertakers at Puteoli include provisions for what happens 'if anyone throws out a corpse', although the issue there may be evasion of the contractor's monopoly more than disrespect to the corpse (Hinard and Dumont 2003, text at 16, ll. I.32 – II.1; discussion at 101–4). Latin tends to use the term *cadaver* for an anonymous corpse which does not get proper treatment (Allara 1995, 77–9; Hinard and Dumont 2003, 103). Martial 8.75 refers to a man with only one little slave who drops dead in the street:

> Four branded slaves carried the worthless corpse (*cadaver*)
> The unhappy pyre receives thousands such.

This is just what would happen to abandoned corpses at Puteoli, although the contractor there was not allowed to use branded slaves (or blind or mutilated ones; Hinard and Dumont 2003, 16, ll. II.6–7).

Ideally, the corpse would be taken home for the post-death rituals to be carried out. One case is recorded of a body being brought home from a long distance away, in a description which clearly tries to reproduce as many aspects of the 'good death' as possible. According to the *Consolatio ad Liviam* (or *Epicedion Drusi*) which is preserved with the works of Ovid, the body of Nero Drusus (the brother of Tiberius) was brought from Germany to Rome in 9 BC by his brother. This is also stated by Dio (55.2.2–3) and Livy (*Per.* 142). The *Consolatio* (89–95) offers consolation in the way in which Tiberius was able to perform the deathbed rituals by reaching Nero Drusus in time:

> But you [Tiberius] saw your brother, on the point of death, at the last moment, and he saw your tears, and as he was dying he felt your chest pressed against his, and he kept his eyes fixed on your face, blue eyes which were swimming gradually to death, eyes which were about to be closed by brotherly hands.

although it also has to acknowledge that Nero Drusus' wife was not there (307–12):

> With his last words as he was dying he lamented your [Antonia's] absence, and his ice-cold tongue formed your name. You unhappily receive not the one he had promised. The one who was sent abroad, your husband, does not return, and will not be able to tell you about the destruction of the Sicambri….

Seneca (*ad Marc.* 3.2) also notes the absence of his mother Livia, who was not able 'to drink in her son's last kisses and the welcome last words from his mouth'. Tiberius' breakneck ride to get to his brother before he died is included by Pliny (*HN* 7.22.84) in a list of exceptionally speedy journeys, and was clearly part of the topos of how Nero Drusus received as much attention as possible for someone who died away from home. It would be interesting to know how the body was preserved during the journey back to Rome, since the sources are clear that it was the whole body which came back, not the cremated remains. Dio (66.26), discussing the supposed murder of Titus by Domitian, mentions a tradition that he was placed in a chest packed with snow. There do not seem to be any references to the use of this method to preserve corpses, but it would be particularly plausible in the case of one being brought to Rome from a cold region, and Nero Drusus' death evidently happened when snow would have been available, since Augustus is said to have met the body at Ticinum 'in deepest winter' (Tacitus, *Ann.* 3.5). An alternative is implied when Silius Italicus (13.458–65) makes the unburied ghost of Appius Claudius (consul 212 BC) ask Scipio Africanus to cremate his body immediately after his death following fighting at Capua, so that he can go to the Underworld, rather than preserve it, presumably by embalming since he asks Scipio to 'keep away the drugs which preserve the body from corruption' (*arce quae putris artus medicamina seruant*), for a funeral at the family tomb. However, this possibility does not seem to be mentioned anywhere else (Spaltestein 1990, 242), although Silius goes on to give Scipio a long speech about disposal methods used around the world. Embalming was regarded as un-Roman (according to Tacitus, *Ann.* 16.6) when it was used for Poppaea, but by the end of the first century AD it was probably acceptable for

Priscilla, wife of the imperial freedman Abascantus (Statius, *Silv.* 5.1) – in these cases, however, it was the method used for final disposal of the body rather than a measure for temporary preservation.

It was more normal for a body to be cremated in the place of death and the remains transported to the place of final burial later (Carroll 2006, 163–4). That is what Ovid requests his wife to arrange (*Tr.* 3.3.64–76). He pleads (*ibid.*, 29–32) that if he dies while still in exile he should at least receive the mercy of being buried under his native soil, and the consequence of that will be that his wife can carry out annual rituals at his tomb (*ibid.*, 81–4). He plays with the idea of his ghost being stranded in Pontus (*ibid.*, 61–4; *E.P.* 1.2.107–12), echoing the apparently widespread belief that the soul continued to be linked with the place of burial even if he did not really share it. The punishment of exile was exacerbated if it was continued after death.

Agrippina's journey to Rome with the ashes of Germanicus after he died at Antioch in AD 19 is a good example of how the consequences of dying away from home could be alleviated, with the reiteration of many of the funeral rituals in Italy as she progressed from Brundisium to Rome (Tacitus, *Ann.* 3.1–3). The ashes are even said to have been carried on the shoulders of centurions and military tribunes, an adaptation of how a body would normally be carried. Martial (9.30), writing at the end of the first century AD, describes how Nigrina brought the remains (*ossa*) of her husband Antistius Rusticus back from Cappadocia and placed them, in an urn, in a tomb. Private citizens had to make their own arrangements about the return of their remains if they did not expect to have a relative with them, as this legal text shows (*Digest* 34.4.30.2 Scaevola):

> A man requested from his heirs that, if he died in a province, 60 [aurei] should be given to L. Titius to arrange for his body to be brought back to his homeland, and he added these words: 'If anything is left over from that money, I want it to be given to him'. The same day he wrote a codicil to his heirs like this: 'I ask you that, if something should happen to me either in a province or on the road, you arrange to bring back my body to Campania and the tomb of my sons.' The question was, did he tacitly take away from L. Titius what was left over of the 60? The reply was that it seemed to have been taken away.

The Latin refers to the return of the *corpus*, not *ossa* or *cineres*, but that is probably because the text is from the time when inhumation had replaced cremation as the norm (Scaevola was active in the reign of Marcus Aurelius). For the same reason, a text attributed to Ulpian (*Digest* 11.7.14.4) specifies that the costs of returning the *corpus* of a person who died abroad could be reclaimed as funeral expenses. L. Titius may represent someone who would be travelling with the testator, or someone who would be sent from home to make the arrangements. In either case, the testator clearly did not expect to be friendless even if he died abroad, but he also realised that in the absence of a close relative who could be relied on, he had to give someone an incentive to bring him home. There was a specific reason, the desire to be buried with his sons. Home in this case was important not for closeness to forebears but for sepulchral union with the man's sons. There is no clear evidence that people thought being buried in the same grave as someone was necessary to ensure reunion in the afterlife, but reunion in the tomb is often mentioned as a consolation in epitaphs.

Epitaphs also record plenty of real life cases like the one from the *Digest*, *e.g.* when Julia Helias, priestess of the imperial cult, died at Rome aged twenty-five, her two sisters arranged for her body to be brought back to Lugdunum and placed in a sarcophagus in a mausoleum (*CIL* XIII 2181). The burial society at Lanuvium (*ILS* 7212) had special provisions if a member died more than twenty miles away: if the society was notified, three members were sent to arrange the funeral there. Evidently transporting the body home for the funeral was not an option for such a distance. If the society was not notified, the expenses of the funeral could be reclaimed from it. In other words, a member dying away from home could hope for the proper rituals, and society membership took the place of family. A slave whose body was not given up by the owner could still have a 'token funeral' (*funus imaginarium*). The law provided protection for the transport of bodies on such occasions (*Digest* 47.12.3.4 Ulpian; see further Cracco Ruggini 1995, n.15):

> It is stated in an edict of the Divine Severus that corpses which have not been committed to permanent burial may be moved. It is ordered that corpses should not be detained or impeded or prohibited from being taken through the territories of towns. The Divine Marcus said in a rescript that people who transport a corpse on the journey of the deceased (*iter defuncti*) through villages or a town did not deserve punishment, even though such things should not happen without the permission of those who have the right to give permission.

One consequence of the change from cremation to inhumation during the second century AD must have been that transferring a corpse became a different process. Since cremation no longer occurred at the place of death, presumably, if the corpse was going to be transferred, there was now no reason to have the funeral rites at the place of death rather than the place of final burial. Embalming and even mummification may have been useful for precisely this reason, to preserve the corpse for a delayed funeral (Carroll 2006, 164 n.78, cites a possible case of a mummified body being sent from Egypt to Rome). It has been suggested that jars found at various sites in Rome containing small fragments of bone may represent symbolic repatriation of a small part of the remains of people who died abroad (Messineo 2001, 37; he also discusses the view that they represent the rite of *os receptum* where a bone was removed before cremation). If so, they would presumably represent inhumation burials since a larger quantity of cremated remains could have been sent with no greater difficulty. The change to inhumation probably reduced the chances of the remains being returned home for final burial, however, since the transportation was now a more difficult process.

Conclusion

For Augustus, *euthanasia* involved dying peacefully at home. The bad death which Ovid was afraid of was going to take place abroad, alone. In both cases, the physical setting of the death was important, both for the way in which the dead were remembered and for the actions of the mourners. Someone who died at home, surrounded by family and friends, could expect their final wishes to be listened to and carried out. They could assume that after death the appropriate rituals would be performed, including in at least some cases the making of a death-mask. Their memory would thus be enhanced. They would have the consolation of expecting it to be preserved through a tomb which relatives would maintain, portraiture which would keep their image alive in the home or the tomb, and posthumous arrangements which would maintain their influence after death. Mourners would be able to carry out their obligations to the deceased, which in itself would be a consolation to them. Fear of dying away from home was thus based not just on sentiment, but also on a clear understanding of what the consequences might be: practical instructions not carried out; the body not adequately cared for; the physical image and thus the memory not preserved; the bereaved unable to mourn properly. Residual fears about the soul being trapped abroad were added to the more certain knowledge that even if a tomb was built it would not be maintained, leading to rapid and inevitable oblivion. Thus Ovid's appeal for his remains to be returned to Rome even if he could not come back from exile while alive represents the one possible alleviation of his inevitable bad death, and the request was made to Augustus, whose death (at least as reconstructed by Suetonius) had all the features of the Roman good death.

Bibliography

Allara, A. (1995) Corpus et cadaver, la «gestion» d'un nouveau corps. In *La mort au quotidien dans le monde romain*, 69–79. Paris, de Boccard.

Altmann, W. (1905) *Die römischen Grabaltäre der Kaiserzeit*. Berlin, Weidmannsche Buchhandlung.

Bettini, M. (2005) Death and its double. *Imagines, ridiculum* and *honos* in the Roman aristocratic funeral. In K. Mustakallio *et al.* (eds) *Hoping for Continuity*, 191–202. Helsinki, *Acti Instituti Romani Finlandiae* 33.

Carroll, M. (2006) *Spirits of the Dead. Roman Funerary Commemoration in Western Europe.* Oxford, Oxford University Press.

Champlin, E. (1991) *Final Judgments. Duty and Emotion in Roman Wills, 200 BC – AD 250.* Berkeley, University of California Press.

Connors, C. (1994) Famous last words: authorship and death in the Satyricon and Neronian Rome. In J. Elsner and J. Masters (eds) *Reflections of Nero*, 225–35. Chapel Hill, University of North Carolina Press.

Cracco Ruggini, L. (1995) Les morts qui voyagent: le repatriement, l'exile, la glorification. In *La mort au quotidien dans le monde romain*, 117–134. Paris, de Boccard.

Crawford, J. S. (1977) Physiognomy in Classical and American portrait busts. *American Art Journal* 9, 49–60.

d'Ambra, E. (1995) Mourning and the making of ancestors in the Testamentum Relief. *American Journal of Archaeology* 99, 667–681.

Drerup, H. (1980) Totenmasken und Ahnenbild bei den Römern. *Mitteilungen des Deutschen Archäologischen Instituts, Römische Abteilung*, 87, 81–129.

Edwards, C. (2007) *Death in Ancient Rome*. New Haven and London, Yale University Press.

Feraudi-Gruénais, F. (2001) *Ubi diutius nobis habitandum est. Die Innendekoration der kaiserzeitlichen Gräber Roms*. Wiesbaden, *Palilia* 9.

Flower, H. I. (1996) *Ancestor Masks and Aristocratic Power in Roman Culture*. Oxford, Clarendon Press.

Flower, H. I. (2006) *The Art of Forgetting. Disgrace and Oblivion in Roman Political Culture*. Chapel Hill, University of North Carolina Press.

Graham, E-J. (2006) *The Burial of the Urban Poor in Italy in the Late Roman Republic and Early Empire*. British Archaeological Reports International Series 1565. Oxford, Archeopress.

Hinard, F. and J. C. Dumont (2003) *Libitina. Pompes funèbres et supplices en Campanie à l'époque d'Auguste*. Paris, de Boccard.

Hope, V. M. (2007) *Death in Ancient Rome. A Sourcebook*. London, Routledge.

Huskinson, J. (1996) *Roman Children's Sarcophagi*. Oxford, Clarendon Press.

Huskinson, J. (2005) Children in Roman funerary art. In K. Mustakallio *et al.* (eds) *Hoping for Continuity: childhood, education and death in Antiquity and the Middle Ages*, 91–103. Rome, *Acta Instituti Romani Finlandiae* 33.

Jackson, D. (1987) Verism and the ancestral portrait. *Greece and Rome*, 2nd ser., 34, 32–47.

Jenkins, I. and Williams, D. (1987) A bronze portrait head and its hair net. *Record of the Art Museum, Princeton University*, 46.2, 8–15.

Jitta, J. and Zadoks-Josephus, A. N. (1932) *Ancestral Portraiture in Rome*. Amsterdam, Allard Pierson Stichting.

Koortbojian, M. (2005) *Mimesis* or *phantasia*? Two representational modes in Roman commemorative art. *Classical Antiquity* 24, 285–306.

Martorelli, R. (2000) Clothing in burial practice in Italy in the early Christian period. In J. Pearce, M. Millett and M. Struck (eds), *Burial, Society and Context in the Roman World*, 244–8. Oxford, Oxbow Books.

Messineo, G. (2001) Dalle necropolis del suburbio settentrionale di Roma. In *Römischer Bestattungsbrauch und Beigabensitten in Rom, Norditalien und den Nordwestprovinzen von der späten Republik bis in die Kaiserzeit*, 35–45. Wiesbaden, Deutsches Archäologisches Institut Rom, *Palilia* 8.

Mielsch, H. and Hesberg, H. von (1986) *Die heidnische Nekropole under St Peter in Rom: Die Mausoleen E-I und Z-Psi*. Rome, Atti della Pontifica Accademia Romana di Archeologia ser.3 Memorie vol.16.

Pollini, J. (2007) Ritualizing death in Republican Rome: memory, religion, class struggle, and the wax ancestral mask tradition's origins and influence on veristic portraiture. In N. Laneri (ed.), *Performing Death*, 237–85. Chicago, Oriental Institute Seminars 3.

Smith, R. R. R. (1981) Greeks, foreigners, and Roman republican portraits. *Journal of Roman Studies* 71, 24–38.

Spaltestein, F. (1990) *Commentaire des* Punica *de Silius Italicus livres 9 à 16*. Geneva, Droz, Université de Lausanne Publications de la Faculté de Lettres XXVIIIb.

Toynbee, J. M. C. (1971) *Death and Burial in the Roman World*. London, Thames and Hudson.

Trapp, F. A. (1977) The emperor's nightingale: some aspects of mimesis. *Critical Inquiry*, 4.1, 85–103.

van Hooff, A. (2003) The imperial art of dying. In L. de Blois *et al.* (eds), *The Representation and Perception of Roman Imperial Power*, 99–116. Amsterdam, Gieben.

van Hooff, A. (2004) Ancient euthanasia: 'good death' and the doctor in the Graeco-Roman world. *Social Science and Medicine* 58, 975–85.

Wallace-Hadrill, A. (2005) Housing the dead: the tomb as house in Roman Italy. Paper given at *Commemorating the Dead* conference, University of Chicago. URL: http://marty-center.uchicago.edu/conferences/thedead/private/wallace-hadrill.pdf (accessed 24 August 2008).

2

Memory and Materiality: Re-embodying the Roman Funeral

Emma-Jayne Graham

'… they shift beneath our grasp, moving with the peculiar malleability of a corpse caught midway between death and putrefaction. It is an ugly task, yet what ugliness it has lies not in the proximity of the dead but in the intimacy it demands of us, this closeness with the flesh and substance of their bodies.'
(James Bradley, *The Resurrectionist* 1996, 4)

It has recently been argued that 'the bodily aspect of death – and its profound impact on the living who must deal with it – is something that archaeologists have very successfully avoided' (Nilsson-Stutz 2003, 131). Although studies of past mortuary practices have incorporated the complex social dimensions of death and mourning into their theoretical and methodological approaches, Nilsson-Stutz points out that this has led to a marginalisation of the biological remains of humans, turning them into 'signs, symbols or indicators' (*ibid.*,, 8; 2008). The disappearance of a living person and the emergence of a cadaver is an event with extreme consequences for the living, with their responses revealing 'attitudes toward the body, the self and other, the dead and the living, culture and nature, order and disorder, and the present, the future and the past' (*ibid.*,, 81). Nilsson-Stutz argues that these responses to the dead body help to structure mortuary events and the memories and identities of the participants, but are often overlooked. Consequently, in order to understand past mortuary practices more fully it is necessary to unite the social and biological aspects of death.

This chapter will explore the potential implications of such an approach for the study of Roman mortuary activities. The implications of considering the physiological and biological aspects of death alongside its social dimension are considerable, but in keeping with the themes of the volume this chapter will focus primarily on the insights that such an approach might offer to the study of memory and its impact upon individual and communal identity. In particular, it will be argued that an investigation of possible responses to the materiality of the cadaver, at specific points during mortuary activities, provides an alternative means of considering the creation and significance of memory during the funeral. Although it may not be possible to access these memories directly, a consideration of the ways in which these might have been affected by the corpse can contribute towards a more comprehensive appreciation of the complexities of the funeral and associated processes of memory and identity formation.

Roman bodies

Several recent publications have approached the issue of the ancient body (for example, Corbeill 2004; Montserrat 1998; Wyke and Hopkins 2005), and the dead body has also received attention, most notably from Kyle (1998) and Hope (2000). Hope's excellent survey of the treatment of the corpse in Rome ranges from proper (or improper) burial, through to corpse abuse and the role of body parts in superstitious magic and medicine, but central to her study is the observation that 'as an inanimate object the corpse could become a powerful symbol, which could be honoured and prized or dismissed and despised by others' (*ibid.*,, 104). This resonates with Nilsson-Stutz's observation that dead bodies are commonly reduced to symbols or metaphors, rather than considered as social agents in their own right. Hope's study emphasises the passive nature of the bodies being treated, and she notes both that '[t]he living controlled dead bodies,' and that 'ultimately the dead were powerless' (*ibid.*,, 125–126). The corpses of ancient Rome were indeed vulnerable to manipulation, and this remains important, but these statements deny the corpse itself an active role in funerary and memory practices by suggesting that the living exercised complete control over the ways in which it was perceived and treated. The examples cited by Hope are admittedly those of unusual or deviant practice, in which the living intentionally exercised their power as living beings over the biological reality of the dead body, however, they demonstrate particularly well the ways in the which the body can be absent as a social actor even in instances where it forms the focal point of discussion (for further comments on the absence of bodies in discussions of the body see Joyce 2005; Meskell 1998, 2000; Nilsson-Stutz 2003, 2008; Williams 2004).

The corpse is also conspicuously absent from scholarship concerned with Roman memory; something that can be explained by the nature of the evidence drawn upon for research into ancient remembrance. An immense wealth of information for Roman concerns with memory, and fears of being forgotten, in the form of monuments, texts and architecture composed or erected after the funeral, provides a large corpus of data for explorations of remembrance activities. Examinations of post-mortem memory have focused largely upon this, stressing especially how memory was relevant to the social and status concerns of the living (see for example Carroll 2006, this volume; D'Ambra 2002; Graham 2006; Hope 1998, 2001). Since it was the living who did the remembering many examinations of the memory process have focused upon the means by which this was achieved (for example, funerary monuments, eulogies, wills, epitaphs and ritual observances), and the extent to which these could be manipulated in order to promote, negotiate or affirm the social, legal, cultural, ethnic or religious identity of the deceased and their surviving family. The body of the deceased has not been afforded a place as a source of evidence in these studies, despite being the focal point of many mortuary activities. This is probably linked to the fact that we possess relatively little evidence for Roman corpses, either in the form of textual writings concerning the body or from archaeological contexts. Ancient bodies survive most fully in the form of inhumed remains, which might reveal something about the treatment of the corpse (how it was dressed and laid out for example), but this is the body *after* deposition and is very different in nature from a fleshed cadaver. This is not the body with which the mourners interacted. The corpse, as we shall see, was a very particular manifestation of materiality and consequently quite unlike a skeleton.

More difficult to explain is the frequent absence of the *living body* within examinations of Roman memory and commemoration (although see Edwards 1996 and Favro 1996). Archaeological studies of other periods have employed theories of performance, phenomenology and embodiment to enrich explorations of memory, but their potential has yet to be fully realised by scholars exploring the mortuary rites of the Roman period (see Brück 2005; Hamilakis 1998; Joyce 2001; Meskell 2005, 1999; Meskell and Joyce 2003; Tarlow 2002; Thomas 2000, 2002). However, the perspectives provided by an embodied approach to funerary activities offer the potential to expand understandings of the complex role of memory within ancient society, by taking account not only of the dead body, but also the interaction of *living bodies* with the cadaver and the impact of these experiences on memory and identity.

Defining the dead body

As Nilsson-Stutz (2003 and 2008) has observed, the biological death of a person brings about a profound change: a social being disappears, and a cadaver emerges. The difference between the living subject and the dead object has often been considered quite distinct, given that the dead no longer possess the capacity to move, think or communicate (see Fahlander and Oestigaard 2008, 5). However, as Nilsson-Stutz (2003, 23) continues, the status of the cadaver is difficult to identify: 'having been nature and culture, subject and object, it is now suddenly neither. Still, for a time, it remains recognizable as the person it used to embody.' This places the cadaver in a unique position, somewhere between object and subject, person and non-person.

Noting the peculiar nature of the dead body as neither subject nor object, Nilsson-Stutz suggests that this renders the cadaver 'a completely liminal category of social actor, as it simultaneously is and is not the person that died, and both is and is not a subject' (2003, 58). This, she argues, aligns with Julia Kristeva's (1982) work concerning the *abject* – something that is neither object nor subject, and is often considered to be polluting and dangerous (see for example Hertz 1960[1907]; Lindsay 2000). However, this is the cadaver immediately after death; it does not retain this ambiguous abject status for long. Nilsson-Stutz (2003, 98) argues that the living transform it from abject to *object* via culturally-specific mortuary rites. By handling and treating the body the living reconceptualise the cadaver and their relationship with the social being that it once was. Through this treatment the cadaver loses its liminal character in the minds of the mourners (although remains liminal in a wider cultural sense) and becomes an object with which the living can interact in a more meaningful way. It is now definable. The experience of being involved in these treatments (whether as participant or onlooker) can also have significance for the reconceptualisation of the identity of the living, as well as their relationship with the deceased (Connor 1995).

This process of transformation is most clearly manifested in the ancient Egyptian tradition of mummification which, through the use of specialist treatment, transformed the cadaver from dangerous liminal abject to a recognisable object, or 'a type of artefact in and of itself' (Meskell and Joyce 2003, 128). Mummification represents a very specific way of transforming the body, but the manner in which the cadaver is treated need not be so dramatic; cleansing and dressing the corpse can also be viewed from this perspective. By treating the body in accordance with these culturally specific expectations, the living reconceptualise the cadaver as an object they can act upon. It is no longer an indefinable abject, but can perhaps, to an extent, now be understood from a similar perspective as other objects with which they interact. Given the close relationship between objects and memory (Jones 2007), it is important to consider how this reconceptualisation of the dead body might impact upon memory, in particular the implications for the way in which we consider the materiality of this specific object and its affect on mourners.

Bodies, material culture and materiality

Literature on the modern and ancient body has increasingly recognised that it can be seen as a *project*, being constructed and understood through encounters with the world, and shaped, formed and embodied as the result of social and cultural action (Shilling 2003, 4; also Joyce 2005; Thomas 2002). This is not dissimilar to the concept of material culture (see Ingold 2007), and studies have stressed the varied ways in which bodily products and parts might come to be considered as material culture as their artefactual nature becomes the focus of attention (including saints' relics, body parts used in magic, exchanged or even consumed; Hamilakis *et al.* 2002, 11–12). The entire body is rarely considered to be material culture, but Joanna Sofaer asks 'why an exploration of material qualities should apply only to objects and not to bodies, especially since objects can be regarded as bodies and bodies as objects' (2006, 67–68). Stressing that the biological aspect of the body is essential, it is Sofaer's contention that 'bodies are *material* and *social*, just as objects are' (*ibid.*,, 85 original emphasis), and because we cannot separate them we should consider them in the same ways as material culture. The body can therefore be perceived as a very specific 'form of material culture' (*ibid.*,, 85), with its specificity lying in its very materiality. The human body, like other objects, is made of material and can be touched, altered, treated, changed and manipulated through, for example, tattoos, piercing, head and foot binding, the amputation of parts, and circumcision. However, the materiality of the dead body is not inert, nor is it stable, since it possesses an inherent dynamism that distinguishes it from many (although not all) other types of object that are seemingly more stable (such as inorganic objects that decay and change more slowly). As soon as death occurs the cadaver begins the inevitable process of putrefaction and decay. The effects of this process may not be immediately evident to mourners but, over several days, the body will begin to undergo detectable changes that affect the senses of the living.

The dynamic nature of the body's materiality may therefore have played a central role in the embodied experiences of the living who encountered it, not only acting as a metaphor for the altered nature of their relationship with that person (Graham 2009), but also from the perspective of sensory experience (Joyce 2001, 2005; Kus 1992; Meskell 2000; Tarlow 2002). The impact of the lingering smell of death, for example, has been noted widely (Kus 1992; Roach 2003; Williams 2004, 2006). The various stages of putrefaction may take some time, depending upon climatic conditions and the treatment of the cadaver by the living, but certain changes are evident within several hours and days of death (see Nilsson-Stutz 2003). For cultures in which a period of lying-in-state is important (such as Rome), these changes may become particularly evident, having a significant impact upon embodied experiences and memories of encounters with the deceased. Given the importance that has been ascribed to memory within Roman culture generally (Edwards 1996; Favro 1996), it is important not to neglect this perspective.

The materiality of memory

The concept of embodiment focuses around the impact of bodily experiences on our understanding of the world. Indeed, Meskell (2000, 13) defines the embodied body as 'a lived experience where the interplay of natural, social, cultural, and physical phenomena are brought to fruition.' This concept has influenced studies of the past by stressing that memories are closely linked with embodied encounters with the world, in terms of their creation and subsequent use and recall, during which they might, for example, play a role in the formation of identity (Fisher and DiPaolo Loren 2003; Joyce 2005). Experiences of the materiality of the dead body therefore have consequences for the study of these embodied memories.

Much has been written about the importance of post-mortem memory perpetuation in the ancient world, focused largely on the role of memory within negotiations for status and identity, and the presentation of these to the wider world, as well as a fear of oblivion in the afterlife (Carroll 2006; D'Ambra 2002; Graham 2005, 2006; Hope 1998, 2001). Less has been written about the ways in which rituals and activities became sedimented within the living body as embodied memories that contributed to the identity of the survivors, perhaps even to the same extent as the public statements made by the funerary monument (Favro 1996; Graham 2009). These practices, which Connerton (1989) might describe as 'incorporating' practices, may for example, have held additional significance for those who did not, or could not, erect a memorial. Taking account of the materiality of the dead body allows us to begin to explore the significance of embodied memory within Roman remembrance and identity. It offers the opportunity to delve deeper into the role played by memory, not only during the funeral but also in the creation of individual and group senses of identity.

A memory cannot be recreated or re-experienced, and although it can be recalled and recounted, it cannot be shared (Cubitt 2007, 66). People may participate in the same activity but their memory of that experience remains personal to them. This is because memory is shaped and constructed in response to an individual's existing knowledge and experience of the world, other memories, and the specific socio-cultural or religious context in which it is formed (Devlin 2007). For a long time memory was considered to be a matter of storage and recall (see Cubitt 2007; Devlin 2007; Jones 2007) but is now more commonly understood as an active process whereby engagement with the world builds up an understanding of relationships with the past, present and future through embodied experience. The senses play an important role in this, as Hamilakis (2002, 122) explains, '[t]he notion of embodiment is based on the idea that our subjectivity is defined by our sensory experiences. We exist in and attend to the world through our senses, our bodily encounters with the world.' Through practice, these ways of being become 'sedimented' in the body as embodied memory (Hallam and Hockey 2001; Jones 2007; Meskell and Joyce 2003). Memories are therefore closely associated with our sensory experience of the world; an observation illustrated most famously by Proust's description of memories being evoked by a Madeleine cake and cup of limeflower tea.

This is where an analysis of materiality meets that of memory, for through sensory experience of materialities, embodied memories come into being. Andrew Jones' recent work on *Memory and Material Culture* (2007) provides a methodology for uniting the materiality of the human body and the concept of embodied memory. Rather than viewing objects in terms of their symbolic value, Jones (*ibid.,*, 19) contends that, 'the materiality of objects is best seen as impinging on people sensually and physically at a fundamental level.' Accordingly, it is the interaction between people and objects that is important, with the latter forming the 'ground for humans to experience memory' (*ibid.,*, 22). Although Jones focuses on 'traditional' material culture (*i.e.* artefacts, structures, and monuments) his arguments can be applied to the human body as a material object.

Inspired by the work of Gell (1998), Jones stresses the importance of *materiality*, noting that it is because of its 'physical immediacy that material culture provides such potent metaphors for the experience of memory' (2007, 43). For Jones, material culture presences the past in the present, not only through the existence of objects, but through the fact that they offer a means to presence the past in a *sensory* manner. Hence the material world not only provides metaphorical links with the past but also presents 'a framework for remembrance,' since, 'it is the social practices in which artefacts are engaged which determines how remembrance is socially experienced and mapped out' (*ibid*.,, 225). Jones stresses that certain objects do not embody specific emotions, but their very materiality might evoke particular sensory appreciations and uses (*ibid*.,, 65). This is important for understanding the role of the corpse in the memory processes of the Roman period, for it allows us to perceive the cadaver as a material object that might facilitate different types of emotionally charged performance and sensory experience. Attempting to explore these different experiences associated with, or brought about by, interactions with the corpse might therefore offer an opportunity to consider the complex relationship between Roman funerary rites, memory and identity from a new perspective.

The performative and sensory aspect of memory has been stressed by archaeologists, sociologists and anthropologists alike (Battaglia 1992; Hallam and Hockey 2001; Kus 1992), and Hurcombe (2007, 539) has recently noted that 'as part of an idea of performance in archaeology, sensory perception and the role of objects for the senses could be a powerful tool for new insights.' This issue has been approached for Anglo-Saxon England by Howard Williams, who has examined the ways in which 'the corporeal presence of the dead provides an agency to affect the experience and actions of mourners and evoke memories of the past' (2004, 264; 2006). Williams points to several ways in which the cremation of the dead body may have impacted upon the memories of mourners, emphasising the fact that 'bodies are foci for mnemonic agency' (2006, 85). Williams stresses the role of the senses in the production of memory: the image of the body on the pyre, the distinctive smell of burning flesh and incense, the sound of gases escaping as the body is heated and physical contact with the cremated remains. In many respects the experience he reconstructs is overly dramatic, but the emphasis placed on the sensory experiences caught up within mortuary activities is instructive. Whether evoking responses of fear, mistrust, disgust, or confusion, loss and sadness, Williams proposes that 'the experience of the cadaver creates such a unique and powerful impact on the senses that it can form the basis of the way in which the dead person is remembered' (2004, 267).

The work of Williams expands upon the ideas of Susan Kus (1992) concerning the need to incorporate sensory experience within theoretical discourses, in particular her observation of the ways in which the smell of the decomposing cadaver influenced the creation of memories and directed the activities of the mourners. The role of the senses, especially smell, in processes of memory have also been examined by psychologists, and experiments suggest that odours are 'equipotent with other stimuli for inducing accurate event recollections, but that odours evoke memories that are more emotionally potent,' and that odours are 'unusually effective contextual memory cues' (Herz and Engen 1996, 306–307; Aggleton and Waskett, 1999). The varied smells associated with the Roman funeral (such as the decomposition or burning of the body, incense and perfumes) may therefore have played a central role in cementing memories of that event in the bodies of the participants, but also in the recall of previous funerals complete with the emotions and individual and collective identities associated with them. These were experiences that not only affected the individual, but also the wider social or familial group.

The term 'social memory' is problematic in many ways (see Connerton 2006; Cubitt 2007; Devlin 2007; Fentress and Wickham 1992; Van Dyke and Alcock 2003), but Cubitt's observation (2007, 16) that social memory is not a product but a process, provides a useful way of resolving these problems. Viewing social memory as a process that draws upon the separate memories of individuals within a particular group to create a sense of a shared past allows us to understand how memory can contribute toward a sense of communal identity (Cubitt 2007, 14–15). Social memory is particularly important when we are dealing with the impact of death, allowing us to access the ways in which a group of individuals not only responded in terms of maintaining or realigning their own senses of self, but also how this affirmed their communal sense of identity. Each person may possess individual embodied memories of the event, but these can be drawn upon in particular circumstances to create a sense of group identity. In light of the potential significance of embodied memories born out of sensory experiences of the cadaver, it is necessary that these be considered in discussions of social memory. In order to explore the possible implications of these observations for past embodied experiences of the materiality of the dead body and their importance for the production of memory, and identities in the Roman world, we can turn to the activities and rituals of the funeral.

Embodied encounters with the corpse: the Roman funus

In the Roman world the period immediately after death was one during which people were compelled to interact with the cadaver. The following discussion will examine how these engagements had the potential to become embodied memories, and their importance for the identity of the living. Exploring the potential responses of two specific identity groups, the family of the deceased and funerary professionals (*libitinarii*), it will highlight the plurality of possible experiences surrounding encounters with the cadaver and the extent to which they might have given rise to distinct identities. For the purposes of this discussion it will be presumed that the deceased is male, but it must be stressed that the deaths of women, children, the very elderly, slaves, the poor, members of particular ethnic or religious groups and so forth may have elicited very specific responses, rituals and emotions (see Hurcombe 2007, 538).

Preparation of the body: the mourning family

Reconstructing the events of a single ancient funeral is notoriously problematic (Noy, this volume; Šterbenc Erker, this volume), but sources refer to a number of activities that appear to have been considered important. Amongst these was the act of *depositio*, whereby the body was moved first to its knees and then the ground (Artemidorus 1.13; Ovid, *Pont.* ii.245; Servius, *Aen.*. 12, 395; Corbeill 2004; Šterbenc Erker this volume). This was a rite which necessitated several people, perhaps both men and women, coming into direct contact with the materiality of the body and being compelled to experience it through the medium of touch, sight and probably smell.

Although the affects of decay will yet to have had a significant impact, death does result in some fairly rapid changes to the body. According to Nilsson-Stutz (2003, 142) death 'is immediately followed by a general relaxation of the muscle tone; the muscles become soft and the joints flexible.' This will have been noticeable to those responsible for moving the body, which no longer felt like a living being and responded in a different way to their attentions. Blood, which is no longer pumped around the body, will settle in accordance with gravity (post-mortem hypostasis) thus giving the deceased a distinctive pallor, and the body will begin to cool, most rapidly during the first few hours (*ibid.*,, 142–143). Roman mourners evidently noted these changes, and Virgil (*Aen.* 6, 218–20; Hope 2007, 97), describing the preparations for the funeral of Misenus, writes: 'Some lit fires beneath the cauldrons to boil water and they washed and anointed the *cold body* of their friend and lamented' (my emphasis). Lucian (*Luct.* 11; Hope 2007, 99), in a satirical comment, notes the anointing of a body 'which is already speeding to decay.' Lucian's account may be exaggerated but provides us nevertheless with evidence that he, and his contemporaries, were aware of the changes that the body underwent, and hints at the possibility that these could play a part in directing mortuary activities. *Rigor mortis* typically sets in between two to four hours after death, beginning at the head and spreading down the body over the course of approximately twelve hours, before gradually disappearing in the same direction (Nilsson-Stutz 2003, 143). It is therefore likely to have been in its very early stages when the body was washed and prepared, and if it had set in would have rendered the activities particularly difficult. Nevertheless, these changes may have affected the way in which the mourners experienced the cadaver, perhaps compelling them to perform the washing and dressing ceremonies before it set in and made them more difficult. Consequently, these changes to the materiality of the cadaver probably had a direct impact upon the embodied experiences of the funeral participants, in particular their sensory experiences. It is therefore important to explore the ways in which the materiality of the Roman cadaver may *potentially* have had an impact upon the mourners who were involved in these processes.

Beyond the distinctive smell of decay, the fact that the dynamic materiality of the cadaver, and its eventual decomposition, elicited responses from the living designed to counter or deny this process in the form of anointing with perfumes, incense, and honey, will have had an impact on the sensory experiences of the mourners (Martial 2.11.54; Persius 6; Lucan 1.7; see Classen *et al.* 1994, 42–44). The smell of these substances was designed to mask those that would eventually emanate from the corpse as putrefaction set in. Rather than experiencing the scent of decay the mourners would experience their encounters with the body in the context of the smell of the incense and perfumes with which it was treated, or perhaps an unusual mixture of the two. Given the power of smell to aid emotional recall (Herz and Engen 1996; Kus 1992; Williams 2004, 2006), the scent of myrrh and other perfumes may have brought to mind previous occasions on which these scents had been encountered. Although these may not have been associated exclusively with funerals (see Classen *et al.*1994 for Roman use of perfumes), the unique combination of incense and decay, coupled with the sight of the corpse (senses do not operate independently; Hurcombe 2007), is likely to have made this the most prominent memory. Not only would this have created embodied memories of the events in which the mourners were participating, but did so in the context of existing experiences and knowledge. Like the smell of the burning body highlighted by Williams (2004 and 2006), the scent of the incense will have brought to mind previous funerals and ancestors, consequently presencing these past events in the present. The body, and the treatment that its presence and dynamic materiality demanded of the living in the form of anointing, thus provided a ground or framework for remembrance (Jones 2007). Sensory experiences of the cadaver are likely to have continued throughout the remainder of the funeral, in particular during the period of lying-in-state (Servius, *Aen.* 5.64), during which putrefaction will have begun in earnest, causing the body to swell, change colour and appearance and emit a distinctive smell (Nilsson-Stutz 2003). Although family members are unlikely to have come into direct contact with the corpse during this stage, it remained on display within the *atrium* for several days and will have continued to affect the senses of the living.

Tradition dictated that the immediate family of the departed took an active role in each stage of the funerary ritual and, in particular, female mourners were required to wash, anoint and dress the body (Virgil, *Aen.* 4.683, 9.486–89; Corbeill 2004; Mustakallio 2005, 182; Lindsay 2000; Šterbenc Erker, this volume). The role of women provides a good example of the way in which different members of a family group may have experienced the same activity in diverse ways. It was women who came into direct contact with the materiality of the corpse as they washed and prepared it and, as a consequence, their memories will have been affected by the sensory and emotional experience this act embodied. Participation in the traditionally female act of preparation affirmed both their identity as female individuals and their place within the wider family group. As Mustakallio (2005, 180, citing Radcliffe-Brown 1964) observes, '[e]ven in the serious moments of funerals, the participants may experience "not merely a negative sentiment of sorrow and loss, but a positive emotion of social bonding".' There may also have been a sensory aspect to this bonding. As Classen *et al.* (1994, 140) observe in their discussion of the role played by smells in creating a sense of communion during rites of passage, 'odour, such as that of incense, helps create the desired fellow-feeling by virtue of the way all concerned become conscious of partaking of and being enveloped in the same smell.' For the female mourners, the embodiment of their encounter with the materiality of the corpse in this context may have created a very specific memory that contributed to their understanding of the world, and their place in it, that was different from that of their male counterparts who acted as spectators. Perhaps, if different roles were assigned to different members of the female group these even acted to structure their understanding of their place within the family hierarchy, with more important women possibly taking on duties considered to be the most important, symbolic or pious.

The links between rites of death and birth in the Roman period have recently been stressed (Corbeill 2004; Hänninen 2005; Mustakallio 2005). The parallels between these rites of passage provide an opportunity to explore how the existing knowledge and understandings that may have been already sedimented within the bodies of female mourners could have been drawn upon during the funeral, in the form of embodied memories, to structure their understanding of the world and the activities in which they were participating. Many of the women, although perhaps not all (depending upon age and marital status), may have had some involvement with the rites surrounding birth, during which the newborn child was placed on the floor in order to check its viability, before being washed (Artemidorus 1.13; Soranus, *Gyn.* 2,10; Varro, *de vita populi Romani* 81; Corbeill 2004; Hänninen 2005, 55). The obvious parallels between this and the act of placing the corpse on the floor in order to check that it was lifeless, before washing and preparing it, are likely to have been recognised by the mourners preparing the corpse (Artemidorus certainly noted them). This may perhaps have brought to mind the occasion on which the deceased had themselves been treated in this way as an infant. Depending upon the relationship the women shared with the deceased, this may have engendered a powerfully emotional response that recalled the earlier life of the deceased, or indeed other members of the family. The occasion of birth was primarily a female-centred event, with few male participants (see Corbeill 2004), so the memories that were recalled by the similar activity of the funeral were again very specific to the women of the family. Male mourners, primarily onlookers, will not have experienced the funeral in the context of these same sorts of memories. Even if, as Artemidorus (1.13) suggests, they possessed knowledge of the events that took place at birth, the fact that they were detached from their performance means that they may have understood their current responses in a very different context. Consequently, their experience of the preparation of the corpse will have been very different in nature to those of the women and served to affirm their identity as male mourners.

Highlighting gendered differences in experience reveals the importance of considering alternative perspectives when exploring the funeral. Family members evidently experienced different degrees of interaction with the corpse depending upon their position within the family, gender, age and responsibilities, as well as traditional custom. Age may have been especially significant, with young or elderly members of the family (male or female) having different roles and responsibilities, or perhaps being excluded from certain activities. Despite this plurality of experience, their actions were always directed by the presence of the cadaver and the fact that it demanded attention. The body lay at the very centre of events and it was the mourner's interaction with it, and the way in which it affected their senses, that created a framework for the creation of embodied memory and identity. This also facilitated the re-negotiation of relationships within the family group, and the affirmation of communal aspects of their identity. Moving, washing, anointing and dressing the corpse brought some members of the family into direct contact with its dynamic materiality, and may have evoked strong emotional responses that had a significant impact upon memories of the event and the deceased. As Williams (2004, 267) has observed, the cadaver is capable of evoking particularly powerful emotional responses, and these will have occurred in the context of existing embodied knowledge, with the encounter between the mourners and the body reviving memories of previous experiences and persons. In this respect the materiality of the corpse, and the adherence to socio-cultural expectations with regards to its treatment, acted as a framework for social memory, as memories were produced, embodied, and perhaps recounted, in an atmosphere of group recollection and communality.

Preparation of the body: the funerary specialist

It was an act of familial *pietas* to gather together to wash, dress and prepare the body for burial, with different members of the family bearing different responsibilities. However, the late Republic and the early Imperial period witnessed the emergence of a group of funerary specialists, referred to collectively as *libitinarii*, who would perform these mortuary acts for a fee (*AE* 1971, n88; Horace, *Epist.* 1.7.3–7; Martial 1.47; Valerius Maximus 5.2.10; see also Bodel 2000, 2004; Hope 2007; Lindsay 2000). In particular, Plautus (*Poen.* 63) refers to *pollinctores,* who would prepare the body and cover the face with powder (*pollen*) in an attempt to conceal the discolouration caused by death. It can perhaps be assumed that powder was also used by the family as part of their own treatment of the body. Bodel (2004, 155) identifies other specialised roles, including a *strator,* who appears with the *pollinctor* (*leges Cumanae* b,I.5; b,I.11). Bodel (2004, 155) suggests that the *strator* had the task of laying out the body, and perhaps dressing and anointing it, ready for its exposition in the *atrium*. Funeral workers suffered from social and physical exclusion as a result of the stigma of death pollution caused by the nature of their work, but perhaps also because their profession entailed gaining profit from other people's misfortune (Valerius Maximus 5.2.10; Bodel 2000, 140–141). Nevertheless, the fact that they existed and continued to find employment indicates that their services were probably used on a regular basis.

There were at least two funerary specialists who could potentially have been involved in the initial preparation of the body: the *pollinctor* and the *strator*. They will, undoubtedly, have performed the same activities as the family, by washing, cleansing, anointing, dressing and laying out the body, which meant that they too came into direct contact with it. These activities will also have become sedimented into the bodies of the specialists as a key component in the way in which they understood the world and their place in it, especially given the frequency with which they performed them. However, there are several ways in which their experiences will have been embodied in a different manner from those of the family, despite performing essentially the same activities. Not only were the *pollinctor* and *strator* more accustomed to handling bodies in various states of decomposition, rendering the materiality of the corpse less remarkable and unusual, but the performance of these acts will not have occurred within the same emotionally charged context as it did for the family. It is unlikely that the specialists shared a relationship with the deceased during their lifetime and, as a result, the context of their interaction with the cadaver was probably very different from that of the family. Corpses were part of their daily existence and, consequently, the feel, smell or sight of the body will not, under normal circumstances, have elicited the same strength of emotional feeling as it would for the family. This is not to say that these specialists were immune to the sensory impact of a dead human being and did not contemplate its wider meanings within an emotional context, but their occupations will have acted to help objectify the corpse simply as providing the ground for their work. For them it was a true material object.

Despite this, it can be argued that the cadaver probably played a central role in the creation of embodied memory for these funerary workers, and was consequently involved in the construction of their sense of identity, both as individuals and as a group. Identity for the mourners was partly reliant upon their relationship with the person who had once been the subject of the cadaver, and their treatment of it consequently involved the re-negotiation of that relationship (Graham 2009). For the funerary specialist it was the material of the cadaver itself, the fact that it required certain treatment, and their regular interaction with it, which defined their personal and social identity, and dictated and created the structure of the world in which they lived. As noted above, funerary specialists were marginalised and excluded from contact with the community they served as a consequence of the nature of their work. They were marked out physically from other members of the community through the manner of their dress and may have been forced to live outside the town limits (*AE* 1971, n.88; Bodel 2000, 2004). This, and their shared qualifications of age and physical fitness, has led Bodel (2004, 154) to propose that there was a strong sense of communal identity and solidarity amongst the *libitinarii*. Embodied experiences of dealing with the dead may also have contributed to the consolidation of a particular communal identity, formed not only as a result of their social exclusion but also through the process of social memory, which drew on these embodied practices. Their world and identities were structured by the very materiality of the cadavers that the community produced since their services would not have been required if bodies were not composed of dynamic material and subject to decay. It is therefore important that we view the activities of the *pollinctores*, *stratores* and other specialists within this context and acknowledge that their identities and memories will have been constructed accordingly.

What is particularly important for the purposes of this study is that despite performing essentially the same activities, the *pollinctor* and *strator* experienced the cadaver in a very different manner to that of the mourning family. The memories of both might have been constructed in response to a sensory experience of the materiality of the corpse, but these were formed in the context of their own specific understandings of Roman society and culture, as well as previous experiences of the dead body. For the *libitinarii*, these memories affirmed a very different understanding of the structure of the social world, and in particular their marginal place within it. The family, on the other hand, constructed their memories in the context of their relationship with the person of the deceased, the emotions of previous funerals and their relative unfamiliarity with the materiality of the corpse. Their memories were probably considerably more emotionally charged than those of the specialists, but the memories of the latter were no less valid or representative of their interaction with the cadaver. This was social memory at work, drawing on embodied memories to construct a communal sense of the past, present and future, and the place of the living within it. The 'memory' of these events possessed by the funerary workers was, however, at odds with that of the family, and although it too may have been used to create a communal sense of the past, present and future, this was completely different to that understood by the mourning family.

The services of funerary specialists appear to have become progressively more popular during the course of the first century AD, and mourning families will therefore have had increasingly less contact with the cadaver, perhaps to a point where they dealt directly with it only rarely (amongst the wealthier classes at least). As a consequence, the embodied experiences outlined above will have changed and the resulting senses of identity may have been very different for all concerned, but especially for those who no longer had to play their previously ascribed role, such as women (see Šterbenc Erker in this volume for how gendered roles may have been maintained). This has important connotations for the ways in which we approach the study of the Roman funeral and demonstrates that even seemingly traditional rites were not necessarily always understood or experienced in a static manner. Not only did individuals and groups experience these in different ways, but over time what they were experiencing altered too, as direct contact with the cadaver was minimised. This has implications for the way in which we understand the significance of these events in various periods, raising the possibility of subsequent changes, but also the relevance of other funerary rites, which may have become increasingly more important or been adapted to compensate for these changes.

Conclusion: re-embodying the Roman funeral

This exploration of possible experiences of the dead body during the Roman funeral demonstrates how participation in the same activities could lead to the creation of competing memories and distinct identities, as a result of existing understandings of the social world and embodied experiences. What is more, the materiality of the cadaver was central to this process by acting upon the senses of the living. It compelled them to act in culturally-specific ways, and provided a material framework for the process of memory. The dead body was more than an inert or passive object to be manipulated by the living; in fact its very material presence may have acted upon the memories of the living in order to construct their sense of self.

It has been argued above that the memories produced and sedimented in the body through interactions between the living and the cadaver played an important role in the maintenance of both individual and collective identity. These observations demonstrate once again that memory could be important throughout the funeral, not only towards the end when attention shifted to the funerary monument or tomb and subsequent events designed to commemorate the dead. They emphasise the extent to which memory, as a process, was involved not only in the perpetuation of the memory of the deceased, but was also closely associated with the rehabilitation of the mourners and their own understandings of their place in the world. Similar arguments have been advanced for other forms of Roman remembrance, including the funerary monument, which could serve as a focus for the creation, maintenance, affirmation and negotiation of the identities of both the dead *and* the living (Hope 1998). Combining these approaches, and exploring the links between them, may allow for the development of a more nuanced understanding of these processes, especially given that embodied memories probably operated in combination with other memories of the person during life, of later elements of the funeral such as the cremation or burial, and of subsequent commemorative activities, to create a complex multi-faceted memory of the deceased. The role of the body has been shown to be particularly significant, both in terms of the agency of the material corpse and the embodied experiences of the living. Given that Roman society was 'a society of memory' (Flower 2002, 159), it is essential to investigate new methods of accessing its different manifestations, including embodiment. It is therefore vital that we begin to examine the very bodies that inhabited, experienced and manipulated the ancient world, both in life and death, in order to comprehend the full extent of the significance of memory as an active process.

It is, of course, impossible to recreate the exact nature of mourning experiences in the ancient world and unfortunately primary sources are limited in what they reveal about this aspect of the funeral. This may mean that any future consideration of embodied memories of the funeral will be severely restricted to 'educated guesses'. However, echoing the sentiments expressed by Kus (1992, 172) that we should not ignore the senses in theoretical approaches, Hurcombe (2007, 540) stresses that 'there is a case for thinking through the range of colours, textures, sounds, smells and tastes available within the societies we study in an holistic way to understand what might draw or deliberately attract attention in that society.' Given that these are likely to have held meaning for the people of the past it is essential that we do not side-line the senses and resulting embodied memories, even if acknowledging that their ability to raise new questions is all that current evidence will allow. It may not be possible to identify the exact embodied responses of participants in a Roman funeral, but an exploration of *potential* responses allows us to glimpse the complex diversity of experiences that might have been possible and to acknowledge the presence of a multiplicity of meanings that could have been attached to them. An examination of the ways in which embodied experiences may have contributed to these broader processes of memory and the maintenance of individual and collective identity can only enrich existing interpretations.

Acknowledgements

I would like to thank Valerie Hope and Janet Huskinson for inviting me to contribute to both this volume and the *Memory and Mourning: Death in Ancient Rome* seminar in Birmingham, during which some early ideas for this paper were first put forward. I am also grateful for their comments on an earlier draft of the chapter.

Bibliography

Aggleton, J. P. and Waskett, L. (1999) The ability of odours to serve as state-dependent cues for real-world memories: can Viking smells aid the recall of Viking experiences? *British Journal of Psychology* 90, 1–7.

Battaglia, D. (1992) The body in the gift: memory and forgetting in Sabarl mortuary exchange. *American Ethnologist* 19(1), 3–18.

Bodel, J. (2000) Dealing with the dead: undertakers, executioners and potter's fields in ancient Rome. In V. M. Hope and E. Marshall (eds) *Death and Disease in the Ancient City*, 104–127. London, Routledge.

Bodel, J. (2004) The organization of the funerary trade at Puteoli and Cumae. In *Libitina e dintorni. Atti dell'XI Rencontre franco-italienne au l'epigraphie (Libitina 3)*, 147–172. Rome, Edizioni Quasar.

Bradley, J. (2006) *The Resurrectionist*. London, Faber and Faber.

Brück, J. (2005) Experiencing the past? The development of a phenomenological archaeology in British prehistory. *Archaeological Dialogues* 12(1), 45–72.

Carroll, M. (2006) *Spirits of the Dead: Roman Funerary Commemoration in Western Europe*. Oxford, Oxford University Press.

Classen, C., Howes, D. and Synott, A. (1994). *Aroma. The Cultural History of Smell*. London and New York, Routledge.

Connerton, P. (1989) *How Societies Remember*. Cambridge, Cambridge University Press.

Connerton, P. (2006) Cultural Memory. In C. Tilley, W. Keane, S. Küchler, M. Rowlands and P. Spyer (eds) *Handbook of Material Culture*, 315–324. London, Sage Publications.

Connor, L. H. (1995) The action of the body in society. Washing a corpse in Bali. *The Journal of the Royal Anthropological Society* 1(3), 537–559.

Corbeill, A. (2004) *Nature Embodied: Gesture in Ancient Rome*. Princeton, Princeton University Press.

Cubitt, G. (2007) *History and Memory*. Manchester, Manchester University Press.

D'Ambra, E. (2002) Acquiring an Ancestor. The importance of funerary statuary among the non-elite orders of Rome. In J. M. Højte (ed.) *Images of Ancestors*, 223–246. Denmark, Aarhus University Press.

Devlin, Z. (2007) *Remembering the Dead in Anglo-Saxon England. Memory Theory in Archaeology and History*. British Archaeological Reports, British Series 446. Oxford, Archaeopress.

Dyke, R. M. van and Alcock, S. E. (2003) Archaeologies of memory. An introduction. In R. M. Van Dyke and S. E. Alcock (eds) *Archaeologies of Memory*, 1–13. Oxford, Blackwell Publishing.

Edwards, C. (1996) *Writing Rome. Textual Approaches to the City*. Cambridge, Cambridge University Press.

Fahlander, F. and Oestigaard, T. (2008) The materiality of death: bodies, burials, beliefs. In F. Fahlander and T. Oestigaard (eds). *The Materiality of Death: Bodies, Burials, Beliefs*. British Archaeological Reports, International Series S1768, 1–16. Oxford, Archaeopress.

Favro, D. (1996) *The Urban Image of Augustan Rome*. Cambridge, Cambridge University Press.

Fentress, J. and Wickham, C. J. (1992) *Social Memory*. Oxford, Blackwell.

Fisher, G. and DiPaolo Loren, D. (2003) Embodying identity in archaeology: Introduction. *Cambridge Archaeological Journal* 12(2), 225–30.

Flower, H. (2002) Were women ever "ancestors" in Republican Rome? In J. M. Højte (ed.) *Images of Ancestors*, 159–184. Denmark, Aarhus University Press.

Gell, A. (1998). *Art and Agency: An Anthropological Theory*. Oxford, Clarendon Press.

Graham, E-J. (2005) The quick and the dead in the extra-urban landscape. The Roman cemetery at Ostia/Portus as a lived environment. In J. Bruhn, B. Croxford and D. Grigoropoulos (eds) *TRAC 2004. Proceedings of the Fourteenth Annual Theoretical Roman Archaeology Conference. Durham 2004*, 133–143. Oxford, Oxbow Books.

Graham, E-J. (2006) *Death, Disposal and the Destitute. The Burial of the Urban Poor in Italy in the Late Roman Republic and Early Empire*. British Archaeological Reports, International Series 1565. Oxford, Archaeopress.

Graham, E-J. (2009) Becoming persons, becoming ancestors: personhood, memory and the corpse in Roman rituals of social remembrance. *Archaeological Dialogues* 16(1), 41–74.

Hallam, E. and Hockey, J. (2001) *Death, Memory and Material Culture*. Oxford and New York, Berg.

Hamilakis, Y. (1998) Eating the dead. Mortuary feasting and the politics of memory in the Aegean Bronze Age Societies. In K. Branigan (ed.) *Cemetery and Society in the Aegean Bronze Age*, 115–132. Sheffield, Sheffield Academic Press.

Hamilakis, Y. (2002) The past as oral history. Towards an archaeology of the senses. In Y. Hamilakis, M. Pluciennick and S. Tarlow (eds) *Thinking Through the Body. Archaeologies of Corporeality*, 121–136. New York, Kluwer Academic/Plenum Publishers.

Hamilakis, Y., Pluciennik, M., and Tarlow, S. (2002) Introduction. Thinking through the body. In Y. Hamilakis, M. Pluciennick and S. Tarlow (eds) *Thinking Through the Body. Archaeologies of Corporeality*, 1–21. New York, Kluwer Academic/Plenum Publishers.

Hänninen, M-L. (2005) From womb to family. Rituals and social conventions connected to Roman birth. In K. Mustakallio, J. Hanska, H-L. Sainio and V. Vuolanto (eds) *Hoping For Continuity. Childhood, Education and Death in Antiquity and the Middle Ages*, 49–59. Acta Instituti Romani Finlandiae vol. 33, Rome.

Hertz, R. (1960 [1907]). *Death and the Right Hand*. Translated by R. and C. Needham. London, Cohen and West.

Herz, R. S. and Engen, T. (1996). Odor memory: review and analysis. *Psychonomic Bulletin and Review* 3, 300–313.
Hope, V. M. (1998) Negotiating identity and status. The gladiators of Roman Nîmes. In R. Laurence and J. Berry (eds) *Cultural Identity in the Roman Empire*. London, Routledge, 179–195.
Hope, V. M. (2000) Contempt and respect: the treatment of the corpse in ancient Rome. In V. M. Hope and E. Marshall (eds) *Death and Disease in the Ancient City*, 104–127. London, Routledge, 104–127.
Hope, V. M. (2001) *Constructing Identity. The Roman funerary monuments of Aquileia, Mainz and Nimes*, British Archaeological Reports, International Series 960, Oxford, Archaeopress.
Hope, V. M. (2007) *Death in Ancient Rome. A Sourcebook*. London, Routledge.
Hurcombe, L. (2007) A sense of materials and sensory perception in concepts of materiality. *World Archaeology* 39(4), 532–545.
Ingold, T. (2007) Materials against materiality. *Archaeological Dialogues* 14(1), 1–16.
Jones, A. (2007) *Memory and Material Culture*. Cambridge, Cambridge University Press.
Joyce, R. A. (2001) Burying the dead at Tlatilco. Social memory and social identities. In M.S. Chesson (ed.) *Social Memory, Identity and Death: Anthropological Perspectives on Mortuary Rituals. Archaeological Papers of the American Anthropological Association* 10, 12–26.
Joyce, R. A. (2005) Archaeology of the body. *Annual Review of Anthropology* 34, 139–158.
Kristeva, J. 1982. *Powers of Horror: An Essay on Abjection*. New York: Columbia University Press.
Kus, S. (1992) Toward an archaeology of body and soul. In J-C. Gardin and C. S. Peebles (eds) *Representations in Archaeology*, 168–177. Bloomington, Indiana University Press.
Kyle, D. G. (1998) *Spectacles of Death in Ancient Rome*. London, Routledge.
Lindsay, H. (2000) Death-pollution and funerals in the city of Rome. In V. M. Hope and E. Marshall (eds) *Death and Disease in the Ancient City*, 152–173. London, Routledge.
Meskell, L. (1998) The irresistible body and the seductions of archaeology. In D. Montserrat (ed.) *Changing Bodies, Changing Meanings. Studies on the Human Body in Antiquity*, 139–161. London and New York, Routledge.
Meskell, L. (1999) *Archaeologies of Social Life. Age, Sex, Class et cetera in Ancient Egypt*. Oxford, Blackwell.
Meskell, L. (2000) Writing the body in archaeology. In A. E. Rautman (ed.) *Reading the Body. Representations and Remains in the Archaeological Record*, 13–21. Philadelphia, University of Pennsylvania Press.
Meskell, L. (2005) *Archaeologies of Materiality*. Oxford, Blackwell.
Meskell, L. M. and Joyce, R. A. (2003) *Embodied Lives. Figuring Ancient Maya and Egyptian Experience*. London, Routledge.
Montserrat, D. (ed.) (1998) *Changing Bodies, Changing Meanings. Studies on the Human Body in Antiquity*. London and New York, Routledge.
Mustakallio, K. (2005) Roman funerals. Identity, gender and participation. In K. Mustakallio, J. Hanska, H-L. Sainio and V. Vuolanto (eds) *Hoping for Continuity: Childhood, Education and Death in Antiquity and the Middle Ages*, 179–190. Acta Instituti Romani Finlandiae vol. 33, Rome.
Nilsson Stutz, L. (2003) *Embodied Rituals and Ritualized Bodies. Tracing Ritual Practices in Late Mesolithic Burials*. Acta Archaeological Lundensia No. 46, Lund.
Nilsson Stutz, L. (2008) More than metaphor: approaching the human cadaver in archaeology. In F. Fahlander and T. Oestigaard (eds), *The Materiality of Death: Bodies, Burials, Beliefs*. British Archaeological Reports, International Series S1768, 19–28. Oxford, Archaeopress.

Roach, M. (2003) *Stiff. The Curious Lives of Human Cadavers*. London, Penguin Books.
Shilling, C. (2003) *The Body and Social Theory*. (Second Edition). London, Sage Publications.
Sofaer, J. R. (2006) *The Body as Material Culture. A Theoretical Osteoarchaeology*. Cambridge, Cambridge University Press.
Tarlow, S. (2002) The aesthetic corpse in nineteenth-century Britain. In Y. Hamilakis, M. Pluciennick and S. Tarlow (eds) *Thinking Through the Body. Archaeologies of Corporeality*, 85–97. New York, Kluwer Academic/Plenum Publishers.
Thomas, J. (2000) Death, identity and the body in Neolithic Britain. *Journal of the Royal Anthropological Institute* 6, 653 – 668.
Thomas, J. (2002) Archaeology's humanism and the materiality of the body. In Y. Hamilakis, M. Pluciennick and S. Tarlow (eds) *Thinking Through the Body. Archaeologies of Corporeality*, 29–45. New York, Kluwer Academic/Plenum Publishers.
Williams, H. (2004) Death warmed up. The agency of bodies and bones in early Anglo-Saxon cremation rites. *Journal of Material Culture* 9(3), 263 – 291.
Williams, H. (2006) *Death and Memory in Early Medieval Britain*. Cambridge, Cambridge University Press.
Wyke, M. and Hopkins, A. (eds) (2005) *Roman Bodies. Antiquity to the Eighteenth Century*. London, The British School at Rome.

3

Gender and Roman Funeral Ritual

Darja Šterbenc Erker

Introduction

Roman funerary practices expressed that someone had died and prepared the dead for leaving the world of the living behind. Family and friends accompanied the dead person towards their new or future dwelling. A complex set of purification rites ensured that the mourning family returned to the world of the living after reinforcing the symbolic boundary between the living and the dead. Funeral ritual in Rome marked therefore a passage from physical to cultural death (Ampolo 1984, 72).

This paper will examine funeral practices and their symbolic meanings with a special focus on the division of ritual control between men and women. I shall argue that some practices in Roman funeral ritual were considered men's, others women's work. Modern authors state that lamentation and mourning, two ways of keeping alive the memory of the deceased, were women's tasks. Here I am going to draw attention to transgressions of this norm in Roman society and the meaning of these transgressions in literary texts. Men also had to mourn for persons of higher social standing in a similar way as women did when they were bereaved of their dead relatives. I will also argue that the ascription of femininity to the traditional rites of mourning reveals a normative construction of the gendered nature of funeral tasks bound to an upper-class morality.

The extant sources on the sexual divisions of ritual tasks in Roman funerals are primarily literary references in poetry and antiquarian writings. The main concern of these authors is to show the characteristics of Roman burial customs and the unique Roman way of worshipping the gods and keeping alive the memory of the ancestors. The late Republican antiquarian Varro stresses that his work on Roman religious lore in the *Antiquitates rerum divinarum* seeks to save the Roman gods and the tradition of the Roman ancestors from oblivion (Varro, *ant. rer. div.* 2a, Cardauns; Augustine, *De civ. D.* 6. 2; Moatti 1997, 109–110). Therefore, Varro understands himself as a saviour of the gods of the *res publica*, a task even more important than the salvation of the cult-objects from the burning sanctuary of the goddess Vesta by Metellus or Aeneas' rescue of the Penates from Troy. By keeping alive the memory of ancient funeral customs, antiquarians and poets remind their fellow-citizens, the *populus Romanus*, of the common practices of the people of Rome and their unique Roman identity. The underlying idea is that these practices must not disappear by mingling with Hellenistic traditions present in the Roman Empire. It is not possible to accept the assertions of Cumont (1949, 11) that ritual gestures lost their meaning for the celebrants at the end of the Republic because these rituals were constantly commented on and re-interpreted in antiquarian works.

This chapter will examine sources ranging from the end of the Republic to the second century AD, as well as several antiquarian texts that refer to Republican and Augustan knowledge on funerals in the city of Rome, such as Servius' *Commentary on Aeneid* from the fourth century AD and the lexicon *De significatione verborum*. This lexicon was written by Verrius Flaccus, a learned freedman of the Augustan Age. A shortened form of the lexicon has survived in fragments *via* S. Pompeius Festus (second century AD) and in the even shorter version of Paul the Deacon (eighth century AD). References to funeral rites in Roman poetry are in fact representations, literary images of funeral sequences. The primary concern of poets was to construct their respective imaginary worlds and *personae* and not to give a full description of the rites. Poetic representations of funerals sometimes pervert Roman social and cultural values centred on the sphere of death; therefore they must be submitted to cautious analysis, as stressed by Houghton in this volume. Modern critics assume that some funeral rites, as depicted in poetry, only reflect literary *tópoi* without having an actual basis in the real life of the Romans. However, the poets had to take into account the audience's experiences which derived from their participation at funerals and gave them the opportunity to recognise descriptions as referring to common funeral rites.

First, I will explore the issues of death-pollution, gender and mourning, followed by an analysis of some practices performed at the moment of dying. Second, some women's tasks will be discussed, such as preparing the corpse and the excessive mourning at the funeral procession. Third, some of the men's tasks (funeral eulogy, sacrifice and purifications) will be examined. Fourth, the task of prolonged mourning will be highlighted, followed by a short analysis of the festivals for the commemoration of the dead. Finally, I will draw some conclusions concerning gendered tasks in Roman funeral ritual and also about the literary practices of the Roman antiquarians.

Death-pollution

By acknowledging the death of a member of their family, the cognate relatives (blood relations as far removed as the sixth degree) became temporarily a *familia funesta*, a family 'under an obligation of a funeral' (Servius, *Aen*. 6. 8; 11. 2). Men and women were prohibited from performing their usual activities; they could not offer sacrifices to the gods or execute any other ritual. For the entire period of the funeral ritual the family members had to cease all participation in sacred, public and economic activities, and were also excused if they did not appear in court. The usual flow of time stopped for the family, the private festival of the dead began (Cicero, *Leg.* 2. 22. 55: *feriae denicales*; Paulus 61L*)*. The male and female relatives of the dead were defiled by a symbolic 'stain', and separated themselves from the other 'pure' members of the community by creating a special separate space for funeral ritual. The separation between the death-polluted and pure was marked by putting branches of cypress at the entrance of the house of the dead. According to Servius, these branches warned the *pontifices* not to enter the house and thereby become death-polluted themselves (Servius, *Aen.* 3. 64). In another passage of his commentary, Servius explains that the cypress branches signalled to those who intended to perform a sacred ritual not to enter. If they entered the house without knowing there was a corpse, they could not perform the planned ritual since they had been contaminated by the death-pollution (Servius, *Aen.* 4. 507). Although these prohibitions were imposed upon both sexes, Servius stresses that the ability to perform the men's, and especially the priests' duties, was removed temporarily by death-pollution. A person who wanted to perform a ritual could postpone acknowledging the fact that he had become *funestus,* Servius mentions the procedure of recognising the fact of becoming polluted by death (*funestatus*) as *funus agnoscere* (*Aen.* 6. 8; 11. 2; Latte 1960, 102).

Lindsay (2000, 153) argues in his article on death-pollution that in Roman funerals several aspects were at stake: the practical concerns over the disintegration of the body of the deceased, concerns about the health of the urban environment and also 'the remnants of age-old taboos'. However, Roman funeral rituals did not focus primarily on the hygiene or the health of the urban environment, but on the subsequent separation of the death-contaminated persons and objects from the world of the dead. 'Purity' and 'pollution' are two categories constructed in relation to religious and social conventions, as Bendlin (2007, 178) argues convincingly. Standards of death-pollution in Roman burials varied according to the social status of the deceased. This feature shows that they were not the same as our modern conceptions of hygiene (on culturally determined different systems of classification of purity and dirt *cf.* Douglas 1966; on discrepancy between modern and ancient Greek hygienic standards *cf.* Bendlin 2007, 179). The lowest strata of the Roman society did not receive any funeral rituals at all, the corpses of the poor were simply thrown into pits (*puticuli*). Dead slaves had to be removed immediately from the city (Law of Puteoli, *AE* 1971, 88. II. 21–23; Dumont 1995, 182–3) whereas the corpse of a freeborn citizen or a magistrate was displayed (*collocatio*) for some time in the *atrium* of his house. Important statesmen were even buried inside the city-walls (Cicero, *Leg.* 2. 23. 58; *cf.* Plutarch, *Mor.* 282f–283a; *Publ.* 23). Cicero mentions famous men, for example, Publicola and Tuberto, who were buried inside the city, but supposes that this happened before the so called Law of the Twelve Tables forbade such burials. Furthermore, Cicero sees in the case of Gaius Fabricius an exemption from the law on account of his merits (*virtus*) for the political community. The location of family tombs inside the city during the Republic increased a family's prestige (Flower 1996, 119). However, this practice was very unusual. The ban on burying inside the city (*urbs*) was connected with its particular religious status, and its boundary was marked by a line known as the *pomerium* (Scheid 1998, 67; Beard, North, Price 1998, 180). According to legend, the *urbs*, the space inside the *pomerium*, was inaugurated by the mythic founder of Rome, Romulus, who received the necessary favourable signs from the gods. To keep the sacred space of the city and its political institutions intact, all contacts with death-pollution had to be avoided; even the army, which was regularly involved with killing and death, was not allowed to cross the sacred boundary.

Funeral rites did not concern 'age-old taboos' as Lindsay (2000, 153) asserts, but religious and social obligations. The pontiffs promulgated regulations concerning burials which concentrated on the social status of the dead and the rights of his family to keep alive the memory of the deceased, and to commemorate his actions. According to Cicero (*Leg.* 2. 22. 55) the pontifical laws addressing the cult of the dead express enormous concern and care about ceremonial details. At the end of the Republic, the rules on regulation of tombs, successive sacrifices and purification rites, aiming at separating the realms of the living and the dead, were at the core of Roman concerns about funerals. Gestures and attitudes changed through the decades and centuries, and were re-interpreted and adapted to new circumstances; the memory of old traditions was kept alive in antiquarian texts. Plutarch records an excellent example of continuity and change concerning burials inside the city of Rome, in expressing the traditional honour of a family. Publicola received a very special honour by being buried inside the city, but Plutarch adds that during his lifetime no one from this family was actually buried there. Instead, a corpse was carried to the family's tomb at Velia and put on the ground, while somebody took a burning torch and held it under the body, then retrieved it, in order to show that the dead person has a right to be buried there, but resigned it (*Publ.* 23. 6).

Lindsay (2000, 169) writes that acts of cleansing in a Roman funeral ritual were originally understood in a religious sense, but they had declined and were little understood in the imperial period. The paradigm of interpreting the decline of religion in the empire has undergone justified criticisms recently, since Roman religion was constantly renewed and re-interpreted (Beard, North, Price 1998, 117–118). Wallace-Hadrill (2005, 64–65) argues convincingly that Republican and Augustan authors who lament the 'decline' and 'negligence' of religion, used this kind of a rhetorical *tópos* in order to discredit the credibility of the *nobiles*. The *nobiles* were considered to be in charge of keeping Roman traditional religion alive. Imperial authors do not write of a decline of purification rites, but testify to their persistence and the necessity of accomplishing these rites. Plutarch writing about the customs of the Romans ('Roman questions', *Mor.* 263e–291c), stresses the enormous importance of the performance of purification rites in the second century AD. He mentions a curious rite which the Romans undertook for those who were said to have died in a foreign country and who received a symbolic funeral ritual *in absentia*. The body could not enter the house by the door, but had to be carried into the house through the *atrium*. Plutarch draws attention to a parallel with Greek customs of the rebirth of a missing person believed to be dead who had already been mourned. In the Roman case, Plutarch understands that if a person who had been declared dead happened to return home alive he had to be brought into the house from the open sky because the purification rites had to be performed under the open sky (*Mor.* 265b). This explanation confirms that purification rites were still duly performed, understood and interpreted at the time when Plutarch wrote his treatise on Roman customs.

Gender and mourning

Men and women in mourning changed their usual behaviour and attitude. According to Servius mourners inversed everything (Servius, *Aen.* 11. 93; Scheid 1984, 137–8); they wore dark funeral clothes, fasted, ceased to comb and wash their hair and neglected their body's hygiene. Plutarch writing in the second century AD mentions that Roman women wore white while attending a funeral (*Mor.* 270e–f; Richlin 2001, 241), whereas they wore dark mourning veils according to the late Republican antiquarian Varro (*vita pop. Rom.*, 107R: *pullae palae*; Cato in Servius, *Aen.* 3. 64). Plutarch is the only author to mention white as the colour of mourning, therefore we cannot be sure whether the mourning colour changed or not. Nevertheless, his statement underlines the general attitude; the wearing of different clothes to non-mourners, and thus inverting the usual clothing style, was still an important feature of the ritualistic display of mourning. Members of the family (slaves included), their clients and friends attended the display of the body (*collocatio*) and expressed their grief. The way in which one mourned, or was expected to mourn, differed not just according to gender but also according to social status, education, time period and place.

Women expressed their grief during the funeral ritual in a threefold way: by lamentation, the singing of dirges (*neniae*), and by crying out with sorrow (*eiulatio, lessus*). The non-discursive expressions of mourning, such as the crying out, are described as feminine practices *par excellence* (Virgil, *Aen.* 4.337–338: *femineo ululatu*; 2.487–488; on womanish wailing *cf.* Richlin 2001, 238), groaning (*gemitus*) on the other hand is associated with men (Statius, *Silv.* 2. 6. 5; Virgil, *Aen.* 6. 220; 9. 499). Lizzi and Maurin understand lamentation, a kind of oral poetry which expressed grief in stereotypic formulas, as primarily a woman's task and stress the difference in the way men and women mourned (Lizzi 1995, 49 et passim; Maurin 1984, 206: 'la lamentation des femmes et le discours des hommes'). But in literary sources describing the mourning of the common people or of a crowd, both men and women were shown to recite laments and express similar gestures of sadness: pulling the hair, scratching the cheeks till blood was flowing, beating the head and (bare) chest, falling on the earth, putting the ashes of the extinguished hearth on the head were all ritual duties (*iusta*) of mourners towards the dead (*e.g.* Apuleius, *Met.* 8. 7; Lucian, *Luct.* 12–13). The historian Tacitus underlines the uniqueness of the mourning of both sexes when Agrippina, the widow of Germanicus, arrived at Rome with the ashes of her dead husband: 'one could not distinguish the laments of the men from the women' (Tacitus, *Ann.* 3. 1. 5: ... *neque discerneres... virorum feminarumque planctus*; Corbeill 2004, 76).

The opinions of Lizzi and Maurin may be influenced by taking for granted gendered descriptions of mourning in normative discourses such as the philosophical treatises of Cicero and Seneca, who described female grief as an exaggerated and negative custom. Seneca draws a line, based on their ways of mourning, between women, barbarians, the ignorant and uneducated, and plebeians, who were 'overcome' by grief on the one hand; and men, the educated and cultured, and civilised peoples, to whom grief was less hurtful on the other hand (Seneca, *ad Marc.* 7. 3; *ad Polyb.* 6. 2). The author ascribes an overwhelming grief to women, who allowed their pain to wear them out. Cicero (*Tusc.* 2.55) stresses the importance of men's self-restraint in grief, in order to fulfill their duties and bear their pain. Wilcox (2005, 242) draws attention to Cicero's claim in a letter to his friend Titius (*Fam.* 5. 16. 6) that by indulging in excessive mourning for his sons, Titius may threaten his manhood.

Seneca and Cicero, who were both writing for elite audiences and setting up philosophically derived ideals, express contempt for mourning gestures, describing them as not dignified for men or as female misconduct. Nevertheless, in some cases men were obliged to perform these excessive gestures. At the death of the warrior Misenus in Virgil's *Aeneid* the fellow soldiers cry and exclaim loudly, especially the *pius* Aeneas who excels in mourning (6. 175–176; 6. 212–213; *cf.* 11. 41, 59). Here, Virgil reflects a rather dignified mourning, which was probably expected of a man belonging to the elite. Mark Antony, mourning the death of Julius Caesar on the *rostra*, let his tears flow to incite the vengeance of his death (Appian, *B Civ.* 2, 146; Kierdorf 1980, 102 suggests that Antony acted like a *praefica* demanding a *vendetta*). Mourning by a person of lower social status for somebody placed socially higher could be excessive; an example of this custom is reflected in Virgil's description of Acetes, the servant of Evander's son Pallas, who honoured his dead master by beating his chest, scratching his cheeks and throwing himself on the earth (*Aen.* 11. 85–87). Such an expression of the last duties (*iusta*) toward the superior was a social obligation and therefore common in hierarchical Roman society. Funerals of leading families attracted an immense number of their Italic clients to Rome, and at the funerals of members of the emperors' family all the citizens of Rome were obliged to mourn (on the funeral of Augustus, *cf.* Fraschetti 1994, 82–83).

Women's and men's gestures of mourning are shown on the relief of exposition (*collocatio*) of a matron in the family's *atrium*, which is one of the reliefs from the Haterii monument in Rome (dated between the end of the first century and the beginning of the second century AD, Lateran collection in Vatican, Toynbee 1971, pl. 9; and Fig. 8.2, this volume). The dead matron lies in state; a man standing at her side is about to adorn her with a garland like a *pollinctor* would do, on his left two women with dishevelled hair beat their breasts. They could be hired mourners or the matron's relatives. Three hunched figures sit at the head end of the bier, their hair is let down and covered with a *pileus*, a liberty cap, a sign of liberated slaves. Rich Roman men and women usually freed some of their slaves in the last will and testament to gain prestige by ostentatious display of their generosity (*cf.* Carroll, this volume). At the bottom of the relief there is a type of procession of two men and two women beating their chests, a sign of *planctus*, ritual mourning which consisted of the beating of chests, heads and thighs. This image reminded the onlooker of the clients and friends who attended the funeral procession. Here we see that both sexes performed the gestures of beating their chests in the context of a funeral for the wife of the rich freedman Haterius.

Ritual practices performed at the moment of dying

I will now describe the sequence of funeral ritual from beginning to end. According to Servius, commenting on Virgil's *Aeneid* (12. 395), a dying person was carried out of the house and laid on the ground. This gesture was the first sign of the dying person being different from the living (Scheid 1984, 119). Putting a dying person on the earth is exactly the opposite gesture to a midwife's putting a newborn baby on the ground, from where the father lifted and recognised it as his legitimate child (Ovid, *Tr.* 4. 3. 46). The symbolism of these gestures is known from Varro's description of the gods active at birth. The goddess Ops gave strength to the newborn who was considered to be taken directly out of the earth (Augustine, *De civ. D.* 4. 11). Varro stresses the symbolism of the earth at birth and death, the earth has born all people and takes them back (Varro, *L. L.*, 5. 64). Therefore putting the dying persons on the earth marked that they were about to return to where they came from. Due to the numerous parallels of women's actions in rituals of birth and death, Maurin and Corbeill see the women involved in funeral ritual as 'midwives to the dead' (Maurin 1984, 200; Corbeill 2004, 89–106). Both scholars argue that women with their gestures and attitudes escorted the dead from the land of the living and ushered the corpse into its new life.

A close female relative of the dying person pressed a kiss on his or her lips. An antiquarian explanation for this gesture was that the woman catches the breath of life which was about to leave the body. Servius (4. 685) writes that in the *Aeneid* Anna kisses her dead sister Dido, the queen of Carthage, in a woman's way (*muliebriter*), so she can catch her soul (*anima*) and transfer it into herself. Servius' statement that kissing the dying person was a woman's task is confirmed by numerous other sources, but in poetry men kiss their dying relatives too. Ovid in his *Fasti* describes Romulus as kissing his brother Remus farewell (*Fast.* 4. 851), and in Lucan's *Pharsalia* a son demands that his father gives him a last kiss (3. 735–737).

The death of a person was confirmed by the gesture of closing the eyes and calling the name of the deceased three times (Servius, *Aen.* 6. 218: *conclamatio*), the calling of the name continued during the entire funeral. In literary sources men and women perform both ritual tasks, but the number of women involved prevails (*e.g.* Ovid, *Her.* 10. 120; *Tr.* 4. 3. 44; Virgil, *Aen.* 9. 486–487; Livy 4. 40. 3). The constant repeating of scenes in Roman literature in which women kiss, hug and call their dead relatives by their names illustrates that these were women's tasks. Nevertheless, they could be performed as well by men, when the writers stress the binding force of family ties and pious relationship with the dying person.

Women's task of preparing a corpse for display (collocatio)

Female relatives of the dead were in charge of the preparations of the corpse for its display (on rites of treatment of a corpse *cf.* Noy, this volume; Graham, this volume). They washed the body with water and anointed it with scented oils, put it into clean and pure clothes, and covered it with a white funeral cloth. The body would be laid out on a funerary couch in the *atrium* of the house with its feet facing the front door. The burning of incense, lighting of torches and playing of funeral music marked the space of the funeral ritual. It was a female task to purify the corpse, women touched the dead body and regulated its passage out of the community whereas men stayed at a distance since the corpse was a source of a death-pollution (Lizzi 1995, 50–51, 58; Corbeill 2004, 106). Mustakallio (2005) argues convincingly against an assumption that the familiarity of women with death (and birth) was a sign of the low and marginal status of women. She draws attention to the high social status of Roman matrons who performed public mourning or received the ashes of the dead members of their family.

Several literary sources underline the competence of women for preparing the corpse for display. A fragment of Ennius' *Annales* (155) mentions women of a high rank (*bona*) who washed and anointed the corpse of the deceased king Tarquinius. Anna in the *Aeneid* bids servants fetch her water so she can wash out the suicide wound of her sister Dido (Virgil, *Aen.* 4. 683). Servius comments on this line saying that near relatives were allowed to wash the corpse and also makes reference to the mother of the dead Trojan soldier Euryalus, who in the ninth book of the *Aeneid*, laments her fate and speaks of the funeral tasks which she could not perform for her son (Virgil, *Aen.* 9. 486–489). The mother regrets that she could not prepare a funeral for her son, that she did not close his eyes, wash his corpse and cover it with a funeral cloth. Significantly, Euryalus' mother at the same time mentions the preparation of the body for its display and the weaving of a funeral cloth (both were considered to be traditional women's work). In several passages, Virgil describes women spinning wool when they are informed about a death in the family, and thus connects two typical female occupations in Rome, wool working and mourning. Although the mother of Euryalus speaks of these tasks as duties she has to complete for her son, Servius Danielis, in the explanation of this line, refers to *pollinctores*, the undertaker's servants (*Aen.* 9. 485; on *pollinctores cf.* Graham, this volume). According to his commentary, the *pollinctores* performed the task (*officium*) of washing the dead. Servius Danielis adds a popular etymology by deriving the name of *pollinctores* out of '*polline*', fine flour with which the face was powdered so that the bluish colour of death would not appear. Lizzi (1995, 50–51, and note 8) concluded that women washed and anointed the corpse in archaic times, but a few centuries later a *pollinctor* took over these tasks; Bodel (2004) also argues that the use of paid undertakers by the elite, at least, increased.

But even if the undertaker's servant, the *pollinctor*, prepared the corpse for display, it does not mean that men intruded into the realm of women's work. In Roman society tasks were divided into socially recognised women's and men's tasks (Maurin 1983, 141; Corbeill 2004, 74–77). One typical task of an aristocratic Roman matron, already mentioned, was the spinning of wool, attested by numerous epigraphic inscriptions honouring the matron's value as a woolworker (*CIL* VI 15346: *lanam fecit*; VI 37965; *Laudatio Turiae* 1. 30–31). But the wool working of an aristocratic Roman matron consisted of supervising her slaves. Maurin argues that the social and symbolic role of wool-work was attributed to the matron whereas her female or male slaves did the real work. The same principle of division of work applies to the task of preparing the corpse. The aristocratic family who organised a funeral in Rome hired *pollinctores* and other undertaker's specialists to perform different funerary tasks, judging by the references in Roman authors to this standard practice (Seneca, *Ep.* 99. 22, Tacitus, *Dial.* 9. 11. 10; Pliny, *HN.* 7. 176). In literary texts like Virgil's *Aeneid,* preparing the corpse was considered a task for the female relatives of the dead, whereas the *pollinctores* did the actual work for a high class Roman family in mourning. The hired undertakers performed both men's and women's tasks during the funeral ritual, their low social position as slaves did not have any effect on the gendered division of the particular tasks. In aristocratic families, women supervised the work of the *pollinctores* and in this way fulfilled their own socially recognised obligation to prepare the corpse. However men could perform this task when there were no women available, such as in Virgil's *Aeneid*, where the soldiers take care of washing and anointing the dead soldier Misenus (6. 229).

The same principle of delegation of work could be applied in the case of hired mourners and the mourning of matrons. The conclusion of Mustakallio that *praeficae* replaced the mourning of matrons of the Roman elite does not hold (Mustakallio 2005, 185). The number of *praeficae* who displayed excessive mourning in public was an important part of the ostentatious funeral ritual (*cf.* beneath) but it did not replace the mourning of matrons. As Richlin (2001, 244) correctly argues, the hired *praeficae* were stand-ins for the closest female kin. Paid undertakers performed many tasks, but the social value of their performance was attributed to the men and women of the family which organised the funeral.

Excessive female mourning in the funeral procession

In the funeral procession, actors walked with ancestral wax masks (*imagines maiorum*) of the father's and mother's and wife's or husband's dead male relatives who had held state offices (at least the office of aedile), and thus displayed publicly the honours the family had achieved (Polybius 6. 54. 3). The hired female mourners (*praeficae*) and musicians followed the masks of ancestors in the convoy walking in front of the bier, with the dead, relatives and friends following it, as is illustrated by the Amiternum relief (Toynbee 1971, pl. 11; Fig. 8.1, this volume).

In a funeral procession it was forbidden for women to mourn 'excessively'. Crying for the departed, screaming, wailing, self-mutilation and lamentations opposed Roman ideals of manhood and a citizen's self-control, since these acts invoked strong emotions and were incompatible with the ideal of the quiet life of the citizen. This was precisely the reason for repeated attempts to remove expressions of mourning from the public sphere.

The *praeficae* were hired to increase the family's mourning and to augment the prestige of the family. Their performance consisted of tearing the cheeks, singing mourning songs (*neniae*) and screaming; these codified expressions of grief were considered by ancient authors to be 'excessive'. The *praeficae* were leaders of lamentations, Paul the Deacon (250L; Richlin 2001, 243) stresses that they 'give the rest the style (or measure) for lamenting as if set in charge of this'. Horace underlines that the hired mourners lament and express the sorrow even more than the ones who mourn for real (Horace, *Ars P.* 431–2). Lamentation of *praeficae* was limited by the Law of the Twelve Tables; 'women shall not tear their cheeks nor have a *lessum*', a kind of sorrowful wailing (Cicero, *Leg.* 2. 22. 59.). These laws controlling display at noble funerals limited the dimensions of private mourning in public spaces. Cicero explains the sumptuary laws as preventing the display of the differences of wealth (*fortunae discrimen*) at funerals (Cicero, *Leg.* 2. 22. 59). Modern authors stress that the limitation of funeral expenses lay at the core of the regulations of Mediterranean *poleis* which reduced the ostentatious display of riches of the elite families and the dispensing of immense amounts of money for their funerals (Ampolo 1984; Seaford 1994, 83; Corbeill 2004, 75).

In funeral processions in ancient Rome, not only the hired mourners, but other women also scratched their cheeks and cried with sorrow; these were typical expressions of mourning (*cf.* the lamentation and laceration of the parents of the girl Psyche in Apuleius, *Met.* 4, 34 and Noy's discussion of Ovid, *Tr.*. 3.3.37–51, this volume). With reference to Varro, Servius Danielis (*Aen.* 3. 67) explains that women tear their cheeks to appease with their blood the spirits of the dead. The Twelve Tables only forbade the performance of such gestures by hired mourners since the intention of the law was the limitation of funeral expenses.

Mourning in public spaces was not stigmatised as 'female' where it did not interfere in relations of competition between particular families. When citizens and their wives mourned for emperors and their families, mourning was regarded as an expression of loyalty and support (Šterbenc Erker 2004, 285 and Šterbenc Erker 2009). The dictator Sulla was mourned by matrons for one year, as Granius Licinianus (36.27), author of a brief History of Rome (second century AD), writes; the emperor Augustus and his wife Livia also received this honour (Dio 56. 43. 1; 58, 2). In this case, the mourning consisted presumably of some exterior signs (wearing dark clothes and no jewellery). An epigraphic record of funerary honours for Augustus' adopted son Gaius Caesar in the Roman colony of Pisa gives an interesting example of the public mourning of men and women. On the day of Gaius' death (the annual *parentalia*, *cf.* below), everybody donned mourning clothes (*CIL* XI 1421, 22: *cunctos veste mutata*) and matrons adopted an attitude of 'half-mourning' (*CIL* XI 1421, 24–25: *sublugere*), which were only external signs of grief.

Men's tasks in funeral ritual: funeral eulogy, sacrifice and purifications

In private funerals, the speech for the dead was held by the graveside, outside the city. In the so called *Laudatio Turiae* (*CIL* VI 37053; *ILS* 8393) a funeral speech for a Roman matron now often called Turia, the husband of the deceased stressed her exploits and merits. The orator mentioned as one of her achievements the fact that 'Turia' took care of the blood revenge over the murderers of her parents (*Laud. Turiae* 1. 5; Thomas 1984, 69; Flach 1991, 52).

Men and women walked together in a procession (*pompa funebris*) which headed to the *forum Romanum*, if the dead person had a right to a funeral eulogy (*laudatio funebris*) as part of a public funeral, or out of the town's walls, to the family tomb, in the case of a private funeral. Only men spoke the funeral eulogy for the dead magistrates in the *forum*, and very rarely for their wives or female relatives, as Julius Caesar did for his aunt (Plutarch, *Caes.* 5; Flower 1996, 124–125). In the funeral eulogy, the orator mentioned the exploits relevant to the political community; first he described the person who was about to be buried and then spoke of his ancestors, those who had received a wax ancestor mask (*imago funebris*). The orator, a son or a relative of the dead person, commemorated the honours of the family's ancestors, their civic virtues and merits (Polybius 6. 54. 3). The orator depicted the loss of the dead person as a loss which affected the whole city. By remembering famous deeds (*exempla)* of the deceased members of the family, who were represented by the *imagines* sitting in the front of the *rostra*, the glory of the family increased from generation to generation. The *exempla* were, according to Polybius, a very important inducement for the young men of Rome to accomplish virtuous actions. The copies of these formal orations were treasured in archives by families of the Roman elite, to preserve the memory of the famous acts of the family's members and demonstrate their nobility. According to Cicero (Cicero, *Brut.* 62), these *contiones* were often false.

There was an immense contrast between the funeral speeches of men and the laments of women; in the funeral speeches men described the death as a loss for the political community whereas in laments women mourned the loss for their families. But women also expressed their grief in a public space; Cicero mentions a custom in which the singing of the mourning song (*nenia*) followed the funeral oration (Cicero, *Leg.* 2. 24. 62), in the case of a public funeral it took place in the *forum*. Ancient writers often described laments of women as flamboyant and uncontrolled (*cf.* beneath Cicero, *Tusc.* 3.62; Richlin 2001). Women praised the deceased and stressed his achievements and deeds just as men did in funeral orations, but women lamented his loss for the family and described the death as tragic through the conventional formulae of oral poetry (Seneca, *Troades* 63 ff; Fantham 1982, 221, 230, 275; Kierdorf 1980, 100–102). According to Nonius Marcellus it was a task of hired mourners to cry and praise the heroic deeds of the deceased (Nonius Marcellus 92L). The women's lamentations and mourning songs were often described in a negative way; Nonius speaks of *nenia* sang by *praeficae* as a 'vulgar and artless song' (Non. 212L: *ineptum et inconditum carmen*), Gellius refers to the voices of the *praeficae* as 'ugly, useless and inane' (*NA* 18.7.3). These pejorative remarks of Roman intellectuals reveal the rejection of the expressions of grief performed by professionals of a low status; the *praeficae* were slaves of the undertaker, or were freed women.

Cicero (*Tusc.* 3.62; Richlin 2001, 231) describes gestures of mourning (throwing ashes on oneself, scratching the cheeks as 'womanish', beating the chest, legs or head) as worthy of contempt, and censures these nonverbal forms of grief. Instead, he stresses a strong will and the philosophical decision not to let grief or sadness touch the soul, reasoning that there is no use in mourning. In their ethical writings, Cicero and Seneca ascribe to women excessive, out-of-control mourning, while it was becoming for a man to mourn with dignity and self-discipline. Corbeill (2004, 76) draws attention to the dichotomy between the emotional control in men and the uncontrolled display of women as being a distinction that bears on moral evaluations of mourning. The description of mourning gestures as excessive female practices was therefore a way to express a negative judgement from the perspective of the Roman upper-class philosophically derived morals in which male virtues played a central part. This was probably a consequence of the mourning customs which connected lamentations with a call for vengeance for a person who had been murdered (on demands for vengeance in lamentations in ancient Greece *cf.* Holst–Warhaft 1992, for Rome see Thomas 1984 and Šterbenc Erker 2004, 273–279). In 52 BC, Fulvia mourned her dead husband Clodius who was murdered after a fight between his gang and that of his political opponent Milo on the Via Appia. Asconius in his commentary to Cicero's speech *Pro Milone* (28.21) mentions Fulvia's tearful mourning over the body of her husband in the *atrium* of their house; she displayed his bleeding wounds to her husband's followers, thus increasing the outrage against Milo. By performing the mourning ritual, Fulvia successfully incited the followers to acts of revenge (*cf.* Fraschetti 1994, 64).

Carrying the bier and setting the funeral pyre on fire were tasks for men. Servius writes in his commentary on Misenus' funeral that according to the custom of the ancestors, male relatives of the dead performed this role (*Aen.* 6. 223; *cf.* Maurin 1984, 195). Metellus Macedonicus' bier was carried by his four sons, Pliny (*HN* 7. 142) remarks that one of them was praetor and the others had been censors or consuls; in this case the family could display the high honours that the descendants of the dead had obtained. The procession of mourners headed to the family tomb. Both men and women put pieces of sacrificial meat, vases with oil, ornaments, clothes, and precious objects on the funeral pyre if the body was to be cremated or in the grave if the body was to be inhumed (Virgil, *Aen.* 6. 221–225; Servius, *Aen.* 6. 225; Suetonius, *Iul.* 84,4). The sumptuary laws of the Twelve Tables limited the offerings to the dead to three veils and a purple tunic (Cicero, *Leg.* 2. 23. 59) in order to restrict the display of the wealth of the family. The heir sacrificed a sow to the goddess Ceres as well as wethers to the family's Lares (Cicero, *Leg.* 2. 22. 55; Latte 1960, 102; Maurin 1984, 206). Separate offerings were directed at the *di Manes* and at members of the family of the deceased and his friends. It was very important that the living did not eat the offerings consecrated to the dead. Festus-Paulus explains, in the aetiology of the *ludi Tarentini,* that women who ate meat consecrated to the gods of the underworld had born dead babies (Paulus 479L). At funerals, the offerings to the *di Manes* were consecrated and offered first, and after this the sacrificial meal for the living was prepared (Scheid 2005, 18; Scheid 1984, 134ff). The division between the food for the living and food for the dead reinforced the imaginary boundary between the realms of life and death.

Sharing a meal at a common table was a way of expressing affiliation with the community and solidarity among its members (*cf.* Detienne 1979, 10). Men and women ate funeral banquets together at the tomb, thus accompanying the dead to his or her future dwelling and purifying themselves of the death-pollution. Paul the Deacon writes explicitly that the funeral meal (*silicernium*), which consisted of a sausage, purified the family of weeping (Paulus 377L; Nonius 68L). This sacrificial meal was just one of several ritual acts which purified the mourning family. Festus (296–298L) mentions a note by Varro's contemporary Veranius Flaccus which mentioned the sacrifice of a sow to the goddess Ceres. This expiatory sacrifice was to take place in the presence of the deceased (the literal meaning of *porca praesentanea* is a 'sow-in-presence') and was aimed at purifying the mourning family. Scheid (2005, 170–174) argues convincingly that the mourners ate the meat of the *porca praesentanea* at the *silicernium*. It is also possible that the goddess Tellus was an addressee of this offering because an heir had to sacrifice both to Tellus and Ceres similar offerings, a 'preliminary' sow (*porca praecidanea*). This expiatory sacrifice (*piaculum*) cleansed the family of death-pollution when a dead person was not buried at all or when any omissions and errors had occurred at funerals held during the last year (Varro, *vita pop. Rom.* 104R; *cf.* Gellius, *NA* 4. 6. 8). After nine days of mourning, during which men and women of the family of the deceased had to cease their usual activities, another meal at the grave, the nine-day feast (*cena novemdialis* or *novemdiale sacrificium*; Porphyry, *Epod. Hor*. 17. 48), and funeral libations (Petronius, *Sat.* 65) to the deceased concluded the period of mourning for the male relatives. Again both sexes took part in the funeral banquet; men and women poured libations to the *di Manes*, the gods or spirits of the dead, in order to mark and reinforce the separation between the world of the living and the world of the dead.

The sacrifice of the sow to Ceres was only one of several purification rites on the day of the burial. Before the pyre burnt down, the participants of the funeral who were not relatives of the dead were permitted to leave. It was a man's task to cleanse them of the defilement of the death. At Misenus' funeral in the *Aeneid* Corynaeus encircled the crowd gathered at the funeral pyre three times, holding an olive branch in hand, sprinkling each person with water and pronouncing the farewell words, *novissima verba* (6. 229–232). Servius explains the expression by a reference to the word *ilicet,* 'you can go' (*ire licet*) which gives the purification of the death-pollution a performative value (on performative value of ritual gestures and words *cf.* Tambiah 1979). According to the commentator of the *Aeneid* the mourners were cleansed of the death-pollution by encircling, therefore he equates the encircling with purification. Paul the Deacon names this purification *suffitio*: 'on return from the funeral those who had participated in the funeral had to step over the fire and were sprinkled with water' (Paulus 3L).

The members of the family had to wait at the pyre till it burnt down, then women gathered the remaining bones as Ovid orders his wife to do at his funeral (*Tr.* 3. 65–70). Pseudo-Tibullus imagines that at his own funeral his mistress Neaera, with her mother, will collect his bones, put them in an urn, sprinkle them with wine, strew them with scented powders and place the urn in the tomb (Ps. Tibullus 3. 2. 9–25). Both poets describe women who perform these ritual tasks as being very close to the deceased (a wife, a mistress), therefore it seems that the gathering of the remains after the cremation was a way of expressing love and loyalty to the dead person. During the funeral of the emperor Augustus, it was his wife Livia, as well as young representatives of the equestrian order (*primores equestris ordinis*), who collected his bones and put them into the Mausoleum (Dio 56. 42. 4; Suetonius *Aug.* 100). Livia, although being the widow of the dead emperor, did not represent the community of citizens of Rome who mourned Augustus and she was therefore accompanied by young equestrians.

Varro and Cicero point to the important purification rite of the inhumation of the deceased's bones. When the deceased was cremated, one of his bones, usually a finger, was cut (*os ressectum*) and laid in the earth. If this rite was not performed, the family was still considered to be death-polluted (Varro, *L L* 5. 23: *familia funesta*) and the place where the deceased was cremated did not have a sacred (*religio*) character (Cicero, *Leg.* 2. 22. 57). The obligation to cast earth on the *os ressectum* is a further example which shows that Roman funeral norms were concerned with purification of the mourning family.

When the mourning family returned home, an heir had to perform a symbolic 'cleansing' (*purgatio*) of the house of the dead by sweeping it with a special sort of broom. This person was called in this context *everriator* (Paulus 68L), from *extra verrere*, to sweep out. According to Paul the Deacon, failure to perform this, or any other ritual faults, was to be expiated by death, presumably by the sacrifice of an animal. Sacrifice and libations to the *di Manes* as well as several purification rites put an end to the mourning of the male members of the family. Male relatives of the family were purified of the death-pollution which meant they could return to their daily tasks whereas women continued their mourning.

Women's task of prolonged mourning after the funeral

According to legend, Numa, the Roman king and law-giver, set a maximum period of mourning, allowing women to mourn their fathers and husbands for up to ten months (Plutarch, *Numa* 12. 3; Seneca, *Ep.* 63.13; Paulus, *Opinions* 1. 21.2–5, Corbeill 2004, 76). Plutarch mentions this law, saying it was not necessary to mourn for children younger than three years, and older children should be mourned for one month for each year lived, but no longer than ten months. The same custom regulated the problem of children born after the father's death, since widows were prohibited to remarry within the ten months after the husband's death. The custom did not become obsolete after the Augustan period as Humbert (1972, 117ff) has argued; on the contrary, it was observed up to the second century AD. In addition to the evidence given by Plutarch and Paulus, a story in Apuleius' *Metamorphoses* confirms that the rule of ten months of mourning remained in place during the second century AD. A widow does not want to remarry before the mourning time of a year is over because she wants to keep her own honour and fears that the enraged *di Manes* of her late husband will harm her new husband (Apuleius, *Met.* 8. 9). The widow refers to an even longer period of mourning than Numa's laws indicate, which limited the mourning to ten months; this feature probably reflects a personal decision which could have been made without concern for the limits set by ancient law.

It was principally a women's task to carry on with mourning after the funeral ritual. Seneca (*Ep.* 63. 13) writes that in the case of men no rules are laid down because to mourn at all is not regarded as honourable. But men who were not bound to such upper-class norms could prolong their mourning after the *cena novemdialis*, and decide for themselves how long they would mourn. Aulus Gellius mentions an actor who prolonged the mourning for his deceased son (*NA* 6. 5. 4) and in an inscription from Rome, a widowed husband says in a poem he will mourn for his wife until he dies (*CIL* VI 15546, line 16). These two texts also refer to individual decisions which did not take into account upper-class morality condemning the prolonged mourning of men.

The period of mourning for women, following the so-called law of Numa, took ten months, which, according to Roman scholars, corresponded to one year in the reckoning of time under the rule of the kings (Ovid, *Fast.* 1. 33–6, 3.133–4; Rüpke 1995, 192–202). Women performed this ritual duty on behalf of the whole family thus enabling men to participate fully in religious and public activities which could not be performed while mourning. Tacitus in the *Germania* describes Germanic customs using distinctly Roman values and reveals the significance of prolonged female mourning. Tacitus states that mourning was appropriate for German women when keeping the memory (*memoria*) of the deceased (*Germ.* 27. 2), thus confirming Roman traditions.

Festivals of commemoration of the dead (Parentalia)

The private rites of the cult of the dead (*Parentalia*) were performed on the anniversary of the death and during the *Parentalia* in February. In private circles, both men and women commemorated the anniversaries of the death of family members by sacrificing animals and bringing offerings to the tombs. These offerings were supposed to placate the *di Manes*, the 'good' gods of the ancestors. Women performed sacrifices only on their own behalf, whereas men could represent the whole family or the political community. Andromacha in Virgil's *Aeneid* (3. 303–305) offers a sacrificial feast (*dapes*) at the grave of her husband and son in her own name in order to commemorate their death. On the other hand, the heir of the dead person or the *pater familias* performed the funeral sacrifices in the name of the whole family (Cicero, *Leg.* 2. 19. 48).

During private festivals of *Parentalia* a close relationship between the celebrants and the dead was established. This close contact is confirmed by Ovid in his depiction of Anna who is about to carry out the rites of *Parentalia* for her sister Dido. Anna weeps over the urn containing her sister's ashes, pours perfumed oils and puts a curl of her hair on the urn, saying farewell three times and kissing the urn (Ovid, *Fast.* 3. 560–564). Although she touches the urn there is no sign of death-pollution; after the corpse was burnt on a pyre, the remaining bones were pure.

The entire city of Rome commemorated the dead ancestors at the festival *Parentalia* in February. According to Macrobius it was necessary to cleanse the *res publica* in February and to carry out duties (*iusta*) for the *di Manes* (Macrobius, *Sat.* 1. 13. 3). The *Parentalia* started on the Ides of February (13th) at noon, when a public priestess, probably the Great Vestal Virgin, offered a funeral libation on the 'tomb' of the Roman heroine Tarpeia on the Capitol (Philocalus' calender, *CIL* I^2, 309, notifies: *Virgo Vesta<lis> parentat*; Lydos, *men.* 4. 24; Scullard 1981, 75). However, this was not a typical woman's task, Vestals were public priestesses and had a special sexual status (Beard 1980 and 1995). For the whole week of the *Parentalia* (13th–21st February) Roman magistrates set aside the 'official' clothes with the marks of their social rank and wore plain, 'civil' clothes, the temples were closed and no public business could be dealt with. Magistrates thus signalled the private character of their existence during these festive days. The suspension of public affairs had a structural similarity with a week of mourning (*feriae denicales*) in the private cult of the dead. The *Parentalia* ended on February the 21st, when all families brought small gifts to the tombs of their ancestors on a festival called *Feralia*. Ovid in his *Fasti* gives a short description of the rites of the *Feralia* which placated the *di Manes*, and their aetiologies (Ovid, *Fast.* 2. 533–570; Šterbenc Erker 2008, 10–15).

According to Mommsen and Wissowa there was a parallel rite of public *parentatio* held on December the 23rd. This day was consecrated to Jupiter like the Ides of February, the opening day of the *Parentalia* in February. The Flamen Quirinalis offered funeral libations (*Parentalia*) in the name of the Roman community at the tomb of Larentia in Velabrum (Paulus 91L, 106L; Augustine, *De civ.* D. 6. 7). There are some similarities between the *parentationes* in February and December; they were both performed by two members of the pontifical college, the Great Vestal and the Flamen Quirinalis. Further, the funeral libations were poured in the name of the whole city of Rome on the tombs of the mythical female ancestors.

Festus writing on sacrifices which were performed for the dead probably points to the funeral libation to Larentia and Tarpeia as a kind of a hero cult (Paulus 91L; Bömer 1943, 78, n. 2 *contra* Wissowa 1912, 235). The aetiological stories about both heroines stress the ambivalent character of these two women in the mythological history of Rome (Šterbenc-Erker 2008, 15–17). The annalistic tradition hesitates between describing them as traitors or saviours of the Roman cause. In the legend of the Sabines besieging the Capitol, Tarpeia opened the door to the enemy and demanded that they give her what they wore on their left arms. Some annalists assumed that Tarpeia wanted golden bracelets, others assumed that she wanted to cheat the enemy's soldiers, demanding as a reward for her favour their shields and weapons, which the Sabines carried on their left arms (Dionysius Halicarnassus, *Ant. Rom.* 2. 40. 2–3 reports on both traditions).

Gellius (*NA* 7. 7) writes about two different versions of the legendary Larentia; Acca Larentia was a prostitute and Hercules' lover; she legated her immense fortune to the people of Rome. Nevertheless, a funeral libation on Larentia's grave was also supposed to keep the memory of Larentia who nourished the abandoned twins Romulus and Remus (Ovid, *Fast.* 3. 55–58). In both cases, ancient historians find it difficult to decide if Larentia and Tarpeia were honoured by public libations for their bad character or good deeds for the people of Rome. Legends of mythical women express the fact that in Roman mythological history, important deeds were performed by men and women. The libations poured on the tombs of mythical heroines, and their antiquarian interpretation, testify to the importance of women who could represent the ancestors of the city of Rome in a public cult, a striking feature in a patriarchical society. In contrast to the texts on politics, antiquarian writings stress the importance of the mythical heroines and depict them as at the core of the society's thinking about the Roman past.

Conclusion

In general the performance of excessive gestures of mourning, like beating the chest or pulling the hair, were considered women's work. References to men's and women's roles in literary texts reveal an ideal model of thinking and acting according to tradition. The gender norms of mourning within the ancient sources were influenced by ideals derived from philosophy within the Roman elite. It was women's work to be in closer contact with the dead and to mourn excessively; these practices enabled men to stay at a distance and to take part in public affairs. This idealised gendered division of tasks was very important in normative discourses. Nevertheless, these normative discourses were not strictly binding in everyday life; men could transgress the realms of men's tasks and accomplish women's tasks, especially mourning gestures. Generally, it can be stated that the social position determined the way in which a person mourned; a client performed a more exaggerated mourning at the funeral of his patron then a patron for his client. The way in which one mourned, or was expected to mourn, differed not just according to gender but also according to social status, education, time period and place.

Men's funeral orations as well as women's lamentations and mourning kept alive the memory of the deceased. In funeral orations men reminded the audience of the famous acts of the deceased and the nobility of the family, whereas women reminded the audience of the loss to their families. When a person was murdered, women used their ritual control of lamentation and incited the mourners to avenge the dead. The case of Fulvia, the widow of Clodius', shows that the mourning of matrons was a source of their ritual and social power.

The description of mourning depends on the perspective the sources take. When they mention prohibitions of female mourning, the sources usually stress the evils of this practice for the *res publica*, and when they approve of it, they see it as a social duty towards emperors or statesmen. Sources on funerals of Roman emperors, and members of their families, testify to mourning by men and women, especially matrons, being expected and encouraged. Exterior signs of mourning were, as in the case of the matrons one year's mourning for Sulla, Augustus and Livia, an important expression of loyalty. At the end of the Republic and under the Empire, matrons had this important social obligation towards the ruling family. Before this time, matrons mourned the dead members of their family, therefore their ritual and social power was limited to the private circle and to the *pompa funebris*. Under the emperors, matrons became subjects of mourning obligations outside their family, which underlines the growth of their social power.

Antiquarians stress that men were responsible for the ritual purification of the participants of the funeral and of the house of the dead. They speak therefore of a gendered division of purification tasks, men performing gestures of sweeping and sprinkling water which enabled the participants or objects (the house of the dead) to leave the context of the funeral and re-integrate into normal society, while women, on the other hand, had close contact with the remains of the dead, touching the corpse.

Anniversaries of the dead (*Parentalia*) and the festival of *Parentalia* in February revived the memory of the deceased ancestors. In a private context, women were responsible for the *Parentalia* on their own behalf, whereas men performed the funeral sacrifices in the name of the whole family, and in public funerals in the name of the political community. Women played an active part in public offerings of the *Parentalia* only as Vestal Virgins. Nevertheless, the implication of the feminine element in public rituals was reaffirmed by the addressees of the public *Parentalia*: among the *di Manes*, the indefinite mass of the gods of ancestors, there were in Tarpeia and Larentia two women who were honoured with funeral libations.

The norms and regulations of Roman funeral rites changed over time. Their archaic meanings were reflected upon in antiquarian texts and given a new significance; the funeral rites changed but did not decline in general. Antiquarians who believe their work to be saving the ancient Roman traditions refer in the first place to the texts of Republican antiquarians like Varro and Cato. Only after referring to traditional knowledge do they mention how the rites and their meanings changed in their own time. Because of this literary practice we cannot conclude that the funeral rites, norms and regulations were no longer understood under the Empire, as Cumont and his followers assert. Authors in the fourth century AD still reflected on Roman funeral rites, rendered their aetiologies, and drew attention to gendered tasks. Their main preoccupation was to rescue and reconstruct a Roman way of life, Roman gods, rituals and cults. In a broader sense they were constructing and re-constructing the Roman identity. The representations of women's and men's work in rituals lay at the core of the question of what it meant to be Roman.

Acknowledgements

I would like to thank Valerie Hope and Janet Huskinson for inviting me to contribute to this volume, their suggestions and improvements of my text. Special thanks to both editors, Elisabeth Begemann and Gwynaeth McIntyre for correcting my English. Some of this material has previously appeared in my Ph.D. thesis, published in Slovenian (Quid lacrimis, */*cf.* Ljubljana 2002); this paper was presented at a congress organised by Barbara Scardigli (University of Sienna) in Pontignano, its final version was written during my research year supported by a fellowship of TOPOI, Berlin.

Bibilography

Ampolo, C. (1984) Il lusso funerario e la città arcaica. *Annalli dell'Istituto universitario orientale di Napoli, Dipartimento di studi del mondo classico, Sezione di archeologia e storia antica* 6, 71–102.

Beard, M. (1980) The sexual status of Vestal Virgins. *Journal of Roman Studies* 70, 12–27.

Beard, M. (1995) Re-reading (Vestal) virginity. In R. Hawley, and B. Levick (eds) *Women in Antiquity*, 166–77. London and New York, Routledge.

Beard, M., North, J. and Price, S. (1998) *Religions of Rome 1; A History.* Cambridge, Cambridge University Press.

Bendlin, A. (2007) Purity and pollution. In D. Ogden (ed.) *The Blackwell Companion to Greek Religion*, 178–189. Oxford, Blackwell.

Bodel, J. (2004) The organisation of the funerary trade at Puteoli and Cumae. In S. Panciera (ed.), *Libitina e Dintorni: Atti dell' XI Rencontre franco-italienne sur l'épigraphie (Libitina, 3)*, 149–70, Rome, Quasar.

Bömer, F. (1943) *Ahnenkult und Ahnenglaube im alten Rom.* Leipzig and Berlin, Teubner.

Corbeill, A. (2004) *Nature Embodied: Gesture in Ancient Rome.* Princeton, Princeton University Press.

Cumont, F. (1949) *Lux Perpetua.* Paris, P. Geuthner.

Detienne, M. (1979) Pratiques culinaires et esprit de sacrifice. In M. Detienne, J.-P. Vernant *et al.* (eds) *La cuisine du sacrifice en pays grec*, 7–35. Paris, Gallimard.

Douglas, M. (1966) *Purity and Danger. An Analysis of the Concepts of Pollution and Taboo*, London, Routledge.

Dumont, J.-Ch. (1995) L'enlèvement du cadavre. In F. Hinard (ed.) *La mort au quotidien dans le monde romain.* Actes du colloque organisé par l'Université de Paris IV (Paris-Sorbonne 7–9 octobre 1993), avec la collaboration de M.-F. Lambert, 181–188. Paris, Boccard.

Fantham, E. (1982) *Seneca's Troades. A Literary Introduction with Text, Translation and Commentary.* Princeton, New Jersey, Princeton University Press.

Flach, Dieter 1991. *Die sogenannte Laudatio Turiae. Einleitung, Text, Übersetzung und Kommentar.* Darmstadt, Wissenschaftliche Buchgesellschaft.

Flower, H. I. (1996) *Ancestor Masks and Aristocratic Power in Roman Culture.* Oxford, Clarendon Press.

Fraschetti, A. (1994) *Rome et le prince.* Paris, Belin.

Holst–Warhaft, G. (1992) *Dangerous Voices. Women's Laments and Greek Literature.* London, and New York, Routledge.

Humbert, M. (1972) *Le remariage à Rome; étude d'histoire juridique et sociale.* Milano, Giuffrè.

Kierdorf, W. (1980) Laudatio funebris. Interpretationen und Untersuchungen zur Entwicklung der römischen Leichenrede. Meisenheim am Glan, Hain.

Latte, K. (1960) *Römische Religionsgeschichte.* Münich, Beck.

Lindsay, H. (2000) Death-pollution and funerals in the city of Rome. In V. Hope and E. Marshall (eds) *Death and Disease in the Ancient City*, 152–173. London and New York, Routledge.

Lizzi, R. (1995) Il sesso e i morti. In F. Hinard (ed.) *La mort au quotidien dans le monde romain.* Actes du colloque organisé par l'Université de Paris IV (Paris-Sorbonne 7–9 octobre 1993), avec la collaboration de M.-F. Lambert, 49–68. Paris, Boccard.

Maurin, J. (1983) *Labor matronalis*; aspects du travail féminin à Rome. In E. Lévy (ed.) *La femme dans les sociétés antiques*, 139–154. Strasbourg, Aecr.

Maurin, J. (1984) Funus et rites de séparation. *Annalli dell'Istituto universitario orientale di Napoli, Dipartimento di studi del mondo classico, Sezione di archeologia e storia antica* 6, 191–208.

Moatti, C. 1997. *La raison de Rome. Naissance de l'esprit critique à la fin de la République.* Paris, Seuil.

Mustakallio, K. (2005) Roman funerals: identity, gender and participation. In K. Mustakallio, J. Hansks, H-L. Sanio and V. Vuolanto (eds), *Hoping for Continuity. Childhood, Education and Death in Antiquity and the Middle Ages* (Acta Instituti Romani Finlandiae 33). Rome, Institutum Romanum Finlandiae.

Richlin, A. (2001) Emotional work: lamenting the Roman dead. In E. Tywalsky and C. Weiss (eds), *Essays in Honor of Gordon Williams. Twenty-five Years at Yale,* 229–48. New Haven, Schwab.

Rüpke, J. (1995) *Kalender und Öffentlichkeit. Die Geschichte der Repräsentation und religiösen Qualifikation von Zeit in Rom.* Berlin and New York, Walter de Gruyter.

Scheid, J. (1984) *Contraria facere*: renversements et déplacements dans les rites funéraires. *Annalli dell'Istituto universitario orientale di Napoli, Dipartimento di studi del mondo classico, Sezione di archeologia e storia antica* 6, 119–132.

Scheid, J. (1998) *La religion des Romains.* Paris, Collin.

Scheid, J. (2005) *Quand faire, c'est croire. Les rites sacrificiels des Romains,* Paris, Aubier.

Scullard, H. H. (1981) *Festivals and Ceremonies of the Roman Republic.* London, Thames and Hudson.

Seaford, R. (1994) *Reciprocity and Ritual, Homer and Tragedy in the Developing City-State.* Oxford, Clarendon Press.

Šterbenc Erker, D. (2004) Voix dangereuses et force des larmes; le deuil féminin dans la Rome antique. *Revue de l'histoire des religions,* 221, 3, 259–291.

Šterbenc Erker, D. (2008) Der römische Totenkult und die Argei-Feier bei Ovid und Dionysios von Halikarnass. In J. Rüpke and J. Scheid (eds) *Bestattungsrituale und Totenkult/Rites funéraires et culte des morts: Regional differences, translocal exchange, imperial trends,*, 9–21, 11–23. Stuttgart, Steiner.

Šterbenc Erker, D. (2009) Women's tears in ancient Roman ritual. In T. Fögen (ed.) *Tears in the Graeco-Roman World,* 135–160. Berlin, New York, Walter de Gruyter.

Tambiah, S. J. (1979) A performative approach to ritual. *Proceedings of the British Academy* 65, 116–142.

Thomas, Y. (1984) Se venger au Forum. Solidarité familiale et procès criminel à Rome (premier siècle av.–deuxième siècle ap. J. C.) In R. Verdier and J. P. Poly (eds) *La vengeance; vengeance, pouvoirs et idéologies dans quelques civilisations de l'Antiquité,* 65–100. Paris, Cujas.

Toynbee, J. M. C. (1971) *Death and Burial in The Roman World.* London, Thames and Hudson.

Wallace-Hadrill, A. (2005) *Mutatas formas*: the Augustan transformations of Roman knowledge. In K. Galinsky (ed.) *The Cambridge Companion to the Age of Augustus,* 55–84. Cambridge, Cambridge University Press.

Wilcox, A. (2005) Sympathetic rivals; consolation in Cicero's letters. *American Journal of Philology* 126, 237–255.

Wissowa, G. (1912) *Religion und Kultus der Römer.* Münich, Beck 2nd edition.

4

Death Ritual and Burial Practice in the Latin Love Elegists

Luke B. T. Houghton

The spectre of death stalks the pages of Latin love poetry: its approach is silent, relentless, implacable (Tibullus 1.10.33–4); it comes to both prince and pauper, to conqueror and captive – in the barque of Charon, Marius sits beside Jugurtha, while Croesus rubs shoulders with the Homeric beggar Irus (Propertius 3.5.13–18). Not wealth, not beauty, not valour can procure exemption from that one eternal night; even the man who bars death's way with iron and with bronze will sooner or later be dragged out head-first from his refuge (Propertius 3.18.25–9). It is a path all must travel, from an emperor's heir and nephew (Propertius 3.18) to a girlfriend's dead sparrow (Catullus 3): for us, warns Catullus, when once our brief light has set, there remains nothing but a single everlasting sleep (5.5–6). And when the elegist has finished moping forlornly outside his mistress' door, or picturing the daily routine of his eroticised rural utopia, or brushing up against his latest object of fancy on the racetrack terraces – indeed, very often before he has finished doing these things – there is little he likes more than envisaging the conduct of his funeral and the place and manner of his burial (Tibullus 1.1.59–68, 1.3.5–10; Propertius 1.17.19–24, 2.13.17–42, 3.16.21–30; Ovid, *Am.* 2.10.35–8).[1]

This profusion of funerary material, combined with the apparent relish with which the lover-poets of elegy savour the details of their imagined obsequies, has made these descriptions a fertile quarry for historians of Roman culture seeking evidence for contemporary death ritual and funeral practice. In a piece on death in Augustan poetry, published in a French volume on death, the dead and the afterlife in the Roman world, Albert Foulon (1987, 355) remarks that 'in this domain above all, literature closely reflects reality, and historians can glean from Tibullus and Propertius more than one pointer for a better understanding of the *pompa funebris*'; and consultation of the references in Édouard Cuq's immensely learned entry for 'funus (Rome)' in Daremberg and Saglio's *Dictionnaire des antiquités grecques et romaines* reveals that Foulon is by no means the first to have held this view.[2] The impression is reinforced by the tendency of commentators (on Propertius especially) to cite parallel passages for the elegists' treatment of funerary ritual primarily – sometimes exclusively – from other elegiac texts, which may demonstrate a consistency in outlook within a single poet's *œuvre*, or between two or more practitioners of the same genre, but does not in itself indicate a shared reliance on any historical reality.

In what follows I shall argue that such an approach is not wholly misguided – for there are indeed reflections of contemporary burial and mourning rituals to be found in the corpus of Latin love elegy, though usually at several removes from their original Roman context; but this material must be handled with extreme caution in attempting to reconstruct practices that might have been observed by the poets' contemporaries in the streets of Rome. It has long been recognised that, to quote Jean-Paul Boucher (1965, 70; see also 67, 71–4), 'a study of the place of death in the elegiac genre is unrepresentative if it does not take account of the original Roman setting'. But an acknowledgement of the importance of this historical setting for a proper social, political and material contextualisation of the genre does not entail the conclusion that elegy provides its readers with a straightforward and reliable reflection of Roman reality (so Guillemin 1940, 108: 'It is...indeed the reflection of life that the mirror of elegy gives back to us'). As we shall see, elegiac evocations of death do not simply mirror the practices of their time, and when details of contemporary usages are invoked, they tend rather to be set up as a foil, to draw attention to the elegists' divergence from accepted norms (for inversion of such norms as a feature of accounts of funerary rituals and traditions in Roman literature generally, see Hope 2007, 94, with references). In other words, the *modus operandi* of the literary critic must be the reverse of that of social historians who comb the texts of the elegists for nuggets of funerary history: we must proceed from what can be surmised about the standard features of Roman funerary custom[3] to see how such material is transmuted into the stuff of poetry, rather than relying on the elegists' own funeral fancies to form an impression of contemporary observances. It is only against the ballast of external evidence, not susceptible to manipulation at the hands of the poet (though often subject to other kinds of distortion!), that we can perceive the habitual inversion of reality observed by Paolo Fedeli (1989, 89) as characteristic of the world of elegy.

In a number of cases, this discrepancy between elegiac fantasy and conventional Roman ritual, and the underlying manipulation of the reader's familiarity with the latter to reinforce the distinctive emphases of the former, has already been amply documented. More than forty years ago L. P. Wilkinson (1966) identified the speaker's preference for small-scale burial rites (*plebei parvae funeris exsequiae*, 24) in Propertius 2.13 as an intimation of the elegist's allegiance to the miniaturist aesthetic of Callimachus (see also Heyworth 1992; Papanghelis 1987, 51–2, 75); and the lover's description of the 'plebeian' funeral he desires is surely very different from the fate which awaited the poorest classes at Rome, unceremonious disposal in the impersonal and unhygienic *puticuli* (see most recently Graham 2007; also Hopkins 1983, 207–11; Cuq 1896, 1392 with nn.24–5, 1397, 1403 with n.26; Carroll 2006, 75–6; Toynbee 1971, 49; Griffin 1985, 150; Rawson 2003, 338). This, in combination with the suggestions of eroticism in Propertius' specification that Cynthia should follow his cortège tearing her naked breasts (27) and plant kisses on his unresponding lips (29: see Papanghelis 1987, 64; Lyne 1998, 536–7 [= 2007, 271–4]; Griffin 1985, 148–9), makes for a singularly unorthodox display of Roman mourning (though for beating bared breasts, see Corbeill 2004, 88 with fig.12, and further refs. n.91). The funeral tableau of 2.13 might even be seen as the purest distillation of the ideals of the Propertian lover-poet – love, literature (of a specifically 'neoteric'/Alexandrian variety: *libelli* [25] recalls Catullus 1), repudiation of wealth (*e.g.* Propertius 1.14, 2.16) and of ancestry (Propertius 1.5.23–4, 2.34.55–6), and the exclusive devotion of the elegiac 'slave' to his single passion (in the epitaph at 35–6). The prominent appearance of these same themes earlier in the poem,[4] as well as in the highly programmatic 2.34, reinforces the impression of the elegist's anticipated funeral as a *mise-en-abyme* of Propertian elegiac values.

Likewise in Propertius 3.16, the lover's desire for separation from the *vulgus* in death as in life – in calculated opposition to common commemorative practice, which created 'streets of tombs' along the thoroughfares leading out of the city (see von Hesberg and Zanker 1987, esp. Purcell 1987; von Hesberg 1994, 38–55; Koortbojian 1996, esp. 231–3; Carroll 2006, 1–3, 48–50) – reflects not only the stance of social separatism consistently advocated by the champion of *nequitia*, but also the poet's distaste for the well-trodden path condemned by Callimachus in the prologue to his *Aetia* (Lyne 1980, 136–7; La Penna 1977, 161):

quod si certa meos sequerentur funera casus,
    talis mors pretio vel sit emenda mihi.
afferet haec unguenta mihi sertisque sepulcrum
    ornabit, custos ad mea busta sedens.
di faciant mea ne terra locet ossa frequenti
    qua facit assiduo tramite vulgus iter.
post mortem tumuli sic infamantur amantum.
    me tegat arborea devia terra coma,
aut humer ignotae cumulis vallatus harenae.
    non iuvat in media nomen habere via.

But if a particular funeral were to follow my fall, such a death would even be worth my buying it for a price. She'll bring me ointments and adorn my tomb with garlands, sitting as guardian at my pyre. Gods grant that she not set my bones in well-travelled ground, where the mob goes its way on a constant track – that's how lovers' mounds are profaned after their death. Let secluded ground cover me with a tree's foliage, or let me be buried hemmed in by heaps of unknown sand: I've no pleasure in having my name in the middle of the road.

The elegist is known not only by the location of his *domus aeterna*, but also by its form and by those who visit it. Cynthia's presence at the grave as guardian (*custos*, 24) is not the least part of its attraction for the lover-poet: so optimistic, indeed, is Propertius' vision of his posthumous rehabilitation in her affections that, so far from posting a *custos* to prevent her lover's access to her, as she did when he was alive (see *e.g.* 2.23.9–10,

14), Cynthia will actually serve as his *custos* herself! Moreover, her usurpation of duties conventionally performed for the departed by family members (for offerings of perfume and garlands at the tomb [23–4], see Lattimore 1962, 134 with n.325, 135–6; Cumont 1949, 44–8) indicates that the company kept by Propertius – or at least by his surrogate monument – after death is to be understood as part of his identity as much as it was in life (see below on Propertius 2.24B.35–8).

These passages will be familiar to any student of Latin poetry, and their divergence from what can be conjectured about contemporary Roman norms is readily apparent from even a limited acquaintance with attempts to reconstruct ancient funerary practice. What I hope to demonstrate here is that this use of funerary ritual as a vehicle for adumbrating poetic and political stances forms a deeper and more persistent current in the genre of love elegy than has previously been observed – to the point where, for reasons I shall hint at later on, these mortuary tableaux offer the fullest realisation of the elegists' distinctive conceptions of the meaning and value of life and art.

The alliance of literary self-definition with opposition to (particularly aristocratic) social convention highlighted in Propertius 2.13 permeates the poet's dealings with death. Near the start of his *œuvre*, Propertius gnomically declares to a rival of higher birth, *nec tibi nobilitas poterit succurrere amanti: | nescit Amor priscis cedere imaginibus* ('nor will your office-holding background help you when you're in love: | Love doesn't know how to make way for ancient ancestor-masks', 1.5.23–4). The *imagines*, which by this time had come to stand as an embodiment of aristocratic values founded on political and military attainment, were wax portrait masks kept in the *atria* of leading Roman families, from where they were brought out and worn in the funeral cortèges of the descendants of those depicted.[5] Although Propertius' use of the term here may mean no more than 'ancestors' in the sense of 'pedigree' (for this general application, see Flower 1996, 32 with n.1), it is tempting to see in the phrase *priscis cedere imaginibus* a more vivid picture of moving aside to let the *imagines* pass on their way in the funeral procession: Amor will not give way before an aristocratic cortège. Propertius' more general disdain for good breeding (see *e.g.* 2.13.10) is here focused graphically upon the specific, concrete picture of the funeral train, as in his rejection of such *imagines* for his own cortège at 2.13.19. Richardson's comment (*ad loc.*), that Propertius would not 'dare refuse his ancestors their honoured place in his funeral had he to consider them', surely misses the point: irrespective of his entitlement to *imagines* (and that a *pauper amator* could indeed have such *imagines* is implied by Dipsas' comment at Ovid, *Am.* 1.8.65–6), this is how the elegist defines himself, carrying over the social antagonism of his poetic *persona* into the sphere of death.

Not only does love have no time for upper-class funerals, the nobility cannot even be expected to show sufficient devotion in love to perform funerary rites for a dead mistress (Propertius 2.24B.49–52):

noli nobilibus, noli consuesse beatis:
    vix venit, extremo qui legat ossa die.

> hic tibi nos erimus: sed tu potius precor ut me
> demissis plangas pectora nuda comis.

> Don't associate with nobles, or with the wealthy: there's scarcely one comes to gather your bones on the final day. I'll be that man for you – but I pray that it'll rather be you who beat your bared breast for me, your hair let down.

Regardless of what Cynthia is being warned not to do with the aristocracy (the text of the verb in line 49 is disputed: see Heyworth 2007, 216–17; Shackleton Bailey 1956, 113), it is clear that it will lead to no reciprocal honours if her association with them is interrupted by death, that most committed advocate of the classless society (*cf.* Horace, *Odes* 1.4.13–14, 1.28.7–20, 2.18.32–4 *etc.*). Only the humble poet will be on hand to oversee her obsequies – but he would much rather she gave him a suitably erotic send-off.[6]

That scenario has already been envisaged earlier in the poem, where Cynthia is pictured uttering over her devotee's bones a valedictory tribute to the lover's constancy that might (despite its implied delivery after the burial) be taken to recall the enumeration of the qualities of the deceased at the *laudatio* delivered by a member of the family at the funerals of prominent Roman citizens;[7] alternatively it could be read as a spoken epitaph (2.24B.35–8) –

> tum me compones et dices 'ossa, Properti,
> haec tua sunt: eheu tu mihi certus eras,
> certus eras eheu, quamvis nec sanguine avito
> nobilis et quamvis non ita dives eras'.

> Then you'll lay me to rest and say, 'These are your bones, Propertius: ah, you were faithful to me, faithful you were (ah!), though you weren't noble by ancestral blood, and you weren't all that rich'.

If we read the lines as a form of *laudatio*, they are soon exposed as a most unusual example of the genre: after the praise of personal excellence (here tailored to reflect distinction in the arena of love), we would expect, following Roman convention, a catalogue of illustrious ancestors and their benefactions and exploits. But the *laudatio* of the elegiac lover reveals quite the opposite – he has no office-holding ancestors (*nec sanguine avito | nobilis*, 37–8) whose glories the orator can associate with those of their successor. In terms of social convention, it is almost an anti-*laudatio*, but for the elegist, whose slogan is *laus in amore mori* ('glory it is to die in love', Propertius 2.1.47, precisely what Propertius is here avowing he will do), the retention of his mistress' love without any assistance from noble birth or financial assets, even when he is reduced to bones, is sufficient guarantee of personal accomplishment.

Indeed, if we consider Propertius' axioms on the nature of love in Book 1, *nescit Amor priscis cedere imaginibus* ('Love doesn't know how to make way for ancient ancestor-masks', 1.5.24) and *nescit Amor magnis cedere divitiis* ('Love doesn't know how to give way to great riches', 1.14.8), we find that, in summing up the poet's qualities in his *laudatio* or epitaph at 2.24B.35–8, Cynthia has enunciated two cardinal principles of the 'life of love' (we might compare the coupling of these two elegiac traits in a programmatic context at Ovid, *Am.* 1.3.7–10). Her précis of Propertius' poetic corpus, spoken over his physical *corpus*, invests the preceding words *tum me compones* (35) with a metaliterary insinuation: the verb *componere* can refer not just to the burial of a body but also to the production of literature – 'compose' in the sense of its English derivative.[8] Cynthia will lay her poet to rest, but she will also 'compose' him, encapsulating two of his fundamental generic traits as an elegist – the lack of distinguished ancestry and of extravagant riches[9] – in the lines devised for her to pronounce over his bones. In this connection it might also be worth noting that *ossa* can be used to refer to the basic constituents (the 'skeleton', as it were) of a literary work, style or argument (see *e.g.* Cicero, *Brut.* 63; Quintilian, *Inst. or.* proem 24, *Decl.* 270); so when Cynthia declares *ossa, Properti, | haec tua sunt* (35–6) followed by a statement of his devotion to her, unexalted ancestry and modest fortune, we find that here she really has composed the *ossa*, the fundamental substance, of his elegiac corpus (the interpretation thus stands even if we retain the manuscript reading *mea* for Porson's *me*: for discussion of the text see Heyworth 2007, 215; Shackleton Bailey 1956, 113).

In this passage we encounter the elegiac *puella*'s usurpation of an activity usually reserved for members of the family of the departed (and male ones at that: on the allocation of rôles in Roman mourning by gender, see Dutsch 2008; Corbeill 2004, 68–72; and Šterbenc Erker, this volume), the delivery of the *laudatio*. As Antony, in the absence of Octavian, pronounced the *laudatio* and led the mourners in ritual lamentation at Caesar's funeral, thereby presenting himself as a member of the dictator's family for political purposes (Flower 1996, 125), so Cynthia here takes over the duty of her lover's next-of-kin, and in doing so is introduced as a provocative substitute for the expected grieving relatives (for mourning as the duty of relatives, see Noy, this volume, under 'Correct disposal of the body'). Again, this is no more than the attentive reader of elegy should expect: the theme of the lover and his beloved as 'family' is one that has surfaced more than once in Propertius' *œuvre* before this point (*cf.* Propertius 1.11.23, 2.6.42, 2.18D.34). The *topos* goes back at least to Catullus (Catullus 72.3–4, with Lyne 1980, 38–41), and can be seen in a less radical form in Tibullus' inclusion of Delia alongside his mother and sister at the lover-poet's funeral (Tibullus 1.3.5–10), a presence picked up on by Ovid in *Amores* 3.9, where both Delia and Nemesis appear at the pyre, with contentious consequences.

An awareness of this characterisation of the personal dynamics of the elegiac relationship helps to illuminate the implications of Propertius' prophecy at 2.1.55–6, *una meos quoniam praedata est femina sensus, | ex hac ducentur funera nostra domo* ('since one woman has plundered my senses, it's from *this* house my funeral will set out'). Contrary to the commentators' inference that Propertius must have died in Cynthia's house for this to happen, the fact is that Propertius – at least in this passage – is not much concerned about the cause and location of his death (for the former, indeed, he offers a range of unlikely mythological possibilities, 2.1.51–4). What matters is the single observation that the speaker's funeral procession will proceed from the house of his *puella*, and from this house rather than any other (hence the emphatic placing of *hac* in line 56). We, and Propertius' first audiences, would expect the cortège to set out from the family home of the deceased (Griffin 1985, 148; as Rawson 2003, 338 notes, 'it was the responsibility of parents to see to a Roman's funeral; otherwise the heir was responsible') – but for Propertius, as an elegist, his family seat *is* Cynthia's *domus*, and the departure of the *pompa* from her house (irrespective of where he has died) strikingly figures the replacement of family values and attachments by the lover-poet's total absorption in his disreputable mistress.[10] Only this can explain the causal connection (*quoniam*, 55) between the two lines of the couplet. *praedata* (55) further situates Propertius' funeral here within the realms of *servitium* and *militia amoris* (*cf.* Ovid, *Am.* 1.2.19, 1.3.1, 2.17.5–6). After the substitution of erotic death for more conventional forms of *laus* a few lines earlier (Propertius 2.1.47–8; Hubbard 1974, 101–2 analyses the likely reaction of a respectable Roman of the late Republic, in the person of Cicero, to this challenge to cherished civic ideals), this first funeral scene of Book 2 programmatically anticipates the even more radical subversions of Roman funerary decorum in subsequent elegies.

In the same way that Cornelia's rewards for a life of fidelity and fecundity are death and funeral rites in the presence of her children (Propertius 4.11.97–64 Heyworth), the crowning glories of the elegist's erotic career will be his death and lamentation in the presence of the beloved. In both cases the funeral reflects the status, activities and affections of the deceased during his or her lifetime, and the ideal of a departure from life in harmony with its previous course seems to have been as much a commonplace in Roman sentiment as in that of later ages (see McKeown on Ovid, *Am.* 2.10.37–8 for references). Such a conception, provocatively transferred to the arena of love, may supply at least part of the motivation behind Tibullus' desire for a terminal swoon in Delia's embrace in the very first poem of his collection (Tibullus 1.1.59–60, *te spectem, suprema mihi cum venerit hora, | te teneam moriens deficiente manu*: '*you* may I look upon when my last hour comes, *you* may I hold as I die in my failing grasp'), and the erotically-tinted funeral he goes on to imagine for himself in the following lines (1.1.61–8), with its tears, kisses, and audience of young men and girls (65–6) – the intended readership of love elegy (see Propertius 3.9.45–6; Ovid, *Am.* 2.1.5–10).

Whatever its relationship to the treatment of the same motif in Tibullus 1.1 (Lyne 1998, 529 [= 2007, 262–3] sees Tibullus 1.1 as a response to Propertius; also Murgatroyd on Tibullus 1.1, intro. [pp.50–1]; doubts raised by Knox 2005, 205–6), Propertius' first exploration of the theme of his own funeral might be seen to embody a similar principle of harmony, even identification, between life and death. Faced with the prospect of shipwreck after abandoning his mistress, the lover's complaints turn to a fantasy of the care his body would have received had he died at home, a far cry from the *parva...harena* ('little sand') that now awaits his corpse (Propertius 1.17.19–24):

> illic si qua meum sepelissent fata dolorem,
> ultimus et posito staret amore lapis,
> illa meo caros donasset funere crines,
> molliter et tenera poneret ossa rosa;
> illa meum extremo clamasset pulvere nomen,
> ut mihi non ullo pondere terra foret.

> If some fate had interred my grief back there, and a final stone were standing over my buried love, she'd have made an offering of her precious hair at my funeral, and would lay my bones softly on delicate roses; she'd have called my name over my ultimate dust, that the earth might be weightless upon me.

Death on land would at least have secured a tombstone for the elegist's final resting-place (*ultimus…lapis*, 20), a lasting monument to his buried love. Some commentators have taken *posito…amore* (20) in the sense in which that phrase occurs at Propertius 1.9.8 (*utinam posito dicar amore rudis!*: 'would that I might be called a novice, my love set aside') and Ovid, *Amores* 2.9.25 (*'vive' deus 'posito' si quis mihi dicat 'amore'*…: 'if some god said to me, "Live, with your love set aside"…'), so that Propertius would here seem to be looking forward to death as a remedy for his unhappy love. But given what follows, Shackleton Bailey (1956, 51) is surely right to insist that 'the force of his appeal is somewhat weakened if he is to be supposed unconscious of Cynthia in the grave or indifferent' – *posito* refers to a literal, physical burial rather than a metaphorical setting aside. We do not have to wait very long to discover through whose agency this burial would have taken place, and indeed the emphatic juxtapositions *illa meo* (21) and *illa meum* (23) reflect verbally the proximity to his *puella* which Propertius so desires even – perhaps especially – in death (see also 1.17.12, *ossaque nulla* tuo nostra *tenere sinu*), and of which he is now deprived by the expanse of sea between them.

The lover fondly goes on to imagine his mistress paying various kinds of tribute to his remains. The surviving evidence is perhaps insufficiently conclusive to demonstrate with certainty that offerings of human hair were actually made at Roman tombs,[11] though the value placed by Propertius on this asset of Cynthia's is shown by his choice of the epithet *caros* (21; McNamee 1993, 225 offers a poetic interpretation of these locks as a symbol of Propertius' verse, equivalent to the *tres…libelli* of Propertius 2.13.25). The next activity in the list, *molliter…tenera poneret ossa rosa* (22), has caused some confusion amongst critics: the meaning of the phrase – mirrored in the enclosing word order – seems to be that Cynthia will lay the poet's bones among roses, but no comparable practice is attested in any description of Roman funerary ritual.[12] We might expect roses to be offered at the tomb, but not as part of the burial itself (though Juvenal does mention roses *in urna*, 7.208), and both Camps and Fedeli (*ad loc.*) attempt to construe *poneret* as *sterneret* in order to achieve the former sense. But *sterneret* occurs nowhere in the textual tradition, though the metre would comfortably have accommodated it here (see Heyworth 2007, 79–80): why has the poet apparently altered the expected ritual in associating it with his funeral at Cynthia's hands?

One clue is provided by the terms in which this ceremony is described. The wish that the bones of the departed might rest *molliter* ('softly', 22) is a recurring sepulchral formula (Lattimore 1962, 71–3 with 72 n.383; Cumont 1942, 355–6; also Ovid, *Amores* 1.8.107–8), and Cynthia's handling of Propertius' bones is in part a realisation of that wish, just as the passage ends with a variation on the conventional prayer that the earth may lie light upon the bones of the deceased (*sit tibi terra levis*), a motif sufficiently common in funerary inscriptions to be represented by an abbreviation – STTL.[13] But *mollitia* is also a characteristic of elegiac poetry (*quaeritis... | unde meus veniat mollis in ora liber*, Propertius 2.1.1–2; also Propertius 1.7.19, 2.34.42, 3.1.19, 3.3.18), and *tener*, the adjective applied to the roses, is used ubiquitously of Amor, of love poems and of love objects in the elegiac genre (Pichon 1902, 277–8). So this treatment is by no means inappropriate for the body of an elegiac poet – but Propertius could equally well have asked for *tenerae rosae* to be placed *molliter* on his tomb, so we are still left with the problem of why he has gone out of his way to bring these roses into direct contact with his dead body.

The answer, I suggest, lies in the inherent eroticism of this funeral, a quality already hinted at in *caros*, *molliter* and *tenera*. Propertius anticipates a burial reflecting the character of his 'life' and writings, and the placing of his bones among roses by the *puella* is a macabre re-enactment of a pursuit we may imagine he enjoyed – or at least hoped to enjoy – in life. The location of the act of love 'among roses' is a commonplace of ancient erotic literature, best known perhaps from Horace's positioning of Pyrrha *multa...in rosa* in *Odes* 1.5.1, but occurring also in a number of other authors (for citations see Nisbet and Hubbard on Horace, *Odes* 1.5.1; according to Putnam 1982, 95–8, this ode is itself permeated by suggestions of death and funerary practice). Cynthia's conduct towards Propertius' bones in death thus replicates the pair's activities in life, and the funeral is once again shown to be the perfect consummation of the 'life of love' (for roses in Propertius' 'missione poetica', see Pellegrino 2004, 140). Attempts to force the expression of these lines to fit what we know of Roman practices fail precisely because Propertius is departing from those practices in order to highlight his own amatory agenda (Hubbard's [1974, 34] description of the scene as 'a bourgeois funeral with all the trimmings, with Cynthia behaving like any conventional and affectionate mortal' is thus very wide of the mark).

This aspiration to an exit reflecting one's performance in life is parodied to outrageous effect by Ovid at *Amores* 2.10.29–36, praying that it may be his good fortune to expire *inter opus* (34), in the midst of lovemaking – 'a consummation', as Lyne (1980, 273) observes with similar wry irony, 'devoutly to be wished' (for a literary interpretation of dying *inter opus*, in the middle poem of the middle book of *Amores*, see *e.g.* Kennedy 1993, 60; Keith 1994, 36–7). The speaker proceeds to imagine some bystander at his funeral remarking on the appositeness of this end to the life it terminated: *atque aliquis nostro lacrimans in funere dicat | 'conveniens vitae mors fuit ista tuae'* ('and let someone in tears at my funeral say, "That death of yours was in harmony with your life"', 2.10.37–

8). The spoken epitaph – or possibly, once again, the *laudatio* – subverts both ritual propriety and the erotic death fantasies of earlier elegists. As so often in the *Amores*, a favourite *topos* of the elegiac genre is reduced to grotesque but hilarious absurdity by being taken to its most extreme manifestation with apparent logical consistency: Ovid trumps his predecessors, and in so doing puts the 'fun' into 'funeral'.

The steadfast adherent of the 'life of love' can expect his constancy to be requited with a suitably elegiac funeral, and it is made clear that for other participants in that life, the treatment to be expected after their demise (as well as their fate in the underworld: see Tibullus 1.3.57–82, Propertius 4.7.55–70) is similarly dependent on their previous conduct. The two possible outcomes for an elegiac mistress are starkly opposed by Tibullus, in an attempt to cajole the grasping and recalcitrant Nemesis into compliance (an attempt he knows will be unsuccessful, 2.4.51–60). Wind and fire are called down upon the house and wealth of the mercenary *puella*, while young men watch the conflagration with satisfied complacency (2.4.41–2). But the elegist can envisage a fate worse than death for his rapacious beloved (43–50):

> seu veniet tibi mors, nec erit qui lugeat ullus
>   nec qui det maestas munus in exsequias.
> at bona quae nec avara fuit, centum licet annos
>   vixerit, ardentem flebitur ante rogum;
> atque aliquis senior veteres veneratus amores
>   annua constructo serta dabit tumulo,
> et 'bene' discedens dicet 'placideque quiescas,
>   terraque securae sit super ossa levis'.

> Or if death comes to you, there won't be anyone to mourn you, or to offer a gift at your sorry funeral. But the girl who's been good, and hasn't been stingy, though she live a hundred years, will be mourned before the blazing pyre; and someone (now rather old), in homage to his ancient love, will present annual garlands at the heaped-up mound, and as he goes off he'll say, 'May you rest well and peacefully, and may the earth lie light over your bones, free from care'.

The dereliction of Nemesis by her well-heeled lovers is comparable to that foreseen for Cynthia from her blue-blooded boyfriends (Propertius 2.24B.49–52, above). More than that, it is a direct reversal of the miserly girl's experiences in life – after her death, there will be no one to give her the gifts she so importunately demanded while alive (so Murgatroyd on 2.4.39–44). The double meaning of *munus*, standard term for funeral tributes to the dead and constant object of craving for acquisitive *puellae*,[14] renders the lack of mourning a particularly appropriate retribution for Nemesis' venal sins during her career on earth. Elegy may profit the lover nothing (2.4.13–20), but poetic justice will not be denied.

The good girl, on the other hand, centenarian though she be, will be rewarded for her generosity and lack of avarice with full lamentation at the pyre and perhaps even apotheosis after burial (Murgatroyd on 2.4.47–8 sees in *veneratus* [47] a suggestion of the elegists' cult of the *puella divina*). The disaffected youths who failed to douse the flames of the miser's house have become the elderly but faithful lover who zealously preserves the memory of his former sweetheart and source of literary inspiration (*veteres...amores*, 47) by offering the conventional tokens of affection at her grave mound. Like the annual offering of flowers (the *annua...serta* of line 48 probably refer to the Roman festival *Rosalia*: see Lattimore 1962, 135–40), the sentiments uttered by the old man as he departs are an integral part of Roman funerary culture, *terra...sit super ossa levis* (50) echoing the ubiquitous sepulchral formula *sit tibi terra levis* (see n.13; for epigraphic parallels to *bene...placideque quiescas* [49], see Carroll 2006, 135–6; Lattimore 1962, 71–3; Galletier 1922, 41, 220). And it is perhaps more than the exigency of fitting the formula (which is already a perfect half-pentameter) into elegiac metre that demands the addition of *securae* (50): the ageing lover wishes his dead *puella* not merely the lightness of repose usually entreated for the dead, but his piety goes further and adds the hope that this rest may be untroubled (for *securus* used of the dead, see Cumont 1942, 356 with n.2, who claims significantly that the epithet signals 'the correct accomplishment of the rites'; also Brelich 1937, 62–5). His commemorative *munera* contrast strikingly in their homely and decorous details with the neglect meted out to the girl who set such store by her admirers' pricier *munera* during her lifetime. However much time has elapsed between the relationship and the girl's demise and her now elderly beau's tribute, considerate behaviour in the context of an elegiac love affair is shown to have ramifications beyond the threshold of life.

In some older scholarship (and occasionally in more recent criticism too), the prominence of material relating to death, burial and the afterlife has resulted in a perception of the elegiac poets, Propertius in particular, as 'morbid' or 'obsessive': the student of elegy has become accustomed to such diagnoses as 'a veritable obsession with death on the part of Propertius' (Foulon 1987, 363; likewise Lyne 1980, 141, 'a preoccupation, even an obsession, with death'), or Tibullus' 'pathological fascination' with death, emanating from 'some arcane psychological source' (Elder 1962, 84, 90). Such psychological stereotyping tends to be predicated, however, on a fundamental misjudgement of the tone in which the theme is handled in this kind of poetry. Elegiac death can be grotesque, colourful or pathetic; but it is rarely sinister (except where the lover-poet's antagonists are concerned), and seldom viewed with anything approaching despair or even apprehension,[15] provided certain conditions are fulfilled. It is not death itself that inspires the lovers of elegy with terror, but the absence of the desired *puella* from their exequies (so Propertius 1.19.1–4), or the prospect of an inappropriate or neglected tomb – or no tomb at all. The elegists' visions of their own decline in the arms of the beloved, their prescriptions for the conduct of their funerals and the erection of their monuments, and their anticipation of the shape of things to come in the hereafter are generally characterised by a mixture of languorous enjoyment, aesthetic exuberance and defiant self-assertion. As A. K. Michels (1955, 171, 179) rightly observed over fifty years ago, there is thus no place for talk of Propertian (or Tibullan, or Ovidian) 'morbidity'.

An important corrective to allegations of brooding, despondency and the like is to be found in Theodore Papanghelis' well-known study *Propertius: A Hellenistic Poet on Love and Death* (1987). Relating Propertius' sensibility to that of his Hellenistic predecessors, on the one hand, and to the decadent-aesthetic movement of the late nineteenth century, on the other, Papanghelis traces a self-indulgent sensuality in his subject's synthesis of love and death, an exquisite enjoyment of mortuary eroticism unencumbered by feelings of horror or foreboding. But this suggested equivalence between the temperament of the Latin elegist and the predilections of the Anglo-French *fin de siècle* cannot on its own account for the popularity of funerary scenes in elegy (Propertius was not, after all, the only Latin love elegist), nor for the use of such scenes as (at least some of) the points of highest visibility for the genre's distinctive literary, social and ethical concerns. One part of the explanation may lie in a theory of the origins of the elegiac genre current at the time, that the couplet had its beginning in – and took its name from – expressions of grief for the departed (see *e.g.* Harvey 1955, 170–1; Luck 1969, 25–7). It is highly likely that Propertius and Tibullus were not the first Latin poets, or even the first elegiac poets, to operate with a dialectic of love and death: scenes of erotic death (and erotic 'death') may already have been established as a *topos* of Latin elegy by their predecessors Gallus and Calvus (see Propertius 2.34.89–92; Virgil, *Ecl.* 10.10; Catullus 96 with Calvus fr. 27–8 Hollis [= 15–16 Courtney]), and there are certainly precedents in Hellenistic poetry for the infiltration of erotic elements into descriptions of death ritual (Papanghelis 1987, 65–70, 78; Fantuzzi and Hunter 2004, 187–90).

But at least equally important for an understanding of the elegists' use of funerary ritual to reflect and summarise their poetic and political programmes is an awareness of the connotations and resonances of these ceremonies in their wider social setting. Like the organisers of the *pompa* at Rome (Flower 1996, 127), the authors of the elegiac *funus* took into account their audience's likely preconceptions and experiences in order to achieve their desired effect – an effect that, as we have seen, can be felt only by recognising the everyday practices with which these scenes invite comparison. The conventional usages evoked by the authors of elegy not merely reflected but also formed an integral part of what it meant to be 'Roman', at least among the city's governing classes. The funeral procession, for instance, with its parade of venerable ancestors, and the *laudatio*, setting the exploits of the individual in the context of his or her family's past achievements, implicated the deceased, the grieving relatives and even the bystanders in a pageant that both affirmed and enacted a set of distinctive social values, as Polybius recognised (Polybius 6.53.1–54.4: *cf.* Flower 1996, esp. 277–8; more generally, Morris 1987, 31–2). Similarly, the erection of a monument, the form and setting of that memorial, and the words inscribed on it all located both commemorators and commemorated within certain established (if idealised) social norms (von Hesberg 1994, 11–12, 238; Feldherr 2000, 228 with Cicero *Off.* 1.54–5; Corbeill 2004, 68, '...funerary practice reflects both the social identity of the deceased and the moral and civic values of the society left behind').

If, then, as Propertius (2.1.47), Tibullus (1.1.69–70) and Ovid (*Am.* 2.7.10; *Ars am.*1.372) all suggest, *mors* is already implicit in *amores* (see Papanghelis 1987, 41–5, 64; Bassi 1994, 53–4 with n.3), it also constitutes a very substantial element in *mores.* The part played by funerary ritual and burial practice in underlining the characteristic features of *Romanitas* offered the perfect medium – and the perfect target – for the elegists, intent on promoting an alternative model of thought and action, to signal their divergence from and opposition to the traditional attitudes and values of (at least one section of) their society. The elegiac poets' use of the death motif is thus comparable to their treatment of other aspects of contemporary culture, such as marriage, slavery and warfare. A regular component of the aristocratic social milieu – often with particular political or ideological connotations – is appropriated to convey the equivalence and even the superiority of the lover-poet's ideals; the ethics of *nequitia* both parallel and undermine the institutions and hierarchies of respectable life. In Roman civilisation, as Vernant remarks of the Greeks, '[t]he world of the dead (or at least what remains of it) presents itself as a reflexion, a more or less direct expression, a more or less mediated, travestied, phantasmogorical image – of the society of the living' (quoted by Garland 2001, x n.1; see generally Morris 1992, 1–30); so the authors of Latin love elegy employ the rites, the relics and (as I have shown elsewhere: Houghton 2007) the realms of death to epitomise their own world of distorted reality, the elegiac 'life of love'. By appropriating and perverting the conventions of the Roman funeral, the creators of elegiac funerary ritual situate themselves in relation to each other, to other spheres of life, and to society at large. Drawing on one of the most formalised and theatrical institutions in Roman public life (for the theatricality of Roman death, see especially Edwards 2007, 144–60), the depiction of its participants' obsequies becomes an important and idiosyncratic means by which, in Conte's words (1994, 123), 'the genre "stages" itself, becomes spectacle'.

Acknowledgements

This paper has benefited from comments from many friends and colleagues: I would particularly like to thank Valerie Hope and Janet Huskinson, who organised the *Memory and Mourning* conferences and offered helpful editorial comments at a later stage, William Fitzgerald, Roy Gibson, Emily Gowers, Michael Reeve, Jula Wildberger and Maria Wyke, and audiences in Cambridge, London and Birmingham, for suggestions and improvements. Some of this material previously appeared in my PhD thesis ('Death and the Elegist – Latin Love Poetry and the Culture of the Grave', Cambridge 2005), supported by the Arts and Humanities Research Council.

Notes

1 On elegiac funerals see generally Pellegrino 2004; Lyne 1998, 527–9, 536–8 (= 2007, 260–3, 271–4); Müller 1995; Pieri 1988; Papanghelis 1987, 50–79. I regret that Erasmo 2008 appeared too late for me to take account of it here.

2 Cuq 1896. In general, the citations from Latin elegiac poetry in Cuq's footnotes appear alongside references to other literary and non-literary sources, and broadly speaking demonstrate what they are marshalled to show; just occasionally, however, the authority given for a particular element of Roman funerary practice consists exclusively of references to the elegiac poets (see *e.g.* 1387 n.16, 1395 nn.28–9, 1398 n.40, 1400 n.8) – though this is not to say that Cuq is necessarily wrong to infer some historical background in these instances.

3 On the difficulty of reconstructing 'the Roman funeral', and the necessity of relying on a hypothetical composite, see especially Hopkins 1983, 203.

4 The power of (Callimachean) poetry, 2.13.3–8; disregard for ancestry, 2.13.10; the poet's *rapport* with his youthful female readership (Persephone, 26) in contrast to *populi confusa…fabula*, 2.13.11–14; devotion to a *domina*, 2.13.14.

5 The classic study of the *imagines* is Flower 1996, who considers the masks both at home and in the funeral procession. See also Noy, this volume (distinguishing *imagines* from death-masks); Rawson 2003, 333–5, 337; Bodel 1999, 260–1, 264, 271–2; Dupont 1987; Hopkins 1983, 201–2 with 202 n.2; Toynbee 1971, 47–8, 56–7, 58, 246 (illustr. 31 pl.12–13); Bömer 1943, 104–23.

6 Griffin 1985, 148 with n.23 – but see Petronius, *Sat.* 111, where beating the bared breast (*nudatum pectus*) is described as an element in common custom (*vulgaris mos*), and Corbeill 2004, 86 with n.84 (quoting Servius auctus on *Aen.* 5.78), 88. Propertius' promise here of a decent burial on Cynthia's demise is in striking contrast to the deficient funeral her ghost claims he actually gave her at 4.7.23–34: Heyworth 2007, 216 n.58.

7 The point is perceptively made by Griffin 1985, 148–9; on the *laudatio* see *e.g.* Kierdorf 1980; Flower 1996, 95–6, 128–58, 273–5; Esteve-Forriol 1962, 48–50 (on Propertius 4.11), 121–3, 131–6; Rawson 2003, 334–5.

8 *OLD* s.v. *compono* 4c, 8. Note also the possible metaliterary suggestion in Propertius 1.11.14, *molliter in tacito litore compositam*, with Commager 1974, 12 and McNamee 1993, 225, 234–5; Ovid, *Am.* 2.17.10, with Keith 1994, 31 and n.20.

9 The rejection of riches, *non ita dives eras* (38), depends on a correction of the MSS' bizarre *navita dives eras*.

10 *Cf.* Griffin 1985, 149; likewise Lyne 1998, 528 (= 2007, 262). Note the emphasis in line 55 on *una…femina*, highlighting the gender reversal in Propertius' appropriation of the sepulchral *topos* of the chaste Roman wife as *univira* (see Treggiari 1991, 233–6; also Propertius 4.11.36, 68).

11 See Ovid, *Fast.* 3.559–64 (Dido's sister Anna); *Consolatio ad Liviam* 97–8 (Livia). Lattimore 1962, 202–3 with 202 n.233, offers parallels from Greek literature, but notes that the lack of epigraphic support suggests a theme by this time exclusively literary; also Cumont 1949, 31, 'son existence même est douteuse à Rome'. Pellegrino 2004, 131–7, citing Greek examples, interprets it as an offering of hair to give vitality to the corpse.

12 Richardson, and Enk, *ad loc.*; Dalzell 1980, 31. Cumont 1949, 44, mentions the burial of the dead on a bed of roses, but gives no examples; *CLE* 1064.4, *cingant suaves ossa sepulta rosae* ('let sweet roses surround the buried bones', on an urn) is not conclusive. For Pellegrino 2004, 137–40, the roses – like the hair in the previous line – confirm the poet's immortality.

13 Carroll 2006, 54–5, 133–4; Lattimore 1962, 65–71; Galletier 1922, 41, 46, 51, 214, 220, 225–6, 227–8, 254. On STTL in elegy (including Propertius 1.17.23–4 and Tibullus 2.4.49–50, below), see Yardley 1996, 269–70.

14 Funeral offerings: *OLD* s.v. *munus* 1d (but no qualifying adjective is required); Lissberger 1934, 72–7. Presents: Propertius 2.8.11, 2.16.15 and 21, 2.21.25, 2.23.8; Ovid, *Ars am.* 1.429, 453 etc.

15 Butler and Barber on Propertius 2.13B intro., for instance, see the latter half of 2.13 as 'written in deep dejection and permeated with brooding anticipation of death'. For exploration of supposed elegiac *Todesangst*, see Drews 1952; *contra*, Papanghelis 1987, 4–5, 78–9.

Bibliography

Standard commentaries are cited by author's name only.

Bassi, K. (1994) Desired silence: *Amor and Mors* in Tibullus 1.1. *Syllecta Classica* 5, 53–61.

Bodel, J. (1999) Death on display: looking at Roman funerals. In B. Bergmann and C. Kondoleon (eds) *The Art of Ancient Spectacle*, 259–81. Washington, New Haven and London, National Gallery of Art.

Bömer, F. (1943) *Ahnenkult und Ahnenglaube im alten Rom*. Leipzig and Berlin, Teubner.

Boucher, J-P. (1965) *Études sur Properce. Problèmes d'inspiration et d'art*. Paris, De Boccard.

Brelich, A. (1937) *Aspetti della morte nelle iscrizioni sepolcrali dell' impero romano*. Budapest, Istituto di numismatica e di archeologia dell'università Pietro Pázmány.

Carroll, M. (2006) *Spirits of the Dead. Roman Funerary Commemoration in Western Europe*. Oxford, Oxford University Press.

Commager, S. (1974) *A Prolegomenon to Propertius*. Norman, University of Oklahoma Press.

Conte, G. B. (1994) *Genres and Readers. Lucretius, Love Elegy, Pliny's Encyclopedia*, trans. G. W. Most. Baltimore and London, Johns Hopkins University Press.

Corbeill, A. (2004) *Nature Embodied: Gesture in Ancient Rome*. Princeton, Princeton University Press.

Cumont, F. (1942) *Recherches sur le symbolisme funéraire des Romains*. Paris, Paul Geuthner.

Cumont, F. (1949) *Lux perpetua*. Paris, Paul Geuthner.

Cuq, E. (1896) FUNUS – Rome. In C. Daremberg and E. Saglio (eds) *Dictionnaire des antiquités grecques et romaines*, vol. 2.2, 1386–1409. Paris, Hachette.

Dalzell, A. (1980) Homeric themes in Propertius. *Hermathena* 129, 29–36.

Drews, H. (1952) *Der Todesgedanke bei den römischen Elegikern*. Unpublished thesis, Kiel.

Dupont, F. (1987) Les morts et la mémoire: le masque funèbre. In Hinard (1987), 167–72.

Dutsch, D. (2008) *Nenia*: gender, genre, and lament in Ancient Rome. In A. Suter (ed.), *Lament: Studies in the Ancient Mediterranean and Beyond*, 258–79. New York, Oxford University Press.

Edwards, C. (2007) *Death in Ancient Rome*. New Haven and London, Yale University Press.

Elder, J. P. (1962) Tibullus: *tersus atque elegans*. In J. P. Sullivan (ed.) *Critical Essays on Roman Literature. Elegy and Lyric*, 65–105. London, Routledge & Kegan Paul.

Erasmo, M. (2008) *Reading Death in Ancient Rome*. Columbus, Ohio State University Press.

Esteve-Forriol, J. (1962) *Die Trauer- und Trostgedichte in der römischen Literatur, untersucht nach ihrer Topik und ihrem Motivschatz*. Dissertation, Munich.

Fantuzzi, M. and Hunter, R. L. (2004) *Tradition and Innovation in Hellenistic Poetry*. Cambridge, Cambridge University Press.

Fedeli, P. (1989) Il poeta lapicida. In M. Piérart and O. Curty (eds), *Historia testis. Mélanges d'épigraphie, d'histoire ancienne et de philologie offerts à Tadeusz Zawadzki*, 79–96. Fribourg, Editions Universitaires.

Feldherr, A. (2000) *Non inter nota sepulcra*: Catullus 101 and Roman funerary ritual. Classical Antiquity 19, 209–31.

Flower, H. I. (1996) *Ancestor Masks and Aristocratic Power in Roman Culture*. Oxford, Clarendon Press.

Foulon, A. (1987) La mort dans la poésie augustéenne. In Hinard (1987), 351–63.
Galletier, E. (1922) *Étude sur la poésie funéraire romaine d'après les inscriptions*. Paris, Hachette.
Garland, R. (2001) *The Greek Way of Death*, 2nd ed. London, Duckworth.
Graham, E-J. (2007) *Death, Disposal and the Destitute: The Burial of the Urban Poor in Italy in the Late Roman Republic and Early Empire*. British Archaeological Reports, International Series 1565. Oxford, Archaeopress.
Griffin, J. (1985) *Latin Poets and Roman Life*. London, Duckworth.
Guillemin, A. (1940) L'élément humain dans l'élégie latine. *Revue des Études Latines* 18, 95–111.
Harvey, A. E. (1955) The Classification of Greek Lyric Poetry. *Classical Quarterly* n.s. 5, 157–75.
Hesberg, H. von (1994) *Monumenta. I sepolcri romani e la loro architettura*, trans. L. di Loreto. Milan, Longanesi.
Hesberg, H. von and Zanker, P. (eds) (1987) *Römische Gräberstraßen. Selbstdarstellung – Status – Standard*. Munich, Verlag der Bayerischen Akademie der Wissenschaften.
Heyworth, S. J. (1992) Propertius 2.13. *Mnemosyne* 45, 45–59.
Heyworth, S. J. (2007) *Cynthia. A Companion to the Text of Propertius*. Oxford, Oxford University Press.
Hinard, F. (ed.) (1987) *La mort, les morts et l'au-delà dans le monde romain*. Caen, Centre de Publications de l'Université de Caen.
Hope, V. M. (2007) *Death in Ancient Rome. A Sourcebook*. London, Routledge.
Hopkins, K. (1983) *Death and Renewal. Sociological Studies in Roman History, volume 2.* Cambridge, Cambridge University Press.
Houghton, L. B. T. (2007) Tibullus' Elegiac Underworld. *Classical Quarterly* n.s. 57, 153–65.
Hubbard, M. (1974) *Propertius*. London, Duckworth.
Keith, A. M. (1994) *Corpus Eroticum*: elegiac poetics and elegiac *puellae* in Ovid's *Amores*. *Classical World* 88, 27–40.
Kennedy, D. F. (1993) *The Arts of Love. Five Studies in the Discourse of Roman Love Elegy.* Cambridge, Cambridge University Press.
Kierdorf, W. (1980) *Laudatio funebris. Interpretationen und Untersuchungen zur Entwicklung der römischen Leichenrede*. Meisenheim am Glan, Anton Hain.
Knox, P. E. (2005) Milestones in the career of Tibullus. *Classical Quarterly* n.s. 55, 204–16.
Koortbojian, M. (1996) *In commemorationem mortuorum*: text and image along the 'streets of tombs'. In J. Elsner (ed.) *Art and Text in Roman Culture*, 210–33. Cambridge, Cambridge University Press.
La Penna, A. (1977) *L'integrazione difficile. Un profilo di Properzio*. Turin, Einaudi.
Lattimore, R. (1962) *Themes in Greek and Roman Epitaphs*. Urbana: University of Illinois Press.
Lissberger, E. (1934) *Das Fortleben der römischen Elegiker in den Carmina Epigraphica*. Dissertation, Tübingen.
Luck, G. (1969) *The Latin Love Elegy*, 2nd ed. London, Methuen.
Lyne, R. O. A. M. (1980) *The Latin Love Poets from Catullus to Horace*. Oxford, Clarendon Press.
Lyne, R. O. A. M. (1998) Propertius and Tibullus: early exchanges. *Classical Quarterly* n.s. 48, 519–44 [= 2007 *Collected Papers on Latin Poetry*, 251–82. Oxford, Oxford University Press].

McNamee, K. (1993) Propertius, poetry, and love. In M. DeForest (ed.) *Woman's Power, Man's Game. Essays on Classical Antiquity in Honor of Joy K. King*, 215–48. Wauconda, Bolchazy-Carducci.
Michels, A. K. (1955) Death and two poets. *Transactions of the American Philological Association* 86, 160–79.
Morris, I. M. (1987) *Burial and Ancient Society. The Rise of the Greek City-state*. Cambridge, Cambridge University Press
Morris, I. M. (1992) *Death-ritual and Social Structure in Classical Antiquity*. Cambridge, Cambridge University Press.
Müller, C. W. (1995) Imaginationen des Todes in den Elegien des Tibull und Properz. *Antike und Abendland* 41, 132–41.
Papanghelis, T. D. (1987) *Propertius: A Hellenistic Poet on Love and Death*. Cambridge, Cambridge University Press.
Pellegrino, C. (2004) Immagini del rituale funebre nelle Elegie di Properzio. In C. Santini and F. Santucci (eds) *Properzio tra storia arte mito*, 131–47. Assisi, Accademia Properziana del Subasio.
Pichon, R. (1902) *De sermone amatorio apud Latinos elegiarum scriptores*. Paris, Hachette.
Pieri, M-P. (1988) L'autocompianto funebre del poeta elegiaco. In *Munus amicitiae. Scritti in memoria di Alessandro Ronconi*, vol. 2, 98–111. Florence, Le Monnier.
Purcell, N. (1987) Tomb and suburb. In Hesberg and Zanker (1987), 25–41.
Putnam, M. C. J. (1982) *Essays on Latin Lyric, Elegy, and Epic*. Princeton, Princeton University Press.
Rawson, B. (2003) *Children and Childhood in Roman Italy*. Oxford, Oxford University Press.
Shackleton Bailey, D. R. (1956) *Propertiana*. Cambridge, Cambridge University Press.
Toynbee, J. M. C. (1971) *Death and Burial in the Roman World*. London, Thames and Hudson.
Treggiari, S. (1991) *Roman Marriage.* Iusti Coniuges *from the Time of Cicero to the Time of Ulpian*. Oxford, Clarendon Press.
Wilkinson, L. P. (1966) The continuity of Propertius ii.13. *Classical Review* n.s. 16, 141–4.
Yardley, J. C. (1996) Roman elegy and funerary epigram. *Échos du monde classique / Classical Views* 15, 267–73.

5

'The Sole Glory of Death': Dying and Commemoration in Dionysius of Halicarnassus

Clemence Schultze

Introduction

> Many owls winged their way about the streets, and the house on the Alban Mount, where the consuls stay while the sacred ceremonies are performed at the feriae Latinae, was struck by lightning. The star known as the comet hung for several days over the capital, and finally dissolved into flashes of light resembling torches. Many buildings in the city were burnt down, including the hut of Romulus: this was set on fire by flaming fragments of meat dropped on it after being snatched from some altar by crows. (Dio 54.29)

Not March 44 BC, but – it can be imagined – a chilly day in another March, two thousand and twenty years ago: the latter part of March of 12 BC. The place is Rome, at the tomb of Augustus – though years before Augustus himself will lie there (Davies 2000, 13). A curtain, presumably hanging on some kind of frame or support, conceals the body of M. Vipsanius Agrippa (Dio 54.28.3); in front of the curtain stands Augustus himself. The *princeps* is delivering the funeral *laudatio* for his contemporary, friend, adherent and son-in-law. Some fourteen lines of it have come down to us, preserved in Greek translation on a papyrus (P. Köln 10; Koenen 1970; Haslam 1980). The lines allude both to Agrippa's *tribunicia potestas* (*dēmarchikē exousia*, line 1) and to the fact that in the provinces he held *maius imperium* (*mēthenos ... exousian meizō*, lines 9–10). In lines 11–12 there is a clear allusion to his high position, back-translated as *dignatus summo fastigio* (from *axiōtheis pleistou hupsous*) and then the text breaks down: there is *hēmeterai* ('our'), there is *tais idiais* ('own' or 'particular'), there is *pantōn anthrōpōn* ('of all men'). Various supplements have been offered, plus their respective back-translations: allusions to offices, virtues, *beneficia* are among the suggestions, based upon Dio's judgement that Agrippa 'surpassed others in virtue (*aretē*)' (54.29.2); but none of these is demonstrable beyond dispute.

Even if the owls, crows and comet which attended the season of Agrippa's death are *non vero,* but merely *ben trovato*, the image of the Imperator delivering the funeral oration was doubtless one to stick in a man's memory. In a conjunction of greatness and relationship, Augustus was speaking of his colleague, friend and kinsman by marriage. It can easily be imagined, further, that somewhere among the onlookers at the back (for surely he could not aspire to a closer view) stands Dionysius of Halicarnassus. His clothing is Greek, for he was not entitled to a toga; his form and face are shadowy – except that, doubtless, his expression is alight with eager interest. For he is beholding, in all its full and formal solemnity, the funeral of one of Rome's grandest contemporary figures, a man equal or superior in military prowess and personal virtues to any of the heroes of the Republic who figure in Dionysius' *Archaiologia Rhōmaikē* (hereafter *AR*).

The treatment of that characteristically Roman institution, the funeral oration, in Dionysius' work reveals much about his historical concerns and methods: the origins of institutions, the interrelationship between Greek and Roman customs, and the role of the historian as recorder of events and assessor of men. To transmit the memory of the past in a right fashion is the writer's prime function, as Dionysius emphasises in the preface (1.1.2): histories are the memorials of the souls (or minds) of their authors, intended to be bequeathed to those who follow afterwards (*mnēmeia tēs heautōn psuchēs tois epigignomenois katalipein*). Unlike things of the body, such works do not vanish with the passage of time (1.1.2). The historian must accordingly be of sound principles, his topic a great one, and his practice careful and truthful (1.1.2–4): these factors guarantee the validity of the things recorded and ensure their beneficial reception by the readers. The latter are conceived by Dionysius, in a later passage of the preface, as the descendants of the great and godlike men of the past: they will in their turn honour and emulate their glorious ancestors (1.6.3–4). The notion that the corporeal dies away (1.6.3; *cf.* 'vanishes' at 1.1.2) is emphasised in both passages by the phrase *tois sōmasin* 'with [their] bodies'. The body dies, but, thanks to the historian, memory lives: his record ensures that the glory of those gone will be immortal – as near to the divine as is possible for mortal nature (1.6.3).

An important form in which memory is preserved in words that link dead and living, deceased and descendants, is the funeral oration. There, in the immediate aftermath of death, come the rituals of bestowal of the body and celebration of the deeds. For Dionysius, the funeral oration originated at Rome and was there practised in a mode actually superior to that of the Greek world. And yet this author, so prolific and so prolix in his composition of speeches, scarcely avails himself of the opportunity offered by the mode of the *epitaphios logos*. Though this may seem surprising, it is in fact fully in accordance with Dionysius' historiographical principles.

Greek and Roman, borrowing and innovation

Dionysius son of Alexandros, of Halicarnassus, (1.8.4) had been in Rome for some eighteen years by the time of Agrippa's funeral (1.7.2); and must, by 12 BC, already have made substantial progress with the historical work, for he was to publish it in 7 BC. And before writing it he had first acquired Latin (1.7.2), which enabled him to read his Roman precursors in the field of annalistic history. He also knew well the pioneering historical work of Fabius Pictor, composed in Greek (1.6.2; 1.79.4; 7.71.1). He mentions, too, that he benefited from what highly learned men (*logiōtatoi andres*) – presumably Roman – with whom he associated could tell him about their past (Schultze 2000). But, although he adopted a year-by-year narrative structure, he did not take the Roman annalistic tradition as his chief model for historical writing. He asserted a historiographical connection with Polybius, a writer whose style he condemned as unreadable (*Lit. Comp.* 4.14–15, with Rhys Roberts 1910 *ad loc.*) but who loomed large as an interpreter of Rome and the Romans to the Greek world. Though the explicit mentions of Polybius in the *Archaiologia* are either passing allusions (1.6.1; 1.7.1) or specific rejections (1.32.1; 1.74.3), Dionysius' choice of a stopping point is at once a compliment to Polybius and a claim to stand in a similar intellectual position: a Greek, who can explain Rome to both Greeks and Romans (Luraghi 2003; Delcourt 2005, 65–69). Where Polybius had started, Dionysius would conclude: 'I take my narrative down to the start of the First Punic War', he says (1.8.2), having begun from the oldest stories of all: (*tōn palaiotatōn muthōn*) (1.8.1). Italy pre-Rome – indeed, actually pre-Troy – is a place of semi-legendary peoples, aborigines and incomers, wanderers and warriors. To link his *Archaiologia* of Rome with Polybius' work is to make an implicit claim to a level of seriousness, both of research and of interpretation.

Broadly speaking, it is the first book which presents the fundamental research: firstly, chronological investigations which determine the accurate date of the establishment of Rome (Schultze 1995); and secondly, the exhaustive (and original) demonstration of the Greek origin of the various *ethnē* who immigrated into Italy (Delcourt 2005, 130–156). This is supported by a formidable array of *testimonia* regarding names, rulers and settlements. Quoted or paraphrased in quasi-antiquarian fashion, these data are deployed to prove that *all* who have contributed to the descent of the Romans and the foundation of Rome are Greeks; and that the Latin language itself is Greek (Gabba 1963). Rome is, accordingly, a Greek *polis* (*Hellada polin autēn*); and, moreover, 'a most hospitable and friendly one' (1.89.1). Book 1 concludes with a resounding endorsement of the Romans:

> It is not just nowadays, when they have full-flowing good fortune as their teacher of fine things, that they have begun to live with regard to *philia*; nor is it from the time when they grasped for the overseas, having overthrown the power of the Carthaginians and Macedonians; but it is from the whole time since they communally settled the city that they lead a Greek life, and they do not strive more notably for virtue now than they did previously. (1.90.1–2)

In the rest of the work, Dionysius promises, he will demonstrate in his coverage of Rome's *politeia* this assertion of the Greekness of their lives and of many of their customs.

For example, he marshals the evidence to demonstrate that *clientela* is an improved borrowing of Greek systems of dependency (2.9.2–3); and that dictators are modelled on Greek *aisumnētai* (5.73.5–74.4). These derivations can appear ludicrous, as when Romulus heartens the Sabine girls captured by his partnerless Roman men, assuring them that marriage by seizure (*harpagē*) is an ancient Greek custom, and a most celebrated one (2.30.5). While Greek models predominate, various other institutions are founded on Etruscan or Italian practice, and some are actually Roman innovations.

In Dionysius' eyes it is plainly no reproach to the Romans to present them as inheritors or borrowers, especially when such borrowing can contribute to the proof of their Greekness. Hence cases where he credits them with being innovators are significant; and those where he judges Roman practice as actually superior to Greek especially so. Striking amongst these is his discussion of the Roman tradition of the funeral oration. He is adamant that the practice of delivering funeral orations originated at Rome; and – despite admitting ignorance as to precisely when it began (see below) – he seemingly regards it as republican in its ethos.

Orations and the funeral context

The delivery of an oration should be separated from the fact of a grand public funeral: Dionysius does indeed conceive that the latter was accorded to at least some of the kings.[1] The main reference to elaborate funeral rites occurs, in fact, on an occasion when for precautionary reasons they are omitted (4.40.5.–6). Tarquinius Superbus forces Servius Tullius to be buried like an ordinary person:

> Tarquinius, fearing that if the corpse were carried through the Forum, as is the Roman habit, wearing royal adornment and the other things which are the custom at royal funerals, some uprising of the people might occur before he had firmly gained control of power, did not allow anything of what is customary to him. (4.40.5)

There is here no mention of the additional danger inherent in the delivery of a funeral oration; but the notion of a cortège, royal clothing and the vaguely adduced customary practices suggests that Dionysius wishes to imply the existence of a set ceremony by the time of Servius Tullius, Rome's most populist king.

The first funeral oration is accorded to L. Junius Brutus the first consul, who has met the death allotted him by the fates (5.15.1–2). As the newly free Republic resists the Tarquins' attempt to regain their former power, Brutus is killed in dramatic hand-to-hand combat with Arruns Tarquinius (*cf.* Livy 2.6.7–9, with Ogilvie 1965, 247–248). Victorious in the battle, Brutus' colleague P. Valerius Publicola returns to conduct the initial triumph of the new regime (5.17.2). Just as Romulus instituted the triumph after his earliest campaign against the Sabines (2.34), so does Valerius continue the practice. Army, knights, people and senate unite in a welcome that is notably characterised by general feasting (2.34.2; 5.17.1–2; Beard 2007, 257–263). The triumph is, as in other writers, juxtaposed with death (Beard 2007, 284–286). Then there comes a marked change of attire and of mood: dark clothing for the mourners, a magnificent bier for the dead man; and the citizen body summoned formally to an assembly.[2] For Brutus, who had been obliged to execute his own sons as conspirators (5.8), the full *polis* now replaces that lost family.

The relevant passage comparing Greek and Roman practice in praising the dead must be quoted in full:

> But on the next day, putting on dark clothing, and putting the body of Brutus, adorned, upon a splendid couch in the forum, he called the people to an assembly and, advancing to the platform, spoke the funeral speech for him.
>
> [3] Whether Valerius first established this custom among the Romans or whether he took over something already in place under the kings, I cannot state for certain. That it was an ancient invention (*heurēma*) of the Romans at the funerals of their notable men to deliver laudations of their virtue and that the Greeks were not the first to establish it, I do know, having learnt it from universal history, handed down by the oldest poets and the most learned historians.
>
> [4] For while they have recounted funeral games, both gymnastic and equestrian, for outstanding men, given by their associates, as by Achilles for Patroclus and, still earlier, by Heracles for Pelops, they do not write of laudations spoken for them – apart from the tragedians at Athens who, flattering their city, made up this tale in respect to those buried by Theseus. For it was late that the Athenians added to their custom the funeral laudation, either for those who died defending their city at Artemisium, Salamis and Plataea, or for the deeds at Marathon. But even Marathon was later than the funeral of Brutus (if, indeed, the speaking of laudations for the departed did indeed first begin then): sixteen years later.
>
> [5] But if anyone (not aiming to discover who were the first to establish funeral laudations) were to wish to understand the custom in itself and in which of the two it is conducted better, he would find that it is applied more wisely among the Romans than among the Athenians. The Athenians seem to have established that these funeral speeches should be pronounced only for those who are being buried on account of war, considering that thus it should be assessed who are good men, on the one factor of their excellence (*aretē*) at the time of death, even though in other regards they are inadequate; [6] while the Romans appointed this honour for all their illustrious men, whether as undertaking leadership in war or as prominent in political matters they have manifested wise counsels and fine deeds; and not only to those dying in war, but also to those who have met their end in any manner whatsoever, considering that it is right to laud good men for every excellence (*aretē*) of their lives and not for the sole glory of their death. (5.17.3–6)

The proof of Roman priority offered by Dionysius is founded on his knowledge of *koinē historia* (Diodorus Siculus 1.1.3 with Burton 1972 *ad loc.*; Marincola 2007, 178). For Dionysius universal history is formed by the twin strands of the works of *sungrapheis* (compilers/historians) and of poets, who are frequently cited, especially in the first book: Agathyllus (1.49.2; 1.72.1); Arctinus (1.68.2); Sophocles (1.12.2; 1.25.4; 1.48.2); Euxenus, who is linked with 'some other Italian *mythographoi*' (1.34.4). Dionysius' argument rests partly on silence. He admits that funeral games indeed go back to the time of Heracles, and were also celebrated during the Trojan War, but claims that funeral orations were not so early. Moreover, despite his respect for poets' evidence elsewhere, he dismisses Athenian tragedians as mere flatterers of their own *polis* when they try to retroject the custom to the time of Theseus (Euripides, *Suppl.*; Plutarch, *Thes.* 29.3–4): the language (*kolakeuontes tēn polin*) is markedly derogatory. In reality, he asserts, it was only lately (*opse*) that the Athenians had adopted the practice – either for Marathon in 490, or in the course of the second campaign (480–79) of the Persian war.[3] It is on the basis of Dionysius' prior chronological work that he can boldly maintain the 'lateness' of the Athenian practice. Described in 1.74.2–6, this almost certainly took the form of a grid correlating consular years, archon years and Olympiads (Schultze 1995, 193–195), allowing Dionysius to state confidently that there is a sixteen year gap between year one of the Republic (508/7 by his reckoning, since his foundation date for Rome is 752/1) and the battle of Marathon.

Then, too, it is not only a case of the priority, but of the actual superiority of Roman practice. Dionysius asserts in an unqualified fashion that the Athenian mode of assessing a man's *aretē* on the basis of his military achievement is flawed: such a man might be totally unworthy in other respects. The Romans' custom is wiser, in that they pay tribute to *all* their outstanding men: the two aspects he specifies are leadership in war and prominence in civil affairs (*politika erga*). As Edwards points out, those likely to qualify are the more senior members of Rome's elite families (2007, 22–23): those who survived the early hazards of warfare and went on to hold high office. The relative weight attributed to politics and to war reflects Dionysius' usual priorities, and, indeed, his promises. In the preface (1.8.2) he announces that he intends to treat the 'whole life' of the ancient Romans – characterised as wars and civil conflicts; forms of constitutions; customs and laws. Although wars are here mentioned first, as befits the traditional subject matter of epic and of history, the other aspects actually predominate in the narrative itself. This is largely owing to a structure, which, while formally employing an annalistic structure with regular mentions of consuls' entry to office and other date markers, in fact comprises larger blocks where, over several years, either external or internal events form the chief topic. (This greatly alleviates the problem of a 'bitty' narrative of the early years of the Republic.) And, since the internal events usually feature pairs or sets of lengthy speeches whereas battle speeches necessarily tend to be briefer, the primacy of internal, civic matters over warfare is asserted.

It is not, however, merely Dionysius' own inclinations in favour of civic life and politics that are at issue here when he stresses the appropriateness of praising the dead man's entire range of activities. He is, of course, quite right to assert that Roman *laudationes* feature deeds of a civic and political nature as well as those of command

and conquest. This is apparent from the earliest preserved funeral *laudatio*, that for L. Caecilius Metellus, consul and dictator, delivered in 221 BC (Pliny, *HN* 7.139–140). In praising him, his son Quintus firstly enumerated his specific offices and 'firsts' (first to lead elephants in a triumph); and then described his ten great achievements or qualities: foremost warrior, best orator, bravest commander, having undertaken the greatest actions under his own auspices, holding the highest offices, supreme in wisdom, considered the leading senator, gaining great wealth by right means, leaving many children, and all in all, *clarissimus* in the state. This exhaustive list has partial parallels in other *laudatio* texts (Kierdorf 1980, 10–21). Of these achievements, three are to do with war, two with office-holding, two with skills or qualities (oratory and wisdom), two with family/*familia*; and *clarissimus* rounds it all off. Dionysius' summary is thus surely founded on the realities of the *laudatio* genre from the third century to the first century BC. In Agrippa's *laudatio* (quoted above), there is, besides the offices and powers mentioned in the extant portion, the likelihood that other offices and qualities were included. Apropos L. Caecilius Metellus, Kierdorf (1980, 18) has percipiently observed that moral qualities such as *industria*, *pietas* and *fides* find no place here: *fortitudo* and *sapientia* are what it is all about; and in this too Dionysius' description resembles the transmitted texts.

Here, then is the first occasion when Dionysius avoids an actual *laudatio*, composed for Brutus and put into Valerius Publicola's mouth for delivery. In fact, he offers only a brief judgment in his own voice at the start of 5.18.1, summarising Brutus as *kratistos*, greatest of all the Romans. Similarly, when it comes to Publicola's own turn, a few years later, Dionysius offers no *laudatio* as such (5.48). In view of the extraordinary frequency of speeches of all kinds (and lengthy ones at that) in the *AR*, this omission cannot be attributed to Dionysius' feelings of modest inadequacy when it happens to be an *epitaphios logos* that is required. The reason lies rather in the historian's responding to the requirement that, having recounted the facts and the deeds, he himself should utter the final judgment.

When it comes to Valerius' turn for assessment (5.48), two elements mentioned are typical of *laudationes*: offices, and triumphs. Valerius has held four consulships and has triumphed twice; furthermore, there is also a characteristic claim to uniqueness, for he has the honour of being one of those who expelled the kings. All that could be lifted from a *laudatio*. But Dionysius goes beyond that genre to something more: in terms reminiscent of the preface, he explicitly refers to the historian's duty to present a totalising judgement, which embraces aspects of a man's life above and beyond those appropriate to a *laudatio*:

> For I consider that it above all befits those writing histories not only to go through the military doings of outstanding leaders and any fine and salutary measures that they have found out and applied for the benefit of their cities, but also to point out their lives, whether these are moderate and sober and adhering throughout to the ancestral practices. (5.48.1)

In Valerius Publicola's case, Dionysius' praise is directed at his avoidance of greed and avarice when circumstances would have allowed him to amass wealth; instead, he lived a life of soberness and self-sufficient frugality. The historian expands on this, offering not just assertion but demonstration. The proof of the frugality is the poverty; the proof of the poverty is the family's inability to bury Valerius in a manner which (so the reader is given to understand) was already fraught with display and expense (5.48.3–4). When the senate learnt of this, they awarded him a public funeral (*ek tōn dēmosiōn … chrēmatōn, cf.* Livy 2.70.7; Plutarch, *Pop.* 23.2). This included a burial place within the city; and the matrons mourned for him as they had for Brutus (a detail which was not actually mentioned at 5.17–18). The splendid funeral itself Dionysius compares to that of a king.

In the surviving portion of the *AR* at least, Dionysius foregoes the opportunity to depict a full Roman funeral, whether a *funus publicum* or one at the family's expense. As to the latter type, the degree of display rendered the funeral a public event in any case (Flower 1996, 95–96). So, apart from the odd allusion intended to point the contrast between true glory and frugal lifestyle, as when Valerius' relatives intend to carry his body out and bury it in a mean and shabby fashion, there is no detailed description of procedure. Dionysius gives little or no notion of the competitive and assertive nature of these funerals – neither of a family's wish to present itself as successful and achieving, nor of the intention (which so impressed Polybius at 6.53–54) of raising the emulative spirit of the young men by the recounting of achievement and the impressive display of office holders brought again to life through their *imagines* (Flower 1996, 91–127). Regrettably, no details of the *imagines* are to be found in the *AR*. Possibly Dionysius thought that all Romans knew this by experience and all Greeks were attentive readers of Polybius. But an additional factor must be taken into account: in the case of both Brutus and of Valerius, there could be no *imagines* – for the consuls of the first year of the Republic obviously lack office-holding ancestors whose *imagines* would be available to exhibit. (Flower 1996, 53–59 discusses the notion of *ius imaginis / ius imaginum.*) This is typical of Dionysius' extreme scrupulosity with regard to matters constitutional and legal.

A case very similar to Valerius' is that of Menenius Agrippa (6.96, *cf.* Livy 2.33.10–11). He too is credited with a military deed (triumph over the Sabines) and a political one (resolving the First Secession by on the one hand persuading the Senate to a compromise and on the other inducing the plebeians to lay down arms and desist from their separatist intentions). Menenius' authority and the degree of trust he enjoys are thus manifest. Since all this was narrated at very considerable length in books 5 and 6, there is no need for Dionysius to recapitulate. But, just as in Valerius' case, he expands upon the funeral – also conducted at public expense. It arises in a slightly different fashion, in that the tribunes decide it would be

> the most shameful of things that such a man should meet with burial in an obscure and wretched manner through poverty; and they urged the people to take on the expense of

> his funeral, each man to contribute towards it such an amount as they should assess. This was welcome to the hearers, and when each man had forthwith contributed the assessed amount, a large sum of money was collected. (6.96.2–3)

The Senate then deem it is fitting to use public funds instead, and place upon the quaestors the task of putting out to tender a large public contract for the funeral.

> ... having adorned his body in the most elaborate manner, and supplying everything else with regard to magnificence, they buried him worthily of his virtue. 6.96.3

And, like Brutus and Valerius (5.48.4), Menenius Agrippa is 'mourned by the matrons for a whole year, laying aside their purple and gold' (9. 27.2, when this funeral is recalled by way of contrast with his son's condemnation, and the latter's poverty (*penia*) is mentioned).

What is apparent from the very similar accounts of these two men's burials is that the explicit judgements of poverty and frugality could not possibly form part of a *laudatio* delivered by a relative within the context of display which characterises a proper Roman elite funeral. Accordingly it must fall to the historian, *in propria persona*, to record the circumstances of the public funeral; he cannot attribute both praise and explanation to a son or close relative of the deceased, engaged in celebration of the dead man. So, both in the case of the *imagines* and that of *laudationes* considerations of appropriateness to the socio-historical context are one determinant of the historian's procedure. The other, of course, is the historian's over-arching responsibility to have the last word in judgement: he is not, after all, a mere neutral device by means of which the memory of doers and deeds is transmitted to passively recipient readers. Writer and reader alike participate in a joint creation of memory: the historian's work is a memorial of his own mind (1.1.2, discussed above). The reception of that work will affect readers' minds – and this should be for their benefit (1.1.2–3). By actively engaging with (*enthumoumenous*) the great men of the past, the readers will be better equipped to make moral choices regarding their own lives (1.6.3–4).

Accordingly, the historian must discriminate; he will not choose to exercise his prerogative of judgement just for any chance notable who happens to die. (In fact one of the ways in which Dionysius departs from annalistic convention is the infrequency with which he 'signs off' a year with a list of the famous men who have died in the course of it.) He limits these 'obituaries' to those whose careers have brought about change (conceived as development, change for the good) in the constitution of Rome. Constitutional change in Dionysius is seen as the gradual perfection over time of the *miktē politeia* (for what Romulus created is already characterised as mixed, though rather primitive and suited to the early stages of development of a citizen body) until it becomes a perfectly mixed constitution, in which all citizens share and participate (Schultze 1986, 130–132). So naturally, the two first consuls qualify on this count; as does Menenius the great reconciler.

Praising a woman: the case of Lucretia

To come now to what may be described as the test cases: exceptions which prove the rule. The first of these is Lucretia. She is a woman – and hence precluded from military or civic service to the city – and she is also an honourable suicide. It is for her that Dionysius comes closest to composing a *laudatio* which is delivered as a speech, by a character in the *AR*. This highly witnessed death of hers, and its consequences, constitute one of the significant turning points of the narrative.

Lucretia's rape took place at Collatia, where she lived with her husband Sextus Collatinus, but Dionysius goes to some trouble to get the poor woman to Rome, causing her to travel to her father's house in order to explain to a *consilium* of family and friends what has befallen her (4.66). She is permitted a few sentences of direct and then of indirect speech (4.66.3–67.1) before she stabs herself: lamentations ensue. At least the fact that the assembled *dramatis personae* are all in Rome means that the display of Lucretia's corpse can follow on quickly (but see Livy 1.58.12–59.1 for real narrative speed). Dionysius requires two chapters of explanation about Brutus and his feigned stupidity (4.68–9); and then allows him a speech which occupies most of 4.70–75. This urges action upon the assembled company, and proposes various constitutional changes that they will put to the demos. It is a fine example of Dionysius' hyper-constitutionality: by the end its author has forgotten that Brutus is not addressing a senate meeting (4.75.4).

At last, then, Lucretia's body is carried out in front of the senate house to be displayed to the people in all its fresh horror: 'untreated for burial and stained with blood' (4.76.3). The location and the fact of display recall Caesar's funeral (Appian, *B Civ.* 2. 143 and 147 (though there are both resemblances and differences here). Brutus then harangues the people for a further seven chapters (4.77–83). A portion of this (4.82.1–4) is arguably the *speech* most resembling a funerary address in what survives of the *AR*. Lucretia is named and identified as daughter and wife (4.82.1); the circumstances of her death are recalled (4.82.1–2); and then she is addressed directly (4.82.3) (as can be paralleled in other *laudationes*, notably that known as the *Laudatio Turiae*).[4] The functions of addressing her are firstly, for praise; secondly, to express the survivors' grief and their compassion for Lucretia's sufferings; and finally to shame the hearers into taking vengeance:

> 'O you remarkable woman, worthy of great praise for your noble disposition! You are gone, you are dead, being unable to endure the tyrant's outrage and despising all the pleasures of life in order not to suffer any such thing again. After this, Lucretia, when you, who happened to have a woman's nature, have shown the mental attitude of a noble man, shall we, who were born men, show ourselves worse than women in excellence?' (4.82.3)
>
> … While Brutus was thus addressing the many people in this way, everything he said was received by them with continual acclamations, to manifest their approval and their encouragement. (4.84.1)

His hearers are affected by varying and diverse emotions: pain and pleasure, anger and fear, as they regard the past indignities and the difficult and dangerous prospect of liberty that is to be gained only by a struggle. This is one of the most striking instances of Dionysius' demonstration (*dēlōsis*) of an event: the historian 'shows' the reader an event; and the reader can thus contemplate the attendant circumstances (terminology of seeing and contemplating, [*horaō, theōria*] are used) so that it comes home to him in a real and vivid fashion. Dionysius discusses this in connection with the Decemvirate and its overthrow:

> For the intellect of every man when led through words to deeds enjoys not only hearing what is said but also seeing what is done. Nor, indeed, what they hear of political actions, are they satisfied with learning the summary and outcome of the events … but they at once demand to be informed also of … what the speeches (*logoi*) were that persuaded them, and what men uttered them, and to learn all the attendant circumstances to those events. Men in politics, among whom I for my part place also those philosophers who consider philosophy as consisting in the practice of fine deeds rather than of fine words, enjoy the comprehensive contemplation of the attendant circumstances: this they have in common with other men. And besides their enjoyment there is in addition the fact that in difficult times they do great benefit to their cities from such experience thus acquired and lead them willing followers to the advantageous, by means of speech. (11.1.3–4)

The death of Lucretia and its aftermath transformed Rome from monarchy to republic – but not by itself: rather because Brutus convinced senate and demos to stand up and struggle for their liberty. Within the totality of his speech, one element is the praise accorded to Lucretia, combined with the evocation of her wrongs. So the *laudatio*-like portion of the speech constitutes one of the *archai* or causes which helped bring about significant political change: it is a causational speech, appropriately included, according to Dionysius' criteria.

Elsewhere (in a First Secession context) Dionysius says

> I might well wonder that some, though they think it necessary to write up accounts of military actions and sometimes spend a great many words on one battle, going through the nature of the places, the particularities of weaponry, the methods of drawing up the lines, the exhortations of the generals, and every other circumstance that gave rise to causing the victory of one side or the other, yet when writing up political commotions and seditions (*staseis*), do not think it necessary to report the words by which the surprising and remarkable events were achieved. (7.66.3)

The seemingly surprising allocation of a *laudatio* to the woman Lucretia is thus explicable; her case must be viewed against that of Coriolanus.

Coriolanus

Whilst Marcius Coriolanus, the Roman anti-hero, receives no funeral speech in Dionysius' work, his funerary rites are described in more detail than any others. Dionysius is not a historian greatly concerned to evoke *Realien:* this is actually the most visual and circumstantial description of such matters ever provided by him.

> When everything was ready, they laid him, dressed in the clothing of a supreme commander, on a couch adorned in a most splendid manner, and ordered the booty, the spoils and the crowns, together with the memories (*mnēmas*)[5] of the cities he had taken, to be carried before his bier. The young men who were the most illustrious for their deeds in war took up the bier, and carrying it to the most notable suburb, placed it on the prepared funeral pyre, the whole city going together in procession with the body with lamentations and tears. [4] Then, when they had slaughtered many victims in his honour and offered up all such first-offerings as men fittingly do at the funeral pyres of kings and leaders of armies, those who had been intimate with him remained there till the fire died down, after which they gathered together his remains and buried them in that same place, constructing an imposing memorial (*mnēma*) by heaping up a lofty mound with many hands helping (8.59.3–4)

In describing the funeral practices, Dionysius elides the differences between triumph and funeral.[6] One specific example is constituted by the depictions of captured cities: this resembles the triumphal practice of carrying pictures or models on litters or floats (Flower 1996, 113 n. 102; Beard 2007, 143–159). In describing these as *mnēmas*, Dionysius implies that they trigger *memories* of Coriolanus' past achievements, just as the tomb-mound itself is a *mnēma* intended to *memorialise* him in the future. Finally, at the very end of Dionysius' treatment of Coriolanus, the author asserts that 'his memory (*mnēmē*) has not become extinct, but he is still celebrated and hymned' (8.62.3). The wording deliberately recalls this earlier interplay between memory and memorial.

Furthermore, the rites accorded to Coriolanus bear some resemblance to Dionysius' presentation of Brutus, insofar as there is an element of surrogacy. Brutus earned a triumph but never lived to celebrate it: hence his colleague Valerius figures almost as a proxy for the dead Brutus. Coriolanus similarly receives posthumously and in exile the triumphal honours which he might have had in his lifetime and at Rome. For – importantly – this is not a *Roman* funeral. Coriolanus has died in the territory of the Volscians, whom he had led so successfully in battle against Rome until the reconciliation mediated by the Roman women's embassy (his wife, his mother and the priestess Valeria). Instead of going back to Rome he has returned to the Volscians to explain this to them, and is stoned to death by them. It would plainly be inappropriate to put a *laudatio* into the mouth of either a Roman or a Volscian. Yet in 8.62.2 it appears that, in some sense, Coriolanus' death does impact upon his homeland in a fashion similar to that enjoyed by great and loyal Romans: Dionysius has him mourned by the Romans, and actually includes a mention of the women laying aside their coloured garments as for Brutus, Valerius and Menenius Agrippa.

The Coriolanus 'obituary' (8.60–62), proffered by the historian in his own person, constitutes by far the longest such evaluation in the *AR*. Its reflective tone would suit a biography rather than a history. In particular, the characterisation of the Coriolanus as the hyper-just man, the one whose passion for justice knows no limits and has no mean, whether he is demanding justice from the plebeians (the original cause of his rift with Rome) or in fulfilling its demands by returning to the Volscians to account for his change of policy and strategy (and getting killed for it) constitutes an element of philosophical reflection rare in Dionysius' work. The apparent anomaly – that the historian provides so lengthy a character assessment not on a great and successful Roman but on an exile and a failure, a might-have-been – can be explained by the interrelationship in Dionysius's history of the tale of Coriolanus (with its assertion of the demos' right to call leading men to account through the institution of popular trial) and the First Secession (the rift and reintegration of the civic body of the whole Roman people). Coriolanus nearly scuppered this reintegration, and yet his later trial, paradoxically, formed a significant step in the development of the mixed constitution. That is why Coriolanus is commemorated.

Conclusion

The way in which Dionysius integrates aspects of Roman funeral practices into his narrative accords with his conception of history and the historian's role. Moreover, his emphasis upon the importance of the *laudatio* and yet the way he eschews presenting particular *laudationes* is not as paradoxical as it seems. He can stress that the *laudatio* is a Roman creation, and admirable in embracing both political and military achievement, while reserving to himself the privilege of a final judgement.

When he asserts in the preface (1.6.3–5) his aim of benefiting three categories of people (the Romans of the past, their present and future descendants, and himself) he implies that memory is more than a mere process of simple recording and transmission. Rather, as the remembered past operates upon the present by means of written histories, it manifests an active power to cause change. The historian is benefited by doing justice to the memory of those great Romans – male and female, successful and flawed alike – who contributed to the city's life and growth: to receive such immortal glory is the nearest that these human beings can come to the divine (1.6.3). But the writer can only do this adequately if his chosen subject and his own moral character are sound: his history is, after all, a memorial of his own mind (1.1.2). His addressees (the descendants, themselves termed godlike – *isotheoi:* 1.6.3) will be changed too by such a history: they will be inspired to emulate their forebears, and to choose lives that are noble. Perhaps, as Dionysius watched Agrippa's funeral, he saw the dead man and himself as participating in a perpetual but fruitful interaction between achievement, memory and judgement.

Notes

1 The kings almost all die or are otherwise removed in circumstances which preclude a funeral; and they mostly lack obvious heirs, children or successors. The deaths of Titus Tatius and Numa are explicitly mentioned as receiving notable burials (2.52.5; 2.76.5); but in the case of those who die in unusual circumstances or by assassination, such as Romulus (variant versions at 2.56), Tullus Hostilius (burnt to death at 3.35); Ancus Marcius (no circumstances, 3.45.2) and Tarquinius Priscus (assassinated 3.73, *cf.* 4.1.1), Dionysius makes no allusion to funeral or burial.

2 The brief account in Livy 2.7.4 includes no reference to an oration; Plutarch, *Publicola* 9.5–7 summarises Dionysius' elements of triumph, quadriga, honours and funeral speech, adding an allusion from Anaximenes 'the orator' to a possible Solonian origin for the practice.

3 Dionysius naturally does not even trouble to mention the Peloponnesian War Funeral Speech of Pericles (Thucydides 2.35–46) which he knew well and (mostly) admired (Thucydides 18; 2 Amm. 16). He is also well acquainted with other examples of the genre: Gorgias' *Epitaphios* (*Dem.* 1); and [Plato's] *Menexenus* (*Dem.* 24–30, *cf.* 32). Demosthenes' own *Epitaphios* is mentioned as spurious in *Dem.* 44.

4 Hope 2007, 106. (*CIL* VI 1527 = *ILS* 8393). Murdia (*CIL* VI 10230 = *ILS* 8394) is not addressed. Kierdorf 1980, 112–116 on women's *laudationes*; 33–49 on l. Turiae.

5 I employ this unusual term deliberately, in order to bring out the word-play between *mnēmē* (memory) and *mnēma* (memorial) just below.

6 There was a real-life parallel to this in the case of the return to Rome of the elder Drusus' body in 9 BC, described by Seneca (*ad Marc.* 3.1) as *funus triumpho simillimum.*

Bibliography

Beard, M. (2007) *The Roman Triumph.* Cambridge MA, Belknap Press of Harvard University Press.

Burton, A. (1972) *Diodorus Siculus, Book 1: A Commentary.* Leiden, Brill.

Davies, P. J. E. (2000) *Death and the Emperor.* Austin, University of Texas Press.

Delcourt, A. (2005) *Lecture des* Antiquités romaines *de Denys d'Halicarnasse. Un historien entre deus mondes.* Brussels, Académie Royale de Belge.

Edwards, C. (2007) *Death in Ancient Rome.* New Haven, Yale University Press.

Flower, H. I. (1996) *Ancestor Masks and Aristocratic Power in Roman Culture.* Oxford, Clarendon Press.

Gabba, E. (1963) Il latino come dialetto greco. In *Miscellanea di studi alessandrini in memoria di Augusto Rostagni*, 199–94. Turin, Bottega d'Erasmo.

Haslam, M. W. (1980) Augustus' funeral oration for Agrippa. *Classical Journal* 75, 193–199.

Hope, V. M. (2007) *Death in Ancient Rome: A Sourcebook.* London, Routledge.

Kierdorf, W. (1980) *Laudatio funebris. Interpretationen und Untersuchungen zur Entwicklung der römischen Leichenrede.* Meisenheim am Glan, Hain.

Koenen, L. (1970) Die *Laudatio funebris* des Augustus für Agrippa auf einem neuen Papyrus (P. Colon. inv. Nr. 4701). *Zeitschrift für Papyrologie und Epigraphik* 5, 217–283.

Luraghi, N. (2003) Dionysios von Halikarnassos zwischen Griechen und Römern. In U. Eigler, U. Gotter, N. Luraghi and U. Walter (eds) *Formen römischer Geschichtsschreibung von den Anfängen bis Livius. Gattungen. Autoren. Kontexte*, 268–286. Darmstadt, Wissenschaftliche Buchgesellschaft.

Marincola, J. (2007) Universal history from Ephorus to Diodorus. In J. Marincola, (ed.) *The Blackwell Companion to Greek and Roman Historiography*, vol. 1, 171–179. Oxford, Blackwell.

Ogilvie, R. M. (1965) *A Commentary on Livy Books 1–5*. Oxford, Clarendon Press.

Rhys Roberts, W. (1910) *Dionysius of Halicarnassus. On Literary Composition*. London, Macmillan.

Schultze, C. E. (1986) Dionysius of Halicarnassus and his audience. In I. Moxon, J. Smart and A. J. Woodman, (eds) *Past Perspectives. Studies in the Greek and Roman Historians*, 121–141. Cambridge, Cambridge University Press.

Schultze, C. E. (1995) Dionysius of Halicarnassus and Roman chronology. *Proceedings of the Cambridge Philological Society* 41, 192–214.

Schultze, C. E. (2000, December) Authority, originality and competence in the *Roman Archaeology* of Dionysius of Halicarnassus. *HISTOS. The Electronic Journal of Ancient Historiography at the University of Durham.* http://www.dur.ac.uk/Classics/histos/2000/schultze1.html (10 August 2009).

7

Bad Deaths, Better Memories

Janet Huskinson

Memory and mourning are both processes which involve deeply personal, often instinctive reactions to death, and yet are also heavily shaped by collective cultural expectations. In Roman memorials the dead are remembered as individuals, and also as people who exemplified socially important qualities in their lives, and in the mode of their death – 'good' or 'bad'. 'Bad deaths' were experiences to be dreaded and especially mourned; yet it was important that those who had died that way were also commemorated in ways that created positive experiences that could at least counterbalance the disaster. This chapter examines the process of creating 'better memories' as it worked out in one particular monument, the funerary altar dedicated by Iulius Secundus to his wife Cornelia Tyche and his daughter Iulia Secunda (Fig. 7.1) who had drowned at sea.[1]

In formulating the notion of 'good' and 'bad deaths' the work of Philippe Ariès has had an important influence. His book *The Hour of our Death*, first published in 1977, was an expansive study of how attitudes to death, burial and commemoration had changed in western society in a thousand years since the early middle ages. The changes he identified essentially relate to two different views of Death, one which saw it as an inevitable part of a natural process and the other as a violent and fearful intrusion into an individual's life. The first of these – which Ariès termed the 'tame' death – allowed individuals to prepare for their end and involved their community in a collective and often ritualised response involving mourners and witnesses (see Graham, this volume). The sense that this kind of Death was all part of a natural process which was both universal and familiar was often suggested through images of sleep and gardens. This was a notion of Death which, according to Ariès (1987, 5, 28) continued from prehistory well into industrialised societies, '… the oldest death there is'. But against its background, he argued, a different attitude began to develop as society came to place more emphasis on individuals and their own lives and destinies. Death was then seen as threatening personal extinction and became something to be dreaded and kept at bay. There was greater concern with the afterlife and with memorials as one way in which the dead might continue to live on in the memories of survivors. Ariès (1987, 95–202, 605–8) discusses this development in terms of eleventh century society, but since one lesson of his study is that attitudes cannot be confined to a single chronological line

Fig. 7.1 Front face of the funerary altar of Julia Secunda and Cornelia Tyche. Paris, Musées du Louvre, MA 1331. (Photo: RMN/Jean-Gilles Berizzi. Reproduced by kind permission of the Agence photographique de la Rèunion des Musées Nationaux.)

of development, this less benign view of Death is to be expected in other societies, particularly those which stress the individual.

Looking for some of these ideas in one particular Roman funerary memorial involves a certain mismatch in methodology since Ariès (1987, xiii) himself deliberately chose to work with a broad, 'chaotic mass of documents' in an approach that he described as 'intuitive and subjective'. But a close reading of a single monument is valuable as it can show in detail how some of his broad ideas come into play. In particular, it can show how the imagery seeks to reconcile the need to record the tragedy that happened with the need to construct more acceptable memories of the women who died and of the loss experienced by those who mourned them – in other words, by taming their 'bad deaths'. After all, universal experience is that 'bad things can happen to good people', and both these aspects need to be acknowledged in constructing the memorial.

The funerary altar dates from the mid second century AD (to judge from the wife's hairstyle) and is said to have been found in the Campus Martius, Rome. Altars like this were usually placed within tomb buildings or precincts and were a popular form of memorial in the late first and early second centuries AD, particularly amongst people from the middle stratum of society. Their decoration offered scope for portraits and inscriptions which could commemorate the lives of individuals, and this was especially important for those moving up the social scale such as freedmen keen to celebrate their newly acquired status and to mourn their dead (Kleiner 1987). The family which erected this altar must have been wealthy but no indication survives of their status, although the wife's second name Tyche was often used for freedwomen (Wrede 1981, 100; *cf.* 97). Only the front of the monument now survives, although the right side panel is known from some sixteenth and seventeenth century drawings (Vermeule 1960, 24, no. 230, Fig. 80; Wrede and Harprath 1986, 98, no. 106).

The front face of the altar forms an *aedicula*, with two slender Corinthian columns framing busts of the two dead women which rest on fronds of acanthus; this format recalls a 'Grabtempel' (Wrede 1981, 86). They are identified by the names inscribed above them as 'Iulia Secunda, daughter' (on the left) and 'Cornelia Tyche, wife' (on the right). The busts are frontal and conventional in appearance. That of the daughter is slightly smaller than her mother's but the supporting foliage has been made taller so that both busts appear to be the same size. Otherwise there are few signs of an age difference: Iulia Secunda is portrayed as a young woman, with a heart-shaped face and with her hair drawn back from a central parting, while her mother has a more elaborate style made fashionable by Faustina the Elder, with side waves and a coil on the top of the head. Both wear mantle and tunic (which falls in deeper folds on the mother's breast than on the daughter's).

The rest of the decoration is carefully coordinated to give each woman her own space whilst presenting them both on virtually equal terms; thus text and images related to Iulia Secunda occupy the left of the panel, and those which celebrate her mother are on the right. Above the simple inscription of their names the curved pediment contains various symbols carved in lower relief. In the centre are two empty chairs, with the letters DM (*Dis Manibus*) set between the legs. To the left, above the bust of Iulia Secunda, are a quiver and a bow, and on the right, above Cornelia Tyche, are a cornucopia, torch, rudder on a globe and a wheel. As attributes of the goddess, Tyche /Fortuna, these obviously pick up on Cornelia Tyche's name, while the quiver and bow link her daughter with the goddess Diana. These links may have been carried through to the sides, to judge from the image of Diana's stag, which was apparently placed halfway down the inscription on the right, on the side adjacent to the bust of Iulia Secunda.[2]

Below each bust is an inscribed panel which records the woman's virtues and her age at death. They show that Iulia Secunda had died at the age of eleven and her mother at thirty-nine (and, incidentally, that there had been more than one child in the family). More about the circumstances of their death is revealed in the expansive, elaborately worded epigram that was originally carved on the right hand side of the altar (*CIL* VI, 20674; translated by Courtney 1995, 162–65, 372–73, no. 174). In rather dramatic terms, which do not record precise time and place, it tells how they had drowned together somewhere off the north-eastern coast of Spain. It also dwells at length on the role of Fate (personified by the *Parcae*) which destined the women to die together on the same day, leaving the dedicant – their husband and father – to outlive them until his own predestined time of death. The initial letters of the epigram's fourteen lines spell out his name, Iulius Secundus.

In discussing the treatment of Death on this monument the sentiments expressed in this inscription make an obvious starting-point. The death it records was sudden and violent, far from tame. The poetic wording dramatically reinforces this point, with references to the force of the sea which killed them (*vi pelagi exanimatas*), and to the great Spanish rivers flowing into their different oceans. As well as evoking the physical horror of their death, this geographical allusion also exposes a further cause of trauma as it locates the tragedy far from Rome, which to judge from the findspot of the monument was probably where they lived. By dying like this they were deprived of the chance to die peacefully at home with due preparation and acceptance (*cf.* Ariès, 1987, 5–10). Their grieving relatives had no chance to make a collective farewell at the bedside, which, for Ariès (1987, 14–22), was an important factor in a 'tame' death.

The significance of such an occasion in Roman attitudes to death is suggested by the number of scenes on funerary memorials which show the deceased reposing on a couch in the company of surviving family members. Some of these specifically depict mourning around the corpse, and often include a pet animal or pair of slippers tucked under the couch to highlight the domestic context of the event (for instance, Amedick 1991, 72–74). Many examples are to be found on children's sarcophagi where it became a popular theme from about AD 130, and in these cases the home setting evokes their natural environment and suggests that their death was a peaceful one contained within the family circle. Yet this is in direct contrast to the sentiment regularly expressed in epitaphs to children (Lattimore 1962, 184–199) which presents their premature deaths as something fundamentally unnatural which caused parents to bury their children. Given the circumstances recorded by this particular memorial this is something that could be said about the death of Iulia Secunda who had predeceased her father, and although the epigram does not make it explicit such a notion of unnaturalness contributes to the idea of destructive Nature set up in the description of the deaths, and this in turn provokes fear and anger in the reader's mind.

In many ways the view of Death presented by this epigram fits with a hostile notion of Death which Ariès termed the 'Death of the Self'. According to him this was 'obtained quite simply by a shift of the sense of destiny towards the individual' (Ariès 1987, 605) which caused the individual to be valued over the community and the achievements and pleasures of this life over the prospect of the world to come. The effect of this was to shift the view of death as a natural and fitting conclusion to all human life to a sense of it as a violent interruption of an individual's activities which threatened to obliterate personal identity. In reaction to this hostile view (as Ariès described 1987, 202–03, 216), there was an increased emphasis on commemorating the dead through monuments and memorials as their survivors sought to counter the threat of their personal extinction by keeping memories of them alive. This was a way of defending the values of life against Death's attack, and also of recording the attainments of particular people. Roman society offers many instances of this process: commemoration of the dead had long been an important practice for patrician families as they sought to consolidate family tradition through recording the *res gestae* of distinguished members, but in the early empire it also became an important concern for certain upwardly mobile sections of society. For freedmen in particular Death posed a particular threat since the demise of a particular family member could well destroy their newly established family, and it is therefore not surprising to discover a strong impetus to commemorate their dead. As has been shown by studies of funerary memorials associated with people of this social stratum (such as Kleiner 1987, 59–71; Wrede 1971 and 1981; Ritti 1977, 386–70), there is repeated stress on the individuality of the deceased and allusion to their particular status and achievements. Portraits, references to professional activities, associations with particular deities, and even onomastic imagery are all brought into play as a way of inscribing memories of the specific hopes and achievements which Death had cruelly ended.

The funerary altar of Iulia Secunda and Cornelia Tyche includes many such features – portraits, divine allusions, name-play – which celebrate the women's individuality and so build up the notion of their lives as something good, destroyed by Death. Yet, as this paper will now argue, these same features also serve to place the women and their lives into a wider, collective context and by asserting some communal or universal values they help to 'tame' the view of Death that is presented: while the particular circumstances make it hard to forget the violent fate suffered by these individuals, care has been taken to foster positive elements as if to create a softer set of memories.

Immediate evidence to support this 'taming' of Death is provided by the existence of the altar itself. Despite the tragic circumstances of the women's drowning, the epigram on the side makes it very clear that they had received a tomb, an emphasis which may well have been intended to comfort those who continued to mourn their distant deaths.[3] Such comfort would have been needed since to die far from home brought a particular anguish, as various epitaphs record; death at sea could bring a double sorrow, through the horror of drowning and the fact that the dead could be deprived of a proper burial by family and friends (Lattimore 1962, 200–202; Carroll 2006, 158; Hope 2009, 60). It was the kind of unexpected death that was particularly dreaded. But this memorial brought Iulia Secunda and Cornelia Tyche back to their home community: it provided them with a 'monumental body' in Rome, even though their physical bodies had perished far away (Llewellyn 1991, 46–53). It gave their surviving family and friends a focus for their memories and mourning, and was a way of 'taming' the violence of their actual deaths. Strangely, the monument (as far as it can be reconstructed from surviving evidence) contains no formal dedication or statement of ownership, and it is only a reading of the inscription on the side that finally reveals the name of the man whose identity makes sense of the relationships '*filiae*' and '*uxoris*' inscribed above the women's busts – Iulius Secundus. One possible explanation is that the altar was originally set on some kind of plinth or within a funerary precinct which bore further inscriptions (*cf.* Kleiner 1987, 24–27).

A second argument for the 'taming' of Death on this altar comes from ideas expressed in the epigram about the workings of Fate (which have already been mentioned).[4] Sudden death (*mors repentina*) which could not be anticipated, was more than merely cruel: as Ariès (1987,10) commented, it had the power to destroy '.... the order of the world in which everyone believed; it became the absurd instrument of chance, which was sometimes disguised as the wrath of God'. In this epigram one might expect that the sudden death which met these women would have been denounced as arbitrary or as an act of an angry god, yet there is nothing of this.[5] On the contrary, the text goes to some length to counter such an interpretation by making long and explicit mention of the destinies which Fate had spun for them and for their survivors. Furthermore, the verse ends with reference to an underlying law which applies to everyone and is inalienable. The use of legal phraseology – *sistere in vadimonium* (to present oneself in court to answer bail) – reinforces the idea of Death as somehow socially sanctioned and non-negotiable. By these the epigram deliberately re-integrates the women's savage and sudden death into the normal order of the universe and of human society.

Similar effects are achieved by the portrayal of the women on the front of the altar, and by the various ways in which they are commemorated there. One striking feature of this is the juxtaposition of their portrait busts with attributes of two goddesses, Diana and Fortuna. This kind of association follows the fashion for representing the dead in the guise of gods which developed from the late first century AD and which was particular popular in freedmen commemorations (Wrede 1981). On this altar the choice of deities seems fairly straightforward: Diana was popular for unmarried girls, whilst Fortuna obviously connects with Cornelia's second name, Tyche.[6] As Wrede (1981, 99–100, 110) has shown there is plenty of literary and epigraphic evidence that women – usually more mature in age – were often associated with Fortuna, whether directly through their names or otherwise: it was a way of inviting good luck and a harmonious marriage. So although actual representations of women as Fortuna are relatively few, the kind of allusions which commemorate Cornelia Tyche here were not uncommon. This memorial is unusual, however, in showing the woman and her attributes separately rather than together in a single portrait figure.[7] More significantly perhaps, it is also unusual in that it appears to be the only recorded example of an onomastic image of the name, Tyche (Ritti 1977; Wrede 1981, 113–14). This type of visual image which alludes to an individual's name has been linked specifically with the same group of people in Roman society who favoured the use of funerary altars and also the practice of self-representation in the guise of gods, and these common factors help to confirm this family as coming from that particular socially aspirational background. It is fair, though, to deduce that the unusual iconographical features in this piece represent a special effort to highlight the notion of Tyche and link Cornelia's second name to the eponymous deity and cosmic force – indeed, given her tragic death and the stress on destiny found in the epigram such a link was surely inevitable. But because Tyche was so regularly seen as a source of good luck and concord in marriage (as is shown by epitaphs discussed by Lattimore 1962, 154–56), the reference to her on this monument also helps to convert bad fortune into good.

Quite what type or level of identification with the deity was intended when such associations were made in Roman portraiture has been a matter of long debate; but it is perhaps best interpreted as a way of signifying special qualities for which the dead were to be remembered – qualities that might be valued by living society but which would somehow transcend death and the material world.[8] Used to commemorate these two women it seems to illustrate a process which Ariès identified (1987, 605–606) as a consequence of the 'Death of the Self', when fearing total annihilation by physical death, people began to think about how their soul might survive separate from the body into the next life. Ariès' discussion of this was set in the context of later Christian eschatology, but it is certainly the case that according to one school of interpretation (as Cumont 1942) a good deal of Roman funerary art should be read in terms of other-worldly symbolism in which concerns to survive or conquer death were paramount. More recent views, however, tend to stress its role as commemorating achievements and status in the past life of the dead, rather than looking forward to some enhanced life after death; they would see self-representation in divine form as a *topos* concerned with qualities prized by contemporary society, and not as a sign of deification in itself. This reading would suggest that the divine attributes juxtaposed here with these women's portraits serve to contextualise them within the values of Roman society, and not to turn them somehow into goddesses.

This conclusion is supported by other aspects of the women's portrayal on the front of the altar: being entirely conventional it serves as a reminder of normal social expectations. In the usual tradition of Roman funerary art their tranquil facial expressions betray nothing of their violent death, while each turns her head slightly towards the other as if to emphasise their personal relationship. All is calmness and propriety. In a similar way each woman is extolled in the epitaph below her image for the usual qualities appropriate to her family position. Cornelia Tyche's virtues include incomparable affection and reverence (*adfectus sanctitatisque*) towards her husband and outstanding *pietas* to her children, while her daughter is praised, in further superlatives, for her precocious beauty, behaviour and learning. Parallels to all these sentiments can be found in many contemporary epitaphs to Roman wives and daughters (such as *CIL* VI 8517; 29580; 34268). The way in which Iulia Secunda is portrayed looking older than her eleven years is also conventional. There are many examples on children's memorials where they are represented like adults in order, it seems, to convey the qualities which they would have consolidated had they lived to maturity. Here some childishness is suggested by the fact that the girl's face is more delicately shaped than her mother's, but her portrait as a whole has an adult composure and composition. Such a mixture of qualities is also frequently found in Roman funerary portraits of children, often more markedly than here. For instance, a young girl of unstated age, shown reclining on the lid of a *kline* sarcophagus in Malibu (Kleiner and Matheson 1996, no. 142), is accompanied by dolls and pet dog, yet has the hairstyle and poise of a much older woman. Pliny (*Ep.* 5, 16.1–6) too commemorates a friend's daughter who had died aged nearly thirteen in similarly ambivalent terms: 'She had the prudence of an elderly lady, the dignity of a matron yet remained sweet like a little girl, with a virgin's modesty.' For such reasons it is possible to conclude that the imagery used to portray these two women is typical of Roman funerary commemoration at this time. In these particular circumstances its very normality serves to bring the remoteness of their death (in terms of its location and its violence) back into the confines of metropolitan Roman society and its expectations of how people should conduct themselves in life and be commemorated after their death. Familarity and collective values take over from the exotic and individual.

In all these various ways the memorial to Cornelia Tyche and Iulia Secunda can be said to 'tame' the violent manner of their death: not only has their extinction as individuals been held at bay, but they have been placed back within the values and memories of their home society. A sense of proper place seems to run throughout the monument, and the formalism of its design creates an orderly and 'tame' effect. As was noted above, each woman has been accorded (literally) her own space, with separate areas designated to receive her epitaph, her portrait, and the attributes of the deity with whom she was linked. This order is an implicit contrast to the chaotic circumstances of their death, suggested in the epigram by references to the force of the water and rather non-specific Spanish location.

Iulius Secundus, their husband and father, is also given his own special space in the acrostic inscription on the side, which is an unusual one since Latin funerary acrostics normally spell out the name of the deceased.[9] This incorporation of his name through the very words of the epitaph gives him a real presence in the processes of death and commemoration: it shows how sometimes 'Survivors of the deceased can also impose their presence and narrative voices on to epitaphs that turn the focus away from the deceased and even the poetic voice toward the survivor expressing their grief' (Erasmo 2008, 173). This explicit identification sets him up to appear like a witness of the tragedy he narrates and a mourner saying a public goodbye to the dead Such roles had an important part in the social aspect of the 'the tame death' described by Ariès (1987, 18–19) which involved the presence of other family members as witnesses along with a certain element of public display. Iulius Secundus is included in the commemoration of his dead wife and daughter by verbal means, just as contemporary funerary reliefs depict living and dead family members together in some act of mourning or commemoration. One example (D'Ambra 1995; Noy, this volume, Fig. 1.2; see also Stuart Jones 1912, 138, no. 65, pl. 23; Kleiner 1987,108, pl. VI, 3 and no. 43), appears to show a son on his deathbed witnessed by his living mother and his dead father whose representation in the scene as a portrait bust seems analogous to the verbal inclusion of Iulius Secundus alongside the two women. So by including himself in the picture Iulius is helping to bring life and death together, as if in some kind of peaceful and balanced resolution.

To sum up, the reading of the altar proposed here shows how many features of its visual imagery and written text serve to 'tame' the historic fact of the women's violent death. In particular they attempt to re-contextualise the women's fate as individuals within the collective concerns of their own community – its social values, its aspirations, and its need to mourn and properly dispose of the dead. In this way the impact of their tragedy can be softened a little; yet as Ariès said (1987, 605),'Death may be tamed, divested of natural forces and ritualised, but it is never experienced as a neutral phenomenon. It always remains a misfortune'. For Iulius Secundus grief would have remained, along with anticipation of his own hour of death. Nevertheless the overall message seems to be that despite the enduring loss of the women, their savage death has been mitigated through elements in the decoration: portraits, inscriptions and general design all seek to reinstate death as something that is part of the regular cosmic and social order and therefore familiar and to be expected.

How effectively this has been achieved can be shown by comparing the treatment of sudden death on another funerary altar, that of Titus Statilius Aper and Orcilia Anthis.[10] Erected by the man's parents around AD 120, (that is about twenty or thirty years before the memorial to Iulia Secunda and Cornelia Tyche) it commemorated a young husband and wife, whose ash urns were probably held in the two cavities on the back.

Although the wife is represented by a bust in the pediment of the *aedicula*, the main visual emphasis falls on the young man who, according to the main dedicatory inscription on the altar's plinth, had died at the age of twenty-two. He cuts an imposing figure in the main panel on the front, tall and dressed in a toga and tunic. The inscription records his profession as architect or surveyor (*mensor aedificorum*), and this is represented by the various tools which replace the usual ritual vessels as decoration on the sides. Furthermore, he is shown standing with a chest and cylindrical scroll-case (or possibly a roll of plans) at his left-hand side, and a tree behind him which indicates some outside location. All this could be read as an image of him working out on site, but such a literal reading is immediately undercut by two other features in the scene: to his right is the standing figure of a small nude boy and between them lies the body of a boar presumably killed in a hunt.

The boar is not so surprising given that the young man's *cognomen* was Aper (boar): its presence sets up some immediate word-play on his name and so enhances the notion of his individual identity, rather as the divine attributes had done for Cornelia Tyche. Indeed the possibility of associating him with a mythological hero is offered – but immediately taken away – in the three line epigram carved above the main inscription panel.[11] This alludes to the story of Meleager's hunting of the Calydonian boar as told by Ovid (*Met.* 8, 260–546) who narrates how Diana had used the boar to avenge herself, and how Meleager who had led the group which killed it, was himself killed after a quarrel about the spoils. The epigram states that unlike the mythological boar Aper was killed not because he was the agent of Diana's vengeance, nor because he was stabbed by Meleager's sword (*non virginis ira nec Meleager atrox perfodit viscera ferro)*, but because he was snatched away by a silent death. In Roman funerary art the hero Meleager became a popular figure to commemorate young men, like Aper, who had died prematurely at their physical peak (Brilliant 1984), but significantly this epigram does not go down this celebratory route. Instead it identifies the dead youth with the slain boar. Though the death which afflicted him is described as silent (*tacita*) other words show that this was no kindly or companionable silence: instead it crept up and brought ruin, snatching his young life (*obrepsit subito fecitq(ue) ruinam/ quae tibi crescenti rapuit iuvenile figuram*) in a way which lacked the heroic style of mythology. He was its innocent victim (*innocuus*); and the imagery by which the epigram conveys this shows a striking similarity to Ariès' (1987, 10–11) description of sudden death, quoted earlier, that it was ignominious and destroyed people's sense of cosmic order, becoming an 'instrument of chance' that was sometimes presented as divine anger.

Like the altar of Cornelia Tyche and Iulia Secunda, then, this monument commemorates the dead through the use of portraits, inscriptions and onomastic references. It too celebrates their individuality and commemorates an end which is reported as sudden and untimely. But while there are features in the women's memorial which arguably serve to 'tame' the savagery of their death, these are hard to find here. It is true that the portraits of husband and wife are conventional in appearance and that the dedication records the social status of the deceased and of the dedicants (his parents) which helps to contextualise the dead young man within his living family.

But the emphasis on him as an individual is very strong, both in the inscriptions and in the visual allusions to his profession (Stewart 2008, 25). The epigram too is heavy with a sense of what has been lost, and with a huge anger at what is presented as a rather ignominious (or at least unheroic) cause of death. Whereas Iulius Secundus spoke of the fates and of universal laws which must be obeyed, here death is shown as an agent in its own right, and one which is scarcely honourable in its actions. Some scholars have suggested that the figure of the nude young boy in the main panel may have represented Death since he seems to have once carried a torch and may have had feathered wings (Kleiner 1987, 215); but as he survives, he does not seem sufficiently menacing to symbolise the *mors tacita* which reduced the young man to the same state as the dead boar placed between them. The presence of this corpse in the main scene which is otherwise dedicated to the celebration of a young man's professional status jars by its sheer incongruity, alerting the viewer to the unexpectedness of the situation. Here, therefore, are signs of the kind of personal extinction which Ariès attributed to the 'Death of the Self'; they are unmitigated by the kind of 'taming' mechanisms that it has been possible to argue for the altar of Iulia Secunda and Cornelia Tyche.

In discussing the nineteenth century Ariès (1987, 609) comments on how up till then the sense of the individual '… had alternated between two extremes: the sense of a universal and common destiny and the sense of a personal and specific biography'. This notion of 'extremes' appears a useful way to sum up the different treatments of death we find on these two altars. Sudden death would have been a regular experience in ancient Rome, with a social impact which compounded personal grief and demanded recognition in its funerary commemoration. One way of managing this was to reconfigure the death as something intelligible in terms of universal laws and society's norms; another was to confront it as some kind of outrage in which individual lives were obliterated as if without cause. Although they had come from the same social background within about thirty years of each other, the memorial to Statilius Aper expresses stark loss and affront, while that to Iulia Secunda and Cornelia Tyche attempts to integrate their deaths into a more reassuring context and so to offer mourners at least the possibility of closure.

Notes

1 Front in Musée du Louvre, Paris, inv. no. 1331. Measurements: H. 1.164, W. 0.929, D. 0.16–0.22. Noses and chins of the busts chipped and restored. *CIL* VI 20674; Williams 1940–41, 47–52; Vermeule 1960, 24, no. 230; Ritti 1977, 283–4 no. 35; Wrede 1981, 227 no. 93, 234, no. 110; Kleiner 1987, 253–256, no. 113; Boschung 1987,105, no. 791; de Kersauson 1996, 302, no. 137.

2 See Wrede and Harpath 1986, 98; Wrede 1981, 227, and Kleiner 1987, 255 for the possibility that the left-hand side was decorated with Fortuna's mirror.

3 According to *CIL* VI, 20674, it had two cavities in its top surface to hold ashes. The epitaph states that 'quas habet...sepulchrum' which makes it sound as if the women's remains were retrieved from the sea.

4 Compare it to another epitaph in which a father mourns the sudden death of his wife and son at sea (as read by Erasmo 2008, 174–76), again using poetic language and another view of the Fates: *CIL* VI 25063; Courtney 1995, 176–77, no. 187.

5 Again, as compared to *CIL* VI 25063 where the bereaved father speaks of being 'robbed' by the Fates despite his vows to the gods.

6 Wrede 1981, 86. For Diana: Wrede 1981, 73, 86, 222–230; Matheson 1996, 189–190. For Fortuna/Tyche: Wrede 1971, 145–46, 164–66; Wrede 1981, 86, 233–236; *cf.* Matheson 1996, 182 and 189 for the range of contexts; and 190 for rarity of having both represented in this way. For other examples of deification on altars: Kleiner 1987, 84.

7 This separation of bust and attributes also occurs in the memorial to Claudia Semne where the attributes of Fortuna are shown in a pediment of the tomb: Wrede 1971, 128–129, Fig. 1. For the use of attributes as a shorthand reference to divinity, Hommel 1954, 44–46 (re attributes shown in pediment of Temple of Fortuna Redux, Rome).

8 *E.g.* Wrede 1971; Wrede 1981; Matheson 1996. Other signs of possible 'deification' have been suggested by Williams (1940–41, 49), Jucker (1961, 27); and Wrede (1971, 165 no. 1) for the chair, and for the acanthus leaves: Jucker 1961.

9 Courtney 1990, 6. *Cf.* Galletier 1922, 316, this is one of only two which spell the name of the dedicant; 315–318 for funerary acrostics generally.

10 Rome Capitoline Museum inv. no. 209. From Rome, Janiculum. Measurements: H: 1.89, W: 0.93, D: 0.79. *CIL* VI 1975; Stuart Jones 1912, 76–7; II,8; Ritti 1977, 290–291, no. 37; Kleiner 1987, 213–216, no. 83; Boschung 1987, 87, no. 326.

11 Galletier 1922, 263–268; *cf.* also 262–3 and 268; Courtney 1995, 164–5, 374, no. 176 for text, translation and commentary.

Bibliography

Amedick, R. (1991) *Die Sarkophage mit Darstellungen aus dem Menschenleben: Vita Privata* (*Die antiken Sarkophagreliefs* ed. C. Robert 1.4). Berlin, Mann.

Ariès, P. (1987) *The Hour of our Death.* Translated from the French by Helen Weaver. Peregrine Harmondsworth.

Boschung, D. (1987) *Antike Grabaltare aus den Nekropolen Roms.* Bern, Stampfli.

Brilliant, R. (1984). *Visual Narratives. Storytelling in Etruscan and Roman Art.* Ithaca and London, Cornell University Press.

Carroll, M. (2006) *Spirits of the Dead: Roman Funerary Commemoration in Western Europe.* Oxford, Oxford University Press.

Courtney, E. (1990) Greek and Latin Acrostichs. *Philologus* 134, 3–13.

Courtney, E. (1995) *Musa Lapidaria. A selection of Latin Verse Inscriptions.* Atlanta, Scholars Press.

Cumont, F. (1942) *Recherches sur le symbolisme funéraire des romains.* Paris, P. Geuthner.

D'Ambra, E. (1995) Mourning and the making of ancestors in the Testamentum Relief. *American Journal of Archaeology* 99, 667–681.

de Kersauson, K. (1996) *Musée du Louvre. Catalogue des portraits romains. II De l'année de la guerre civile (69–69 après J.-C.) à la fin de l'Empire.* Paris, Réunion des musées nationaux.

Erasmo, M. (2008) *Reading Death in Ancient Rome.* Columbus, Ohio, Ohio State University Press.

Galletier, E. (1922) *Étude sur la poésie funéraire romaine d'après les inscriptions.* Paris, Hachette.

Hommel, P. (1954) *Studien zu den römischen Fig.urengiebeln der Kaiserzeit.* Berlin. Mann.
Hope, V. (2009) *Roman Death. The Dying and the Dead in Ancient Rome.* London, Continuum.
Jucker, H. (1961) *Das Bildnis im Blätterkelch: Geschichte und Bedeutung einer römischen Porträtform.* Olten, Urs Graf-Verlag.
Kleiner, D. E. E. (1987) *Roman Imperial Funerary Altars with Portraits.* Archaeologica 62. Rome.
Kleiner, D. E. E. and Matheson S. B. (eds.) (1996) *I Claudia. Women in Ancient Rome.* New Haven, Yale Univerity Art Gallery.
Lattimore, R. (1962) *Themes in Greek and Roman Epitaphs.* Urbana, University of Illinois Press.
Llewellyn, N. (1991) *The Art of Death. Visual Culture in the English Death Ritual c.1500-c.1800.* London, Reaktion.
Matheson, S. B. (1996) *The divine Claudia:women as goddesses in Roman art.* In Kleiner and Matheson 1996, 182–193.
Ritti, T. (1977) Immagini onomastiche sui monumenti sepochrali de età imperiale. *Atti della accademia nazionale dei Lincei* XXI, 4, 258–397.
Stewart, P. (2008) *The Social History of Roman Art.* Cambridge, Cambridge University Press.
Stuart Jones, H. (1912) *The Sculptures of the Museo Capitolino.* Oxford, Clarendon Press.
Vermeule, C. C. (1960) The Dal Pozzo-Albani drawings of Classical antiquities in the British Museum. *Transactions of the American Philosophical Society* 50, 1–38.
Williams, P. L. (1940–41) Two Roman reliefs in renaissance disguise. *Journal of the Warburg and Courtauld Institutes* 4, 47–66.
Wrede, H. (1971) Das Mausoleum der Claudia Semne und die bürgerliche Plastik der Kaiserzeit. *Römische Mitteilungen* 78, 125–166.
Wrede, H. (1981) *Consecratio in formam deorum: vergöttliche Privatpersonen in der römischen Kaiserzeit.* Mainz, von Zabern.
Wrede, H. and Harprath, R. (1986) *Der Codex Coburgensis. Das erste systematische Archäologiebuch.* Kunstsammlungen der Veste, Coburg.

6

'Causa ante mortua est quam tu natus es': Aspects of the Funeral in Cicero's *Pro Rabirio Perduellionis Reo*

Eleanor Brooke

This paper presents a reading of a speech by Cicero which is often dismissed as an arcane oddity: that given in defence of Rabirius on a charge of *perduellio* – treasonable behaviour towards the state – from early in 63 BC, Cicero's consular year. It is certainly one of the more unusual speeches, and indeed trials, for which we have evidence in the late Republic, concerning as it did events which had taken place over thirty years before. Cicero himself makes much of this circumstance in order to discredit his opponents: one of his main lines of argument is that they should never have brought such a case in the first place. On his presentation, this is a trial which comes thirty-seven years too late. The whole thing should have been firmly buried: instead, its audience was faced with ancestor masks and dead statesmen as active participants and key witnesses.

I will argue here that this imagery comes to dominate the speech, and that Cicero's primary approach is to explore the process of establishing public memory, and its inherent susceptibility to change. He makes use of language and settings associated with the traditional aristocratic funeral in order to demonstrate for his audience the problems that might be faced in attempting to guarantee a posthumous reputation in the face of marching time and revisionist future generations; and provides an active enactment of an obligation which he himself invokes, for each living generation to stand as surety for the dead. The extent of Roman concern throughout the Republic's long history with fashioning and disseminating remembrance of individuals has frequently been demonstrated in its varied aspects, from the Scipionic epitaphs to the tomb of the baker Eurysaces: from *imagines* displayed in the homes of the elite to annual rites of celebration held for the dead.[1] Cicero in this speech endeavours to draw on, and thereby confirm, the emotional power of the dead and the continued significance of their memory, and makes use of these to construct for himself as well as for his client a strong public identity.

Background

Rabirius was on trial for his part in the murder of people's tribune L. Appuleius Saturninus, which had occurred in 100 BC during the sixth consulship of Gaius Marius. Increasingly violent popular support for Saturninus had prompted the Senate to pass the hotly contested *senatus consultum ultimum* (hereafter referred to as the SCU): and this backed Marius and his fellow consul L. Valerius Flaccus in taking any steps necessary to restore order at Rome.

It was under the banner of this decree that the events here under discussion took place. An armed force was led through the city against Saturninus and his supporters: eventually they were barricaded on the Capitol, and their supplies cut off. At this point Marius is said to have promised them safety if they surrendered, although sources and critics alike disagree as to how genuine this offer of clemency might have been. In any case, it was never put to the test: the barricades were stormed, and the Capitol reclaimed by the senatorial forces. In the process, Saturninus and Glaucia were taken prisoner: before their fate could officially be decided, they were attacked and killed by an angry mob.

Our main account of Rabirius' trial comes from Dio, who explains events as follows:

> Caesar himself was judge together with Lucius Caesar, for the charge against Rabirius was no ordinary one, but that of *perduellio*, as it was called; and they condemned him, although they had not been chosen according to precedent by the people, but by the praetor himself, which was not lawful. Rabirius appealed, and would certainly have been convicted by the people also, had not Metellus Celer, who was an augur and praetor, prevented it. When nothing else would cause them to heed him and they were unconcerned by the fact that the trial had been held in a manner contrary to custom, he ran up to the Janiculum before they took any vote at all, and pulled down the military flag, so that it was no longer lawful for them to reach a decision...On that occasion, when the signal was pulled down, the assembly was adjourned and Rabirius was saved. (37.27.1: tr. E. Cary, Loeb 1914)[2]

Thus far, the narrative is complex enough: accounts vary as to who was responsible for the actual blows that killed Saturninus, and the extent to which he and his followers had already attempted to surrender to consular forces. Such uncertainties, however, become much more pronounced once we turn to the trial of Rabirius itself, due in part to the conflicting evidence provided by various historical sources – not only Dio's, but also that of Suetonius (*Iul.* 12), in which he suggests that Rabirius would have been acquitted – and in part to the introduction of three striking and unusual features in the handling of the defendant's summons to court.

The first of these is the actual method by which the charges were brought. Rabirius' accusers had resurrected the archaic procedure of appointing two *duumviri* to preside over the case and pronounce sentence upon him, instead of the more recently employed custom of giving such jurisdiction to the popular tribunes. The last recorded trial for *perduellio* under the duumviral procedure is that of Manlius Capitolinus in 338 BC, although as an accusation brought before the tribunes it is thought to have appeared as recently as 87 BC.[3] Cicero uses this archaism in order to discredit the prosecution, laying emphasis on the barbaric nature of the entire proceeding and associating it, somewhat disingenuously, with Tarquinius Superbus (§13). His main complaint is that under this procedure, Rabirius had been declared guilty without trial by the *duumviri*: only then did he have the right of appeal to the people (*provocatio*) to which Dio refers, and which allowed him to put his case in a *contio* before its merits were assessed in the *comitia centuriata*.[4]

It is also striking, and unprecedented in Roman legal history, for an accusation to have been brought so long after the original events upon which it is based: and it is the uncertainties inherent in the concept of the SCU which are widely held to have enabled such a prosecution. Despite Cicero's attempts in this speech to associate the SCU with ancestral values and practice, it had in fact first been employed only twenty years before Saturninus' death, to cover the measures taken to deal with Gaius Gracchus in 121 BC. There too the final outcome had been Gracchus' death, at the hands this time of senators and *equites*. The presiding consul L. Opimius was tried and acquitted of his murder almost immediately afterwards.

The wording of this decree is, however, ambiguous and imprecise, so far as it can be reconstructed: unfortunately much of our evidence for its exact nature comes from Cicero's account of it with reference to Rabirius and Catiline, in his not unweighted speeches.[5] Little indication seems to have been given as to where responsibility lay for the actions carried out under its sanction, and how far beyond the bounds of everyday legality they could be extended: it is not even clear whether final accountability for these lay with the consuls who carried them out, or the senate whose ultimate decree it had been in the first place. In addition, the SCU only had the power to suspend the law for an undefined period of emergency, which in itself made judgment of the actions taken during this period even more difficult: since the criteria by which these would usually have been evaluated were the very objects under suspension.

It is not only the bringing of this prosecution in the first place which is both unique and problematic: even the resolution of the trial itself adds a further layer of confusion. The episode on the Janiculum remains a mystery. Indeed, although several other sources do refer to the *comitia centuriata* as remaining assembled only as long as a guard was posted on the Janiculum, in no surviving ancient history except Dio's is there any allusion to an occasion on which this flag is specifically said to have been lowered: much less so, to it having been lowered simply to stop an assembly, with no enemy in fact approaching. Dio merely attributes this custom to an unspecified date in the distant past, with no other information as to its origin or practice.

The setting for our version of the speech comes from the second attempt to try Rabirius on this charge: having previously been found guilty by a board appointed to investigate the death of Saturninus, presided over by Julius and Lucius Caesar, he appealed to the people for a different verdict. Rabirius' chief prosecutor at this second hearing, T. Labienus, was nephew to one of those killed fighting at the side of Saturninus.

However, despite this family connection providing key motivation for the prosecution, the political context for this trial went far deeper than one man's desire for restitution. What was at stake here was a more lasting threat to the senatorial order: the potential risk of future conviction, no matter how much time had elapsed, for actions originally sanctioned by an SCU. This would have the consequence of undermining it altogether, and thus eliminating one of the senate's main constitutional props. Similarly, from the point of view of the trial's non-elite audience, senatorial entitlement to issue an SCU with no recourse to the people, and to claim operational immunity for the actions carried out during the period of its application, effectively removed any restrictions as to how they could be treated, and threatened the traditional right of the Roman citizen to a fair trial before condemnation.

Trial as Funeral

i. The imago

The occurrence of all these features together in one trial is a combination unprecedented in our records of the Republic, combining as it does the aggressively new with the long obsolete. However, an additional aspect of this trial which is likewise striking, and equally central to its conduct, has received comparatively little critical attention: the portrait, or *imago*, of Saturninus which the chief prosecutor Labienus produced in court. This was a particularly daring move because as a result of his death in 100, Saturninus' images had been banned from public display (§24–5). Such a punishment was reserved for those who had been declared to be enemies of the state, and marked their official erasure from the annals of history: it was no longer permissible for their picture to be produced in public or displayed privately.[6] The use of such a prop appears not to have been an isolated incident: Quintilian refers to an unnamed defendant's production of her husband's *imago* in court (6.1.40), although he remarks that its effect was not what had been intended: instead of moving the jury to sympathy, it produced in them fits of laughter.[7] However, no date is provided for this latter trial, and no evidence survives of any attempt in the later years of the Republic to exhibit in court the prohibited image of someone disgraced as the author of violence and sedition: indeed, Flower (2006, 83) refers to this treatment of Saturninus as the first occurrence of such a ban against anyone at the time of his death. It seems difficult, then, to underestimate how powerful and remarkable such a spectacle must have been. Quintilian, who provides us with our only other source for Labienus' action, seems to regard such a tactic with disapproval: he refers to the use of the mask in this particular trial as something better suited to the theatre ('scaenae', 6.1.49) and adds favourably that Cicero dispelled its effects 'graviter', with dignity, and by simple *oratio*.

It is my contention here that it is the appearance of this mask, and the attendant imagery which would have rendered it so persuasive for Labienus' audience, which came to dominate the rest of the proceedings: and that its associations with funerary practice, as strongly suggested by the setting for its production and by Cicero's treatment of it as a device, provide us with one way into the more general concern expressed in Cicero's defence of Rabirius with questions of public commemoration of and honour for the dead. Cape (2002, 137) notes in the speech the occurrence of certain elements of the kind of *laudatio funebris* elsewhere recorded as common to the aristocratic funeral at Rome. This paper will argue that it is these elements which come to shape and define the entire oration, and that Cicero steadily builds up a nexus of associations with funerary practice which serve to cast the entire *Pro Rabirio* as an alternative form of *laudatio funebris* for Rabirius pre-mortem, as well as for all those Romans who can be shown to have shared with him the glory of Saturninus' defeat and death. The audience will by the end of proceedings have been confronted, through the speeches of both sides, with the dead in a variety of forms. Cicero himself acknowledges this in the opening sections of his defence, in a declaration which comes to be programmatic for the speech and indeed trial as a whole: he describes the case itself as dead ('mortua', §25), and presents this as one of the reasons why it should never have been set in motion.

It is unfortunate that the majority of our sources for the aristocratic funeral are dated either considerably before or considerably after the period under discussion: and that for the final century of the Republic we have little contemporary evidence as to how such ceremonies might have been conducted. The most detailed account of the traditional funeral procession is to be found in Polybius' *Histories*, although his description has often been viewed as an idealised version of events: significantly, he does not tie his account to the burial of a particular individual, but presents it as something more general in scope. It will be useful to cite his account in full:

> Whenever one of their leading men dies, when the funeral has been arranged, the body is carried with every kind of honour into the Forum to the so-called *rostra*, where it is usually propped up for all to see, but rarely is it laid down. The whole mass of the people stand round to watch, and an adult son if he can be present, or if not some other relative, mounts the *rostra* and delivers a speech about the virtues of the dead man and the successes achieved during his lifetime. As a result the people, not only those who shared in the deeds but those who did not, remember what happened and picture it. Both share the same feelings to the extent that the loss seems not to be confined to the mourners but to be a public one which affects the people. Then after the burial of the body and the performance of the customary rites, they place the image of the dead man in the most public part of the house, keeping it in a wooden shrine. This image is a mask, which is made to resemble closely in both the shape of its face and its colouring the features of the dead man. The masks are displayed during public sacrifices and they compete in decorating them. And when a leading member of the family dies, the masks

> are taken to the funeral, and are there worn by men, who seem most like the original, both in height and their general appearance. These men are dressed according to the rank of the deceased: a toga with a purple border for a consul or praetor, an all-purple toga for a censor, and one embroidered with gold for a man who had celebrated a triumph or done something similar. These men all rider in chariots with the rods and axes and other symbols of those in power according to the dignity of rank and status achieved by each man in his lifetime. When they reach the *rostra* they all sit down in order on ivory stools. It is not easy for an ambitious and virtuous young man to see a finer spectacle than this. For who would not be impressed at the sight of the masks of all these men who have won fame in their time, now gathered together as if alive and breathing? What spectacle could be more noble than this? Moreover the man who gives the speech over the man who is about to be buried, when he has finished the eulogy, begins to praise the others present, relating the successes and achievements of each, beginning with the oldest. As a result of this, since the reputation for virtue of good men is constantly renewed, the fame of those who did some noble deed is immortal and the glory of those who have served their country becomes well known and is an inheritance for posterity. But the most important result is that it inspires young men to undergo anything for the common good in the hope of winning the glory that follows the brave deeds of men. (Polybius 6.53–4, tr. V. Hope)[8]

Cicero tells us little about how Labienus might have chosen to present Saturninus' *imago* to his audience, and provides no indication as to how this stunt might have been received. Indeed, the actual nature and form of this portrait is another problematic element in this already problematic trial, and has produced disagreement amongst critics. Was it in fact a funerary mask, in the mould of those paraded at aristocratic death rituals, or would it have been closer in appearance to another form of portraiture? Both Cape and Tyrrell treat this as if it were identical to an ancestor mask, and read the speech accordingly: for Cape, it forms one of those elements of the *laudatio funebris* which he infers in Labienus' speech. However, Flower (2006, 83–4) points out that Saturninus had not reached the curule aedileship and was thus unqualified for such a mask, and asks rather whether it could have been a special kind of portrait made after his death (*cf.* Noy, this volume). Despite this strong objection, it seems to me that even if this were not an *imago* in its strict funerary sense, the associations here created for it through the context in which it was produced would have been enough to suggest a resemblance in function to that of an actual funerary mask. The parading of a dead man's image, the juxtaposition of oratory with that image, and above all the occurrence of these events on the Rostra – the customary location during the aristocratic funeral for displaying the body of the deceased, placing each actor-ancestor on his own curule chair, and the *laudatio funebris* – combine to create this impression. To present, then, any image, whether technically funerary or not, of Saturninus in this way would have had the likely effect of assimilating that portrait to the kind of *imago* paraded after death, and would have produced from it some of the same effects. A reading of this event, therefore, in terms of our other evidence for the public appearances of funeral masks will be useful in providing us with a broader perspective here, and in enabling us to assess its potential outcomes.

The most obvious, and arguably the most immediate, of these stems from the overwhelming association of the funeral mask with mourning publicly expressed: and thus it can be inferred that Labienus was aiming to alter or heighten the emotional tone of his prosecution, and to evoke in his audience the kind of response to Saturninus' *imago* which Polybius suggests for their production in the context of a funeral. The evocation of grief amongst Labienus' audience would have functioned as a powerful directive for their eventual judgement on the case: analogous perhaps to that occasioned by the frequently attested tactic of exposing the battle scars of a war hero on trial, or the powerful topographical associations which so influenced the last trial to make use of *duumviri* – that of Manlius Capitolinus.[9] The response of the spectators at Polybius' standardised aristocratic funeral would, if replicated here, have ensured the sympathy of this crowd for Saturninus and thus for Labienus' prosecution: and would have ensured that Cicero, when he came to speak, would have been forced to dispel and redirect it.

It is also evident from the passage by Polybius that public funerals functioned largely as an expression or affirmation of Roman values, as well as providing both the participating family and the ring of observers with a powerful sense of historical continuity. The achievements of individual ancestors and their magistracies were celebrated in the *laudatio*: the chronological arrangement of the *pompa funebris* laid emphasis on the passing down of virtues from generation to generation, as well as on the unbroken achievements of that particular family within the wider scope of Roman history: and the intended effect on the viewer, as Polybius is at pains to point out, is to inspire them also to the emulation of such deeds and virtues. Flower (1996, 277) writes of the funerary spectacle as inviting 'a dialogue with citizens both during the procession and during the eulogy', which 'affirmed a shared view of the past and the whole community's attitude towards it.', whilst Gowing (2005, 14–15) discusses the funeral and the kind of commemoration contained therein as vital for the continuation of Roman society. Such an approach to the aristocratic funeral also informs the work of Dufallo (2007, 118, 127), Ochs (1993, 93–5), Hölkeskamp (2006, 483) and Bettini (1991, 167–183) among others: and the notion of the funeral as representative of Rome's shared and collective past finds vivid expression in Virgil's Parade of Heroes in the sixth book of the *Aeneid*.[10]

To produce the *imago* of Saturninus, then, reserves for him a place in this normative ritual, and provides him with the kind of funeral of which his actual fate deprived him. The potential result of this restoration, and at the same time one of the wider consequences of these proceedings, is to provide the Roman people with an alternative narrative and evaluation of the events of 100 BC: to change, in other words, history as it had been written in and about that year by the repeated process of denying Saturninus any form of public honour after death. The aristocratic funeral, with its procession of *imagines*, provided its audience with a literal rendering of both gentilician and Roman identity: the established traditions of the city were played out and confirmed – almost, indeed, re-lived – in the parade of its previous generations.

It is thus clear that by the time Cicero stood up to speak, the trial of Rabirius had already been framed in funerary terms: and that this formed at least one of the strands by which Labienus sought to ensure the simultaneous rehabilitation of Saturninus and the condemnation of the man accused of having killed him. How, then, was Cicero to respond?

ii. The active dead: mourning and memorialising

In order to neutralise the effect of the *imago*, Cicero adopts two broad ways of dealing with it. First of all, he seeks to provide this move to rouse popular feeling with a different kind of framework altogether, reminding his audience of the previous precedents laid down for engaging with Saturninus' mask. Cicero makes a number of connections between the portrait as displayed here, and the more usual setting for such a display – the aristocratic funeral. This *imago* is here first associated with grief, in §24:

> at C. Decianus, de quo tu saepe commemoras, quia, cum hominem omnibus insignem notis turpitudinis, P. Furium, accusaret summo studio bonorum omnium, queri est ausus in contione de morte Saturnini, condemnatus est...
>
> But Gaius Decianus, whom you so often mention, was condemned during his prosecution -undertaken with the fullest support from all good citizens – of Publius Furius, a man infamous for all kinds of disgraceful behaviour, because in his speech he was bold enough to regret the death of Saturninus...

Furthermore, Cicero casts the actions of these previous supporters of Saturninus in terms very similar to those used of such *imagines* in a funerary context, arguing that they too indicated a desire to honour or even to imitate the dead man: he refers to the judgement passed on Sex. Titius, condemned for the possession of a similar *imago*, as applying to

> ...qui hominis hostilem in modum seditiosi imagine aut mortem eius honestaret, aut desideria imperitorum misericordia commoveret, aut suam significaret imitandae improbitatis voluntatem.
>
> ...anyone who, by means of the *imago* of a man who had been seditious in the manner of a public enemy, either made that man's death respectable, or roused longing in the ignorant with an appeal to pity, or indicated his own desire to imitate such wickedness.(§24).

Through mention of previous attempts to restore Saturninus to the status he had been denied, and, likewise, to treat him in terms of funerary honours, Cicero represents that of Labienus as the latest in a series: and thus provides guidance for the response of his own audience. Just as those attempts had been damaging for their authors, so too should Labienus' far bolder action receive identical rejection.

Moreover, this suggestion is compounded by the manner of Cicero's reference here to the fact of this portrait being produced by Labienus 'in rostra'. He makes use of repeated imagery of sailing and shipwreck to describe the situation of those who had been so condemned, and this even serves to turn the familiar iconography of the Rostra against Labienus. The naval victories to which the Rostra's name is so often attributed (Livy 8.14.12) become the 'naufragium' of those who attempt to support Saturninus.[11]

This handling of the *imago* of Saturninus functions as culmination for a series of references throughout the speech which serve to associate Labienus and the prosecution with excessive or wrongful mourning. §14 is devoted to a comparison between Labienus and Gracchus, ostensibly prompted by that made in Labienus' speech:

> Scilicet tibi graviorem dolorem patrui tui mors attulit quam C. Graccho fratris, et tibi acerbior eius patrui mors est quem numquam vidisti quam illi eius fratris quicum concordissime vixerat, et simili iure tu ulcisceris patrui mortem atque ille persequeretur fratris, si ista ratione agere voluisset, et par desiderium sui reliquit apud populum Romanum Labienus iste, patruus vester, quisquis fuit, ac Ti. Gracchus reliquerat.

> No doubt, for you the death of your uncle was a heavier grief than was Gaius Gracchus' for his brother; for you the death of that uncle whom you had never seen was more bitter than was for Gaius Gracchus that of the brother with whom he had lived in perfect amity; you are avenging the death of your uncle by a code similar to that with which Gracchus would have pursued recompense for the death of his brother, if on this reckoning he had wished to act; and this man Labienus, your uncle, whoever he was, left among the Roman people a longing equal to that felt for Tiberius Gracchus.

Cicero here unleashes his most sarcastic tone, and a series of rhetorical questions forces the point home: Labienus is taking his grief to an excessive level, and should not, therefore, be thought worthy of comparison with Gaius Gracchus. Such criticism has a threefold effect. First, it shows up Labienus' supposed claim to be following in Gracchus' footsteps as misinformed, at best, and thus makes a direct attack upon his status as *popularis* speaker: and second, it suggests that Labienus' instigation of this accusation was based either on an excess of family feeling, or on a feigned grief which serves as cover for different political aims. To undermine Labienus' motivation for bringing such a charge could serve to discredit the whole prosecution.

However, as its third effect, this passage also compounds the portrait Cicero draws throughout of Labienus as someone who simply has no idea about how the rules and traditions of Rome prescribe the handling of death, in any of its forms. This is demonstrated consistently through the speech. For example, whilst Cicero upholds ancestral standards on the execution of Roman citizens, the bloodthirsty Labienus breaks them with ease:

> ...fateor atque etiam, Labiene, profiteor et prae me fero te ex illa crudeli, importuna, non tribunicia actione sed regia, meo consilio, virtute, auctoritate esse depulsum. (§17)

> ...I confess, Labienus, or indeed, even declare and display, that you were driven back by my purpose, virtue and authority from a course of action that was cruel, inappropriate, and more suited to a king than to a tribune.

Labienus chooses association with those Cicero categorises as deserving of a shameful death, while Rabirius and all worthy men took the cause of virtue and wise government:

> quid tandem C. Rabirium facere convenit? utrum inclusum atque abditum latere in occulto atque ignaviam suam tenebrarum ac parietum custodiis tegere, an in Capitolium pergere atque ibi se cum tuo patruo et ceteris ad mortem propter vitae turpitudinem confugientibus congregare, an cum Mario, Scauro, Catulo, Metello, Scaevola, cum bonis denique omnibus coire non modo salutis verum etiam periculi societatem? (§21)
>
> What, finally, was it fitting for Gaius Rabirius to do? To lie in hiding, tucked away and concealed, and to cover up his own cowardice with the protection of darkness and walls? To make his way to the Capitol and there to join up with your uncle and with the others who were fleeing towards death on account of their shameful lives? Or to come together with Marius, Scaurus, Catulus, Metellus, Scaevola, and ultimately with all good citizens, an alliance not only of safety but also of danger?

This does not, however, form the only strand of Cicero's opposition to the tactics of the prosecution. Although he makes no attempt to produce a funeral mask or similar in his own speech, he nevertheless sets out, as Cape (2002, 137) puts it, to appropriate the funerary associations conjured up by Labienus, and to utilise them for his own client. Cicero creates his own links to the dead: and it is tempting to read this as providing some kind of corrective to the dramatic strategy of his opponent. He too lays claim to them: not as *imagines*, but as participants.

From §20 onwards Cicero gives his own account of the events under consideration. He describes the passing of the SCU as a necessary senatorial response: and the threat to the Republic which Saturninus embodied is repeatedly emphasised. If Cicero is to be believed, every good man in Rome was on the side that Rabirius took: and they are all equally implicated in the single possible crime that Rabirius had committed, which was to bear arms against Saturninus. It is this point which provides the only real argument which Cicero makes against Labienus' accusation, although he makes it with force and with copious illustration: this is to be a defence not only of Rabirius, but of his contemporaries also. He asks

> Nam si C. Rabirius fraudem capitalem admisit quod arma contra L. Saturninum tulit, huic quidem adferet aliquam deprecationem periculi aetas illa qua tum fuit; Q. vero Catulum, patrem huius, in quo summa sapientia, eximia virtus, singularis humanitas fuit, M. Scaurum, illa gravitate, illo consilio, illa prudentia, duos Mucios, L. Crassum, M. Antonium, qui tum extra urbem cum praesidio fuit, quorum in hac civitate longe maxima consilia atque ingenia fuerunt, ceteros pari dignitate praeditos custodes gubernatoresque rei publicae quem ad modum mortuos defendemus?

> For if Gaius Rabirius was guilty of a capital offence in bearing arms against Lucius Saturninus, at least his youth at the time might provide him with some means of mitigating the danger of this accusation. But as for Quintus Catulus, possessor of great good sense, remarkable character and singular humanity, and the father of this man here present; or Marcus Scaurus, notable for his austerity, good counsel and sagacity; or the two Mucii or Lucius Crassus or Marcus Antonius, who was at that time positioned on guard outside the city, all of whom in counsel and ability had long been indispensible to the running of this state; or the others of equal standing, guardians and protectors of the state – how are we to defend them, now that they are dead? (§26)

and follows this up with two similar questions in succession:

> L. Flaccum, hominem cum semper in re publica, tum in magistratibus gerendis, in sacerdotio caerimoniisque quibus praeerat diligentissimum, nefarii sceleris ac parricidi mortuum condemnabimus?
>
> Are we to convict the dead Lucius Flaccus, who always conducted himself most scrupulously in state affairs, and in the conduct of those magistracies, priesthoods and ceremonies for which he was responsible, of terrible wrongdoing and of murder?
>
> C. Marium, quem vere patrem patriae, parentem, inquam, vestrae libertatis atque huiusce rei publicae possumus dicere, sceleris ac parricidi nefarii mortuum condemnabimus?
>
> Are we to convict the dead Gaius Marius, whom truly we might address as the father of his country, indeed the parent of your liberty and of this state, of wrongdoing and a terrible murder? (§27)

There are some elements here which evoke the aristocratic funeral with equal potency, but in support of Cicero's own case this time. Individually, these features can be found elsewhere in a number of Cicero's other works: but together, as here, they form a compelling picture. Such an approach by Cicero is not an overt one, and should be regarded rather as creating the atmosphere of the aristocratic funeral, than as a direct mapping of that form onto this.

The first of these elements is simply the form of situation in which Cicero places himself. His audience is confronted with an orator speaking on behalf of the dead: a subject presented in a state of transition between life and death (§37) – an impression which would no doubt have been furthered by the tradition of defendants wearing mourning, and the connections implicit therein between trial and funeral: and a group of dead men treated as if alive and in attendance, whose own reputations are under discussion and interlinked with the verdict passed on the defendant. This can be seen to echo almost exactly Polybius' description of the ingredients of an aristocratic funeral. It can further be inferred that the involvement of the people and their sense of loss, mentioned also as a key aspect of such a funeral by Polybius, might also have reflected the kind of effect Cicero intended for his speech, and the sympathy he would have been hoping to evoke for his client. In both situations, the participation of the citizen body is vital: their appreciation of the virtues and achievements of the dead are an integral part of the affirmative nature of Roman funeral ritual, and this can be seen to correspond closely to their more immediately practical role as potential voters on the subject of Rabirius' guilt or innocence.

Cicero's treatment of the dead also adds to this impression. He calls upon them as witnesses (using the phrase 'testor', §30), and thus implies their actual involvement in the trial, acting as approving spectators for Cicero and Rabirius. This seems to form part of the function of ancestors at funerals: Flower describes them in such a context as 'participants in a public drama' (1996, 129). Furthermore, the language used by Cicero here is suggestive of that used by Polybius: he is not just defending the dead, but advocating that they should be honoured ('ornabimus', §30). Polybius describes the decoration of such *imagines* on public occasions: the term used, κοσμέω, corresponds closely in meaning to *ornare*.

Cicero also associates this honour closely with praise of the virtues and achievements of the best-known figures among the many dead that are mentioned: Marius, Catulus, Crassus, Antonius. Here the process is not strictly chronological, as in a traditional funeral oration, but in order of seniority: the culmination is Cicero's praise of both consuls at the end of §25. These snapshots of their achievements are focused around the events of 100 to ensure maximum relevance to the matter at hand. The concern which he expresses for their enduring reputations after death, and their remembrance in Roman public life, echoes one of the most vital functions of the aristocratic funeral: that of cementing the reputation of individual families through praise of their services to the state, and thereby providing a wider re-statement of Roman self-identity (*cf.* Blösel 2000, 37–45; Flower 1996, 127, 147–8). The status of the dead is expressed in the *Pro Rabirio* as something which should be a cause for consideration and celebration among the living and dead alike:

> neque quisquam nostrum in rei publicae periculis cum laude ac virtute versatur quin spe posteritatis fructuque ducatur. itaque cum multis aliis de causis virorum bonorum mentes divinae mihi atque aeternae videntur esse, tum maxime quod optimi et sapientissimi cuiusque animus ita praesentit in posterum ut nihil nisi sempiternum spectare videatur.
>
> There is not one of us who, when at times of danger for the state he behaves in praiseworthy and resolute fashion, is not guided by the hope and expectation of posterity's reward. And although there are many reasons that the minds of good men seem to me both divine and immortal, this is chief amongst them: that the spirits of all the best and wisest men anticipate the future to such an extent that they seem to gaze upon nothing but eternity. (§29)

It is this central concept of post-mortem honour, both individual and collective, which is enacted in the publicly observed funeral procession and *laudatio*.

This impression is further underlined by Cicero's treatment of Rabirius at the end of the speech. There the focus is not on Rabirius' being spared for life, but for the kind of death ('the opportunity to die honourably; honeste moriendi', as reconstructed in the fragmentary §37) which Saturninus has specifically been denied ('mortem eius honestaret', §24). He wants nothing more than a traditional burial ('patrio sepulchro' and 'legitimo funere'): to be treated and remembered as a Marius, not as a Saturninus. The suggestion seems to be that it is this speech, and its hoped-for outcome, that will guarantee the terms of Rabirius' remembrance and post-mortem treatment: Cicero asks his audience, through a vote for acquittal, to allow Rabirius the kind of funeral which is being evoked for him here.

On this reconstruction, then, the different participants in the aristocratic funeral find their counterparts here: Rabirius appears in the role of the recently deceased, whilst Marius with his senatorial colleagues represent Rabirius' ancestors. But Cicero too must have a place in this self-assembled '*gens*'. I would argue that his appearance as *laudator* shows him playing two parts simultaneously, both of which serve to direct his audience as to what they are witnessing. On the one hand, the funeral speech would, in Polybius' account, have been delivered by the member of the next generation of the family who bore the closest relation to the deceased, and would provide ideally the opportunity for his first public appearance as orator. That Cicero takes this role here is signposted by his repeated declarations of *aemulatio* with respect to both Rabirius and Marius: and in particular, his claim that if he were ever placed in the same position, he would do what Marius had done (§35). Imitating, equalling, even replicating one's ancestors was a key aspect of aristocratic identity, as the elogia of the Scipiones in particular demonstrate for us: and a number of sources (including once again Polybius) draw attention to the role of these ancestors, most particularly at times when their *imagines* were made visible and public, in rousing their descendants to virtuous behaviour. In marking himself out as potential imitator of those who had opposed Saturninus in 100, and of Marius in particular, Cicero positions himself as their heir.

Such a tactic allows Cicero at this crucial pinnacle of his career to indicate what kind of consul he would be: that he would draw on a variety of influences to shape his political conduct, and follow a pattern, already laid out in Rome's recent history, of service to the state and allegiance to the senatorial order. As a *novus homo*, his concern with his own ancestry is evident on numerous occasions in his public career: and received traditional emphasis in the inaugural consular speeches delivered at the start of this same year (*Leg. agr.* 2.1–5). Elsewhere in his speeches Cicero develops the idea that certain historical figures belong not so much to individual families as to the state: and that these are in a sense 'up for grabs' to all whose character and achievements are sufficiently worthy to emulate or appeal to them (*e.g. Verr.* 2.4.81). Here Cicero appropriates the language of *nobilitas* to establish his own links to figures from the previous generation, and casts his consulship in terms of an ideological, rather than genealogical, succession to those here mentioned. He was to repeat this strategy with varying levels of success throughout his career: and the concern he shows here for the reputations of the dead mirrors that for his own immortality in later public speeches.

On the other hand, if we consider that it is Cicero as consul who is delivering this speech with its funerary overtones, another aspect emerges: the *Pro Rabirio* comes to resemble the kind of *laudatio funebris* delivered at a funeral sponsored by the state, at which the highest ranking public official would preside. This would serve to elevate the otherwise undistinguished Rabirius into someone deserving a state funeral precisely because, not in spite, of the events of 100. Cicero devotes much of the early part of the speech, as well as its concluding sentences, to a declaration of intent as regards his position as consul (§2–3, 6), and makes much of the concept that in defending Rabirius, his private interests as advocate and his public ones as consul, namely the continued well-being of the Republic, have fortuitously coincided (§38). In speaking, then, from this position, he is able to give a forceful display of his own *auctoritas* as orator for and about the dead.

The funeral provides Cicero with the chief means for constructing his own political persona in this trial, as well as that of his client: and it allows him to deal with some of the more problematic aspects of his defence through a reversal of the tactics employed by the prosecution. In addition, however, it also becomes evident that it is precisely these funerary associations which allow Cicero to formulate his main argument for Rabirius' defence in the way that he does: namely, that the conviction of Rabirius is at the same time the conviction of those great citizens, now dead, who likewise participated in the demise of Saturninus and his followers. We have already seen the lengths to which Cicero goes in order to eulogise these men and to present them as a cohesive group, unified in their aim of preserving the state: and it is this ratification of Marius *et al.* which Cicero presents as being under threat from the prosecution. The funeral comes to serve here as both indicator of and metaphor for an extreme anxiety about changing the past, and the attempt here by Caesar and those others responsible for the prosecution to rake up and rewrite events from thirty-seven years before. Cicero issues in the *Pro Rabirio* a strong warning against this, and lays out for his audience its serious consequences: that the established reputations of those already dead – which would often have been cemented in the very type of funeral ceremony here evoked – would be threatened:

> an non intellegis, primum quos homines et qualis viros mortuos summi sceleris arguas…?
>
> But don't you understand, first of all, which men, and what kind of citizens, you are accusing of the worst of crimes, now that they are dead? (§26)

A reading of the speech in these terms provides us with one way in to an examination of a type of argument in Ciceronian oratory which seeks to create and draw upon a pervasive concern about the inevitable changeability of memory and personal reputation, particularly his own.

iii. Marius

This is particularly suggestive in the case of Marius, whose own death and forms of commemoration were themselves extremely problematic. The concluding years of Marius' career, and in particular their association with opposition to the senate, judicial murder and civil war, complicates a wholly positive final assessment of his achievements. However, by praising Marius here in the context of a quasi-funeral oration, Cicero is able to portray his career in such a way as to remove the undesirable elements. The funerary motif ensures a sense of finality in terms of an appraisal of Marius, and Cicero can thus suggest for him a post-mortem reputation which entirely edits out anything damaging. This is particularly emphasised by his stress here on the concord between Marius and his fellow consular Catulus, which may have served to obscure the detail that it was in fact Marius who had later been responsible for Catulus' suicide (Cicero *De or.* 3.9; Velleius Paterculus 2.22.4; Valerius Maximus 9.12.4.). To present them as unified in purpose here also reduces the potential for comparison between Marius' actions in 100 and those towards the end of his career, when he was even more directly responsible for the deaths of Roman citizens and magistrates: it would go some way towards ensuring that an audience did not associate the Marius of the civil wars with the consul who had presided over Saturninus' death. This is vital for the overall strategy of Cicero's defence, according to which Rabirius' guilt is only to be measured in proportion to that of those others who had been involved in the conspiracy: negative associations for Marius, prominent here as leader of the senatorial forces against Saturninus, would have been potentially fatal for Cicero's case.

The presence here of Marius in a funerary context also suggests a particular facet of a previously established connection with Julius Caesar: and this serves to add another dimension to an already politically fraught situation. Under Sulla, Marius' *imagines* had been banned in the same way that Saturninus' are shown here to have been. They were displayed in public again for the first time either four or five years before this trial, at the funeral of none other than Caesar's aunt, and Marius' wife, Julia. The significance of this act has been widely observed: in returning to the memory of Marius after a marked interval, and in claiming him so definitely as part of his own ancestry, Caesar has been viewed as making a strong claim of self-identification – casting himself, in other words, as emulator or even embodiment of his uncle-by-marriage (*e.g.* Sumi 2005, 44; Flaig 2004, 93–4; Flower 2006, 104–5). For Cicero's audience in 63, the most recent and most striking point of reference for Marius in a funerary context would have been this one. In praising the dead Marius, then, and in recalling him to the courtroom as quasi-ancestor for Rabirius, Cicero constructs for himself a role analogous to that earlier claimed by Caesar: and this has a number of effects.

First of all, it serves as apparent buttress for the claim made in Cicero's opening speeches after his election to consulship of 63 BC, in opposition to the agrarian laws put forward by Rullus, that he would be a *popularis* magistrate (*Leg. agr.* 1.23–7). Marius was by this time established as a favourite figurehead for the Roman people, and their strong emotional reaction to the reappearance of his *imago* in 68 is documented by Plutarch. A number of sources both ancient and modern attribute to Caesar's resurrection of Marius a desire to win popular favour and establish himself as people's champion (*e.g.* Plutarch, *Caes.* 5; Flower 1996, 124; Culham 2004, 156): and it is difficult to avoid the notion that Cicero is aiming at a similar effect for himself.

The involvement of Caesar in the conviction of Rabirius would also make him complicit in the accompanying condemnation of Marius which Cicero presents here as its inevitable outcome: and thus we are provided with a retrospective reading of Julia's funeral in 68 as a misleading signifier for the public relationship between Caesar and Marius. The warning issued by Cicero to his audience at §25 of Rabirius' defence, and quoted above, has therefore particular force if applied to Caesar in the context of his previous identification with Marius. Cicero provides his audience with an alternative genealogy for Marius, replacing that of the Julian clan with what Wiseman (1971, 107–112) refers to as 'spiritual' ancestry: unity in death with a group of men whose actions and virtues reflect one's own.

However, it quickly becomes apparent that this very warning, and Cicero's attempt to defend Rabirius through a re-assertion of the status quo and the reputations already established for his deceased contemporaries, in fact serve to highlight a paradox within these rival claims over the way in which the events of 100 BC are to be remembered and narrated. This paradox in itself illustrates precisely why Labienus' rehabilitation of Saturninus could have been so threatening, and could easily have been successful – because in the case of Marius, it had been. Cicero's evocation here of the *imagines* Marius was denied, and likewise their first reintroduction to public view, reminds his audience that despite Cicero's claim to be defending the uncomplicated *gloria* and *fama* of Marius along with that of all the *boni*, he is in fact appealing to a tradition or convention that simply did not exist. What Cicero presents through the medium of the funeral as an unproblematic and established way of honouring and remembering Marius is really nothing of the kind: and in making such a claim the centre of his defence of Rabirius, he is at the same time forced to remind us that Marius' posthumous memory at Rome had likewise until recently been in exactly the same state as that of Saturninus. The funeral itself, then, becomes a battleground: the site of a struggle over the lasting public position of those involved in the events of 100 BC, and by extension over the way in which those events are to be remembered.

Conclusions

The trial of Rabirius thus presents its audience with an evaluation of the past framed in terms of two competing funerals, each of which enforces a rival narrative of the events of 100 BC, and the existence of one of which is shown by Cicero to undermine that of the other. It is thus the task of the audience to confirm one of these as their 'final' narrative, although the very existence of this prosecution so long after the events with which it is concerned, and the choice by Cicero of an defensive approach which illustrates its potential damage to established Romans after their deaths, are in themselves a demonstration of the impossibility of confirming any such narrative as unproblematically finalised, or closed to further evaluation by posterity. It is, therefore, perhaps fitting that no official verdict was ever passed on Rabirius, and by extension on the privileging of one funeral reconstruction over the other: the dissolution of the trial served to suspend judgement on the events of 100 BC once again, and left open the question of how far the SCU might be held in the future to protect those acting under its mandate.

Yet this did not prevent Cicero from making use of the Saturninus affair as a parallel for his own handling of the Catilinarian conspiracy later in the year, as well as for his defence of Milo in 52 BC. In this speech too, funerary features become important for both sides. Milo is cast in the role of Marius and Cicero together, providing the next stage in the 'ancestral' chain established for the first time in *Pro Rabirio* in this particular form and in defence of broadly similar acts (*Pro Milone* §83). On this occasion too the prosecution's use of funerary references is undercut by Cicero's defence speech, and references moreover to another Roman whose burial rites had differed in substance from the kind offered as model by Polybius: to Clodius, whose impromptu funeral and its destruction of the senate house was to become a powerful symbol for his supporters and enemies alike.[12]

Pro Rabirio provides us with a virtuoso demonstration of the manipulation of one particular trope towards one particular end: the funeral becomes here in Cicero's hands an evocative metaphor, and spectacular rhetorical tool. However, its wider application too is key. In this speech Cicero both suggests to his audience and guides them away from anxieties inherent in the paradox of post-mortem honour at Rome: that the deeds of the living stem primarily from a desire to establish permanent memories, whilst their authors must remain aware that the dead are inevitably dependent on the living for continued and positive *fama*. His emphasis here on the presence of the dead, and his summoning of them into the courtroom as part of a wider deployment of funerary imagery, serves to put on trial the memorialising process itself, as well as providing Cicero with a powerful means of delineating his own public identity through the past.

Acknowledgements

This paper forms part of a wider and ongoing PhD project: for which I should like to acknowledge the support of the AHRC. I am grateful to my supervisor, John Henderson, and to Henriette van der Blom, for their remarks on earlier drafts: and to the audiences at the Memory and Mourning conference – especially the organisers, Valerie Hope and Janet Huskinson – for their comments and suggestions.

Notes

1 By a number of scholars, of whom I cite only a representative sample here. On the importance of post-mortem memory as a continued part of individual Roman identity, see Edwards 2007 (especially the introduction and chapter 5); Gowing 2005; Lavagne 1987; Dupont 1987; Carroll 2006, 30–58. On the Scipionic *elogia*, see van Sickle 1987; Coarelli 1972, and on the tomb of Eurysaces, see Petersen 2003. Flower's 1996 treatment remains the standard work on Roman *imagines*. On funerary rites: Toynbee 1971, 50–64, and the references on pp. 8–9.

2 Dio's account is, however, extensively debated in Tyrrell's commentary (1978, 37ff).

3 The reliability of these accounts is problematised by the fact that our evidence comes for the most part from Livy, who was writing after 63 and whose account of these older procedures may have been based to a greater or lesser degree on the treatment given to them by Cicero in 63. Liou-Gille 1994 provides an examination of the similarities between Livy's treatment of Horatius and the trial of Rabirius, and postulates that the Rabirian affair is likely to have influenced Livy's account. For the conviction of Q. Lutatius Catulus on this charge in 87 BC, see Alexander 1990, 60: although the identification of these proceedings as stemming from an accusation of *perduellio* remains questionable.

4 The doubtful nature of this resurrected procedure has led to a great deal of debate amongst scholars: for a variety of versions, compare Tyrrell 1978, 10–35; Phillips 1974; Magdelain 1973; Liou-Gille 1994.

5 The first documented use of the term *senatus consultum ultimum* is not to be found describing these events, but much later – in the *Bellum Civile* of Julius Caesar (1.5), where it is employed to refer to the decree passed against him during his struggle with Pompey. The similarities between the wording of the decree there given and that attested both in 121 and 100 BC have led scholars to group them under the heading of the SCU: see Lintott 1999, 158–69 on the problems inherent in establishing a firm definition.

6 Our evidence for this actually occurring is limited as regards the republican period. For its application to Cn. Calpurnius Piso in the first century AD, see Flower 1996, 24–31, 56–7, 103.

7 Although, as Noy points out elsewhere in this volume, this *imago* was more likely to have been a death mask: which in itself illustrates the broad application of the term.

8 For more detail on the *laudatio* see Kierdorf's standard treatment (1980).

9 For Manlius' trial, see Livy 6:17:4: Vasaly 1993, 16. For Aquilius, see *Verr.* 2.5.3; *De or.* 2.194. Cicero also makes use of this ploy here for Rabirius in §36.

10 See in particular Hardie who refers to this as an inversion of the *pompa funebris*, Hardie 1993, 104.; Feeney 1999; Dufallo 2007, 118; also Luke Houghton's discussion in this volume of the significance of funerary ritual.

11 The traditional setting for the centuriate assembly would be outside the *pomerium* (Tyrrell 1978, 41). Morstein-Marx argues that there is no reason why Saturninus' *imago* should not have been produced at an earlier meeting in the Forum (Morstein Marx 2003, 60), and the Rostra reference here should most likely be taken as a literal one.

12 Dufallo offers a brief reading of the *Pro Milone* through its evocation of the dead Clodius (Dufallo 2007, 30–4). See too Sumi (2005, 43–5, 50) on the unconventional conduct of Clodius' burial rites.

Bibliography

Alexander, M. C. (1990) *Trials in the Late Roman Republic*, 149 BC–50 BC. London, University of Toronto Press.

Bettini, M. (1991) *Anthropology and Roman Culture : Kinship, Time, Images of the Soul.* Trans. J. van Sickle. London, Johns Hopkins University Press.

Blösel, W. (2000) Die Geschichte des Begriffes mos maiorum von den Anfängen bis zu Cicero. In B. Linke and M. Stemmler (eds) *Mos maiorum : Untersuchungen zu den Formen der Identitätsstiftung und Stabilisierung in der Römischen Republik*, 25–97. Stuttgart, F. Steiner.

Cape, R. W. (2002) Cicero's consular speeches. In J. M. May (ed.), *Brill's Companion to Cicero: Oratory and Rhetoric*, 113–158. Leiden, Brill.

Carroll, M. (2006) *Spirits of the Dead: Roman Funerary Commemoration in Western Europe.* Oxford, Oxford University Press.

Coarelli, F. (1972) Il sepolcro degli Scipioni. *Dialoghi di archeologia* 6, 36–106.

Culham, P. (2004) Women in the Roman Republic. In H. I. Flower (ed.), *The Cambridge Companion to the Roman Republic*, 139–159. Cambridge, Cambridge University Press.

Dufallo, B. (2007) *The Ghosts of the Past : Latin Literature, the Dead, and Rome's Transition to a Principate.* Columbus, Ohio State University Press.

Dupont, F. (1987) Les morts et la mémoire: le masque funèbre. In Hinard 1987, 167–172.

Edwards, C. (2007) *Death in Ancient Rome.* London, Yale University Press.

Feeney, D. C. (1999) History and revelation in Vergil's underworld. In P. R. Hardie (ed.), *Virgil, Critical Assessments*, Vol. IV, 221–243. New York, Routledge.

Flaig, E. (2004) *Ritualisierte Politik: Zeichen, Gesten und Herrschaft im Alten Rom.* Göttingen, Vandenhoeck & Ruprecht.

Flower, H. I. (1996) *Ancestor Masks and Aristocratic Power in Roman Culture.* Oxford, Clarendon Press.

Flower, H. I. (2006) *The Art of Forgetting: Disgrace and Oblivion in Roman Political Culture.* Chapel Hill, University of North Carolina Press.

Gowing, A. M. (2005) *Empire and Memory: The Representation of the Roman Republic in Imperial Culture.* Cambridge, Cambridge University Press.

Hardie, P. R. (1993) *The Epic Successors of Virgil: A Study in the Dynamics of a Tradition.* Cambridge, Cambridge University Press.

Hinard, F. (ed.) (1987) *La mort, les morts et l'au-delà dans le monde romain.* Caen, Université de Caen.

Hölkeskamp, K. (2006) History and collective memory in the middle Republic. In N. Rosenstein and R. Morstein-Marx (eds), *A Companion to the Roman Republic*, 478–495. Oxford, Blackwell.

Hope, V. M. (2007) *Death in Ancient Rome : A Sourcebook.* London, Routledge.

Kierdorf, W. (1980) *Laudatio funebris: Interpretationen und Untersuchungen zur Entwicklung der römischen Leichenrede.* Meisenheim am Glan, Hain.

Lavagne, H. (1987) Le tombeau, mémoire du mort. In Hinard 1987, 159–166.

Lintott, A. (1999) *Violence in Republican Rome.* Oxford, Oxford University Press.

Liou-Gille, B. (1994) La perduellio. *Latomus* 53, 3–38.

Magdelain, A. (1973) Remarques sur la perduellio. *Historia* 22, 405–422.

Morstein-Marx, R. (2003) *Mass Oratory and Political Power in the Late Roman Republic.* Cambridge, Cambridge University Press.

Ochs, D. J. (1993) *Consolatory Rhetoric: Grief, Symbol, and Ritual in the Greco-Roman Era.* Columbia, University of South Carolina Press.

Petersen, L. H. (2003) The baker, his tomb, his wife, and her breadbasket. *The Art Bulletin* 85, 230–257.

Phillips E. J. (1974) The prosecution of C. Rabirius in 63 BC. *Klio* 56, 87–101.

Sumi, G. (2005) *Ceremony and Power: Performing Politics in Rome between Republic and Empire.* Ann Arbor, University of Michigan Press.

Toynbee, J. M. C. (1971) *Death and Burial in the Roman World.* London, Johns Hopkins University Press.

Tyrrell, W. B. (1978) *A Legal and Historical Commentary to Cicero's Oratio pro C. Rabirio perduellionis reo.* Amsterdam, Hakkert.

Vasaly, A. (1993) *Representations: Images of the World in Ciceronian Oratory.* Oxford, University of California Press.

Van Sickle, J. (1987) The elogia of the Cornelii Scipiones and the origins of epigram at Rome. *American Journal of Philology* 108, 41–55.

Wiseman, T. P. (1971) *New Men in the Roman Senate, 139 BC–AD 14.* Oxford, Oxford University Press.

8

'The mourning was very good'. Liberation and Liberality in Roman Funerary Commemoration

Maureen Carroll

The death of a slave-owner was an event which could bring about the most important change in status in the life of a slave. If the last will and testament of the master contained the names of any fortunate slaves to be released from servitude, these individuals went from being objects to subjects of rights. Works of contemporary literature and art reveal that it was considered a matter of great prestige to have a large number of freed slaves in the funeral procession of the *patronus*. With mourners made up of freshly manumitted slaves, effectively displaying gratitude and sorrow, a fine funeral and 'good mourning' were assured (Petronius, *Sat.* 42). The manumission of slaves also was a sign of the owner's magnanimity and humanity, character traits that were worth publicly displaying on his tomb.

Freedmen as a group, particularly in the context of self-presentation, social status and social mobility expressed in funerary commemoration, have been the focus of much scholarly debate, some of it very recent (Zanker 1975; Kleiner 1977; George 2006; D'Ambra 2006; Koortbojian 2006; Petersen 2006). The relationship between the freedman and his patron, however, has been less explicitly explored in terms of funerary art and commemoration and in the combination of this evidence with a body of Roman sources reflecting contemporary thought, literature and law. This paper therefore assesses the significance of testamentary manumission in the context of social competition and funerary display, both during the ceremony surrounding the death of the master and thereafter when monuments, texts and rituals played an active role in preserving memory. Relevant funerary monuments are examined that illuminate the relationship between the liberated and the liberator, with death as a significant threshold to the transformation of status. In this context, the role of freedmen in preserving the memory of their patrons and commemorating their relations with them will be explored. The evidence ranges chronologically from the late Republic to the second century AD.

To free or not to free: slave law and manumission

According to Roman law, 'the primary distinction in the law of persons is this: that all men are either free or slaves. Next, free men are either *ingenui* or *libertini*. *Ingenui* are those born free, *libertini* those manumitted from lawful slavery' (Gaius, *Inst.* 1.9–11; Buckland 1975, 62). There were three legally attested ways in which slaves could be made into freedmen (Cicero, *Top.* 2.10; Gaius, *Inst.* 1.17; *Digest* 1.5.1–2; Buckland 1975, 72–76; Watson 1975, 86–92; Kaser 1980, 73–74):

Manumissio vindicta: A slave could be freed by a unilateral declaration of the intention of the master to free the slave, the master applying the *vindicta* (rod) himself in the presence of the magistrate and his lictor.

Manumissio censu: A slave could also be freed by presenting himself as a free citizen for enrollment in the list of citizens during the census every fifth year; this required the consent of the master.

Manumissio testamento: Upon his master's death a slave could be set free, in which case this was stipulated in the owner's will. The heir of the testator was bound to perform the manumission, so both the dead *dominus* and the new heir became the *patronus* of the *libertus*.

Of all the ways of freeing slaves, testamentary manumission was the most common because it had real advantages for the master (Buckland 1970, 442, 460; Watson 1967, 194; Gardner and Wiedemann 1981, 147; Horsley 1998, 52–53). The owner retained the services of slaves to the very last moment, and he could manipulate his slaves by making the contents of his will known in advance, ensuring compliance to his demands and threatening changes to the will if necessary. Only with *manumissio testamento* could the *dominus* impose a formal condition for the slave to fulfil before he was eligible for freedom and citizenship. This might have been a cash payment to the master's heir, a prescribed number of years service for the heir, or the production of children (for female slaves).

Rome in the first century BC was a melting pot of Romans and foreigners, some free-born, many of servile origin, although estimates on the size of the latter population group are difficult (Noy 2000, 15–19, 31–52; Scheidel 1997). Dionysius of Halicarnassus, a Greek working in Rome in the late first century BC, found it unacceptable that so many slaves, especially those of dubious character and guilty of criminal activity, could become freedmen (*Ant. Rom.* 4.24). Even if the situation is somewhat exaggerated by Dionysius, Augustan legislature on the regulation of manumission suggests that the balance between free and servile elements of the population was genuinely delicate and that slaves might too often be freed for the wrong reasons (Bradley 1984, 89–90). Particularly the number of slaves manumitted at the death of their master from this time on varied according to the proportion of slaves in the household and according to their merits and loyalty. An important law of 2 BC, the *lex Fufia Caninia*, limited any owner on the number of slaves he could liberate, forcing the *dominus* to be selective

(Gaius, *Inst.* 1.42–46; Buckland 1975, 78). Those who owned between two and ten slaves could free up to half of them; owners of ten to thirty slaves could manumit a third; owners of thirty to a hundred slaves could free up to a quarter; and a fifth could be liberated by those who owned one hundred to five hundred slaves. The law forbade the manumission of numbers greater than a hundred, 'but if you only own one or two slaves, you are not covered by this law and there are no restrictions upon your freedom to manumit'.

This law put constraints on the wealthy Roman from making his funeral an occasion of conspicuous display, illustrating both his vast slave-holdings and his *humanitas* in giving slaves their freedom. This pertained not only to the aristocracy, but also to those who emulated the elite in this regard. We might think here of the fabulously wealthy Gaius Caecilius Claudius Isodorus, a freedman whose estate included 4116 slaves and whose funeral in 8 BC cost over a million sesterces; this kind of ostentatious display will almost certainly have involved an impressive procession of mourning freedmen (Pliny, *HN* 33.47.135). The *lex Fufia* did not hinder manumission, but it curbed the creation of too many *liberti orcini* (freedmen of the deceased) who had no strong obligatory ties to the family and the community (Fabre 1981, 23–36; Gardner 1991, 27–29, 37). In contrast, masters could free as many slaves as they wanted to while they were alive, which was looked upon favourably as strengthening the social bonds between freedmen and their patrons. Under Justinian, however, the *lex Fufia* was repealed 'as an obstacle to freedom' because it was deemed 'inhuman to take away from a man on his deathbed the right of liberating the whole of his slaves' (*Digest* 1.7; Buckland 1975, 82).

A few years later in AD 4, a new law of Augustus 'set a limit to manumission' which was to keep the Roman people free of the 'contamination….of servile blood' (Suetonius, *Aug.* 40.3–4). This legislature, known as the *lex Aelia Sentia*, was aimed at limiting the unjustified emancipation of those who had served for an insufficient number of years, or who were below the accepted age for manumission, or were otherwise unworthy (Gaius, *Inst.* 1.13–19; Buckland 1975, 78–80). A slave had to be over thirty years of age and be owned by quiritary right; he had to be set free by the rod, by census or by will; and slaves under thirty and manumitting slave-owners under twenty had to have their actions accepted and confirmed by a council. As for those who were unworthy, 'slaves disgraced…by whatever method and at whatever age they are manumitted…never become either Roman citizens or Latins…'

The state was now being far more prescriptive regarding eligibility for manumission. The automatic right to citizenship upon being freed was now denied to many, although the law did allow citizenship to be acquired in a range of exceptions which had to be approved by a special council or *consilium*. When manumission transformed the slave into a Roman citizen, limiting the numbers of freed slaves and regulating the power to manumit was an important mechanism designed to exclude unworthy slaves whilst retaining the desirability of freedom and the reward of citizenship for those who were willing and able to assimilate themselves 'within the existing social status quo' (Bradley 1984, 93).

Freedmen, funerals and mourning

As we shall see, freedmen constructed tombs for their former owners and they helped to perpetuate the memory of their patrons by performing funerary rituals year after year. These were long-term benefits of manumission for the patron and his family, but there were other benefits and advantages that came to the fore immediately after death and in a very public way. I am referring here to the participation and actions of liberated slaves in the funeral procession (*pompa funebris*).

The ostentatious and liberal manumission of slaves, particularly in the context of the funeral, was not always looked upon favourably. A blistering commentary on the practice and a cynical evaluation of the reasons behind some of the apparent generosity of slave-owners was delivered by Dionysius of Halicarnassus (*Ant. Rom.* 4.24) in the latter part of the first century BC, before the new laws limiting manumission came into being. '[In the past] most [slaves] were given their freedom as a reward for good conduct, and this was the best way of becoming independent of your owner...but this is not the situation today...[Some gain freedom] as a result of their owner's frivolity or silly desire for popularity. I personally know people who conceded freedom to all their slaves after their own deaths so that as corpses they would be acclaimed good men, and so that there would be lots of people wearing the felt liberty caps on their heads to follow their biers in the funeral procession.' Bradley (1984, 87–91) suggests that the *lex Fufia Caninia* was passed to limit the numbers of manumissions by testament to curb precisely this practice.

One of the main reasons for the actions of such liberators appears to have been their desire for a funeral of some extravagance, with great numbers of grateful freedmen attesting to their generosity and acclaiming them good men (Treggiari 1969). Slaves might be told in advance of the death of the master that they were to be freed, the master thereby ensuring that his slaves remained on their best conduct and most compliant. Perhaps the best known literary depiction of testamentary manumission as a means to control slaves and win their affection can be found in Petronius' *Satyricon* (71–72) in which the rich freedman, Trimalchio, had his will read out during his dinner party, informing the guests which of his slaves were to be freed when he died and what they were to inherit. Already the slaves show their gratitude, giving a hint of the show of grief and mourning the owner could expect at his funeral: "[A]nd if I live [my slaves] shall soon taste the water of freedom. In fact I am setting them all free in my will. I am leaving a property and his good woman to Philargyrus as well, and to Cario a block of buildings, and his manumission fees, and a bed and bedding..........I am making all this known so that my slaves may love me now as if I were dead." They all went on to thank their master for his kindness, when he turned serious and had a copy of the will brought in, which he read aloud from beginning to end, while the slaves moaned and groaned.........the whole household filled the room with lamentations, for all the world like guests at a funeral.' Although within the realm of comic fiction, this story is rooted in the contemporary practice in the early empire of making funerals, as vehicles of self-promotion, popular spectacles that promoted public participation (Bodel 2000, 262–263).

A dead man's clients and his *liberti* would march in his funeral procession. The more clients, the more important the dead man appeared, and one's freedmen were one important group of these clients. In the so-called Will of 'Dasumius' of AD 108 from Rome, the testator requested specifically that freedmen be his pallbearers (*CIL* VI 10229; ILS 8379a; Bradley 1984, 97; Champlin 1991, 139–141; Gardner and Wiedemann 1991, no. 158). According to Persius (Sat. 3.106), *liberti*, clearly only recently freed by will and referred to as 'day-old Roman citizens', often were used as pallbearers:

> A fine processional with trumpets and tapers too,
> Our poor fellow now looking quite relaxed
> All made up with powder and some sweet smells
> High on a bier with feet turned toward the door,
> Borne out by his slaves (smiling day-old Roman citizens).

A funerary relief of the late first century BC from Amiternum (Fig. 8.1) portrays the *pompa funebris* and the public display of mourning of a family (Toynbee 1971, 46–47, pl. 11; Flower 1996, 98–99, pl. 6; Bodel 2000, 264–265, fig. 1). It depicts the deceased man on a canopied bier, accompanied by the distraught family, musicians and professional mourners. Eight pallbearers are depicted, indicating that this family could afford more than the four pallbearers of a pauper and more than the six bearers encountered in middle-class circles (Martial 2.81, 6.77, 8.76), but we are not looking at an aristocratic funeral procession of overt extravagance. Given that the surviving written documents specify the role of freedmen as pallbearers at the funeral, we might hypothesise that these figures on the relief were of freed status. The wailing women on the relief might also be former slaves lamenting the passing of their patron, although they could equally be hired mourners. There is no doubt, however, that the women on one of the reliefs of around AD 100 from the tomb of the Haterii in Rome (Fig 8.2) are grateful and mourning freedwomen gathered around the deceased *patrona* who is not carried in a cortège, but who lies in state in her home (Giuliano 1968; Sinn and Freyberger 1996; Bodel 2000, 267–270, figs. 2–3; Leach 2006). Three hunched figures sit at the head end of her bier in a pose of public mourning, their hair worn open and looking dishevelled. It is obvious that they are no longer slaves, but *liberti*, as they wear the cap of liberty (*pileus*) on their heads, the headgear given to newly liberated slaves as a sign of their changed status (Appian, *Mith.* 2). Such a cap is the central motif of symbolic significance on the reverse of coins issued by M. Junius Brutus in 43–42 BC in Greece after his participation in the assassination of Julius Caesar (Sydenham 1952,

Fig. 8.1 Funerary relief from Amiternum showing a funeral procession. Drawing: J. Willmott.

Fig. 8.2 Funerary relief from Rome (Tomb of the Haterii) showing the deceased lying in state and mourning dependents around her. Note the three freedwomen with caps of freedom on the lower right. Drawing: J. Willmott.

No. 1301, pl. 30; Crawford 1974, no. 508.3, pl. LXI). The *pileus*, flanked by daggers, and accompanied by the inscription EID MAR, expressed the liberation of Rome from the tyranny of Caesar on the Ides of March.

Who carried the bier and who walked in the procession as a mourner may have differed slightly in the aristocratic funeral from less prestigious ceremonies such as that represented in the relief from Amiternum. At funerals of the nobility in Rome, significant numbers of *liberti* must have accompanied the body, but even other members of the aristocracy might accompany the bier, and they might even wear a cap of liberty (Flower 1996, 91–127). Livy (30.43, 30.45.5, 38.55), for example, tells us how the praetor Q. Terentius Culleo, marched in the funeral cortège of Scipio Africanus in 183 BC wearing a *pileus*, a symbol of the freedom that had been granted by Africanus to him and other Roman captives held by the Carthaginians in 201 BC (38.55). Clearly at the funeral of Aemilius Paullus, consul and victorious general over Macedonia in 167 BC, the pallbearers were men from other nations and Roman citizens as well, and both the young and old had roles to fulfil. Plutarch (*Aem.* 39) tells us: '...his funeral procession called forth men's admiration, and showed a desire to adorn his virtue with the best and most enviable obsequies. This was manifest...in good will and honour and gratitude on the part, not only of his fellow citizens, but also of his enemies...Young and strong of body assisted by turns in carrying the bier, while the more elderly followed with the procession calling aloud upon Aemilius as benefactor...'

Perhaps the desire to have as many participants as possible in the funeral, in emulation of the funerals of the aristocracy, prompted others of lesser status to liberate quantities of slaves according to the last will and testament, who would guarantee those things that society appreciated and valued in the funeral cortège of Aemilius Paullus: a public display of mourning, admiration, honour, gratitude and the portrayal of the deceased as a benefactor. An aristocratic funeral would involve families of similar status, magistrates and officials, throngs of onlookers and, of course, the public parading of wax ancestor masks, the masks sometimes being worn by actors to impersonate famous family members (Flower 1996). Especially for a freedman, who had no illustrious ancestors and who had held no public office apart from those reserved for freedmen, a well-attended, theatrical *pompa funebris* would have helped to compensate in death for inequality in life.

Manumissio testamento had one great advantage, beyond the retention of the services of slaves to the very end and the possibility of applying a condition to their liberation. Testamentary manumission brought the slave-owner prestige and public recognition at his funeral, with freshly freed slaves following or carrying his corpse and noisily proclaiming his liberality and magnanimity. The fictional freedman Chrysanthus, friend of Trimalchio, had freed some of his slaves by *manumissio testamento* (Petronius, *Sat.* 42). According to a friend of Trimalchio's who, along with the freed slaves and the wife of Chrysanthus attended the funeral, 'the mourning was very good'. Petronius and many other Romans will have witnessed this spectacle often enough in real life.

Manumission in funerary inscriptions and written wills

It is not uncommon to find epitaphs that make reference to the tombs having been built by freedmen for their patrons, but it is far less common to find references to *manumissio testamento* in such inscriptions. Nevertheless, such texts exist and they are informative about manumission, at least from the point of view of the *libertus*. A funerary inscription of AD 86 belonging to Lucius Vafrius Epaphroditus in Rome, for example, reveals that he was freed at the age of thirty according to the will of Lucius Vafrius Tiro, centurion of *Legio XXII Primigenia*, on the tenth day of the kalends of April when Domitian was consul for the twelfth time (*ILS* 1985). He died a little over a year later, sadly unable for very long to enjoy his freedom. In Córdoba Lucius Calpurnius Salvianus also was granted freedom according to the will of his *dominus* in the first century BC (*CIL* II^2/7.432=*CIL* II 2265). Typically, the brief, but key, details are that liberation had taken place according to the last will and testament and that the individual's status had irrevocably changed for the better, resulting in freedom and Roman citizenship. To memorialise this change in status, these details were inscribed in a permanent medium on public display.

More precise and detailed information on the manumission of slaves from the point of view of the master can be found in another kind of document, the last will and testament itself (Kaser 1980, 289–299; and see Noy, this volume). Several wills survive in fragmentary form only because they were transcribed onto marble tablets and fixed to the tomb as a permanent record of the original (and perishable) written document. The so-called Will of 'Dasumius' of AD 108 from the Via Appia in Rome is one of them (*CIL* VI 10229; ILS 8379a; Bradley 1984, 97; Champlin 1991, 139–141; Gardner and Wiedemann 1991, no. 158). It preserves some of the provisions this slave-owner made for at least some of his dependants on his death. Excerpts cited below clearly demonstrate the power of the master to determine the fate of individuals of differing sexes and professions, whether to free them or, in line with the *lex Aelia Sentia*, to deny them liberty.

> [Also I ask that freedom be given to] Sabinus the accountant and My[...] subject to their rendering accounts, along with their women. Likewise [...] the cook and Crammicus [the...] and Diadumenus the accountant, [...] the treasurer [along with his woman, whom he is to] have in faithful marriage.
>
> I likewise ask that...you set free...the steward [on rendering of] account [and ...]es and Eutyches the older valet. [In addition I give and bequeath to my] maternal aunt Septuma, wife of Secundinus, [my slaves...Menecrates, Paede]ros. [I ask that you do not] manumit Menecrates and Paederos, [but] keep them [in the same occupation as long as they live since] through no fault of mine they have so gravely [offended...by injurious] and unacceptable [behaviour].

This kind of *ante mortem* regulation of testamentary manumission is also recorded in the marble titular inscription above the door of Gaius Publius Heracla's tomb in the

Vatican necropolis (Tomb A) beneath St. Peter's basilica in Rome (Mielsch and Von Hesberg 1995). Since the tomb was constructed prior to Heracla's death, as was the epitaph, the legal instructions in it refer to the future. It states that legal control of his monument will be given to his freedmen and freedwomen and to 'those whom I shall have freed by will, as well as those who are freed conditionally (*in statu libertatis*)' (*AE* 1945, 136; Gordon 1983, 142–143). Heracla will have freed these individuals, subject to a condition, although we do not know what it was.

Occasionally a person's will was added to or modified from the original terms, and in that case a codicil was written that needed to be witnessed, signed and sealed to be valid (Kaser 1980, 298; Dropsie 1996). A passage from the Will of 'Dasumius' refers to just such a procedure: 'Anything I leave in notebooks [*codicilli*] or in any other form, written and sealed, I wish to be entirely valid, as if I had left them in my will, written and sealed…' A codicil could contain some addition or alteration to the intent to manumit, as it appears to be the case in an inscription from Ostia. Here Marcus Manlius Diligens names specific individuals as well as, more generally, those freedmen and freedwomen whom he will have freed as part of his will or those named in a codicil (*CIL* XIV 382). An epitaph of the late second century AD from Cefalù in Sicily also preserves an *exemplum codicillorum* recording the emanicipation of an *alumnus* and a slave (*CIL X* 7457; *ILS* 8377).

Finally, thanks to the preservation of details of the will in a permanent medium, we have a direct reflection of the *lex Aelia Sentia* of AD 4 prohibiting the *manumissio* of slaves under the age of thirty, unless by agreement with a *consilium*, in a marble epitaph from Ostia (*CIL* XIV 1437; *ILS* 1984; Gardner and Wiedemann, 1991, no. 45). Decimus Otacilius Hilara had his will made to include the testamentary manumission of two sons born as slaves before he and his co-freedwoman were manumitted; one of the sons was young enough to have required his freedom to be conferred on him in *consilio manumisso*.

Tombs and memory

Tombs and grave markers of all shapes and sizes lining the roads outside Roman settlements were among the most visible and public monuments across the empire (Toynbee 1971; Purcell 1987; Von Hesberg 1992; Koortbojian 1996; Carroll 2006). The funerary monument, according to Roman legal sources, was designed to preserve memory (Ulpian, *Digest* 11.7.2.6, 11.7.42). Although there were many people in the Roman empire who, for various reasons, were not commemorated with permanent stone memorials, about 200,000 funerary inscriptions survive, reminding us of the importance attached to the perpetuation of memory. The texts on Roman tombs were a source of information on each individual, and they were intentionally chosen by the deceased or those close to the deceased to negotiate and display status and to commemorate a network of personal relationships the dead enjoyed. What was or was not included in the epitaph reflected an intentional and manipulative selection of details and information to make the life of the deceased visible and memorable (Hope 2001, 24; Flower 2006, 1).

Both patrons and freedmen are well represented in funerary commemoration. Images of freedmen and freedwomen and monuments by and to them are one of the most ubiquitous forms of funerary display in the Roman world (Zanker 1975; Zanker 1992; Kleiner 1977; Dexheimer 2000; George 2006; Leach 2006; Petersen 2006). The 'deliberate shaping process' of choosing particular aspects and circumstances of an individual's life can be seen very clearly here (Hope 2001, 24). A freed slave, and particularly his children who were fortunate enough to be born outside slavery, would have been keen to have that crucial status publicly memorialised in a funerary inscription (Weaver 1991). Patterson (1982, 40) calls the state of being enslaved 'social death', but this phase of a slave's existence ended with manumission. Social resurrection from this point in time needed to be negotiated, and the reality of one's life compensated for; the tomb was an ideal public arena for the transition from having extra-societal status to operating autonomously within the fabric of Roman society. Both the owners of slaves and those freed by them were concerned to have a proper memorial as a reflection of their 'essence and dignity' (*substantia et dignitas*) (*Digest* 11.7.2.6, 35.127), and they used funerary monuments as a public form of self-representation, depicting themselves either as liberal and generous patrons or as faithful and honourable freedmen. The advertisement of a slave-owner's grants of freedom to slaves in the texts and images of funerary monuments reflected not only his *substantia et dignitas*; it also underlined his *humanitas*, especially if the slaves were particularly deserving of freedom. One is reminded of the approval Quintus felt when his brother Marcus Cicero finally freed and made an *amicus* out of his slave Tiro who was worthy, trusted and in possession of considerable literary skills (Cicero, *Fam*.16.16). The idea that loyal service deserved manumission certainly crops up in literary sources, although, in reality, this did not necessarily greatly influence the regularity of grants of freedom (Wiedemann 1985, 164–165).

Patrons provide for their freedmen

The surviving wills of the Roman period demonstrate that the owners of slaves made concerted efforts to leave specifications about their tombs, their entitled inhabitants and their maintenance. They often determined which of those freedmen and freedwomen would have the right and privilege of sharing the family tomb of the *patronus*. Both freedmen manumitted by the testator himself or by his legal offspring could be eligible for this inclusion in the burial community. Freedmen thereby would be assured a decent burial and a permanent monument to perpetuate their memory and display their new social status. From the first century AD funerary inscriptions appear frequently that advertise the provision by the patrons of a place in the family tomb for freedmen and freedwomen; even the possibly as yet unborn offspring of the freedmen and freedwomen are included. In a fairly typical titular inscription of the second century AD from Portus (Fig. 8.3), the patrons Publius Varius Ampelus and Varia Ennuchis emulate dozens of other tomb owners in that cemetery in admitting their household or *familia* into their last place of rest (Baldassare *et al.* 1996, 71–77, figs. 25–26; Hope 1997, 75, fig. 5). The formula *libertis libertabusque posterisque eorum* –for their freedmen and freedwomen and their offspring- is a standard one used for this type of legal document. Since slave women rarely were manumitted before the age of thirty, when they were most fertile, freedwomen had their genetic contribution to the next and subsequent generations of free-born offspring 'severely curtailed' (Scheidel 1997, 167–168). Married couples in the freedman group may often have remained childless or had only few children who may not have survived to inherit (Gardner 1998, 56). The frequent inclusion of *liberti* in the burial community of people who were freedmen and freedwomen themselves is very likely related to this situation and one way in which heirs to the estate and protectors of the tomb could be found. Providing and paying for a monument for one's freedman might also have acted as an 'incentive [for all freedmen] to be loyal to their

Fig. 8.3 Tomb inscription of P. Varius Ampelus and Varia Ennuchis from the Isola Sacra cemetery at Portus providing a place of burial in the tomb also for their freedmen and freedwomen and their children. Photo: M. Carroll.

patrons', as an epitaph from Forlì reveals (*CIL* XI 600; Gardner and Wiedemann 1991, no. 43). Not only the prospect of liberty, but also the promise of one's own memorial, therefore, could be dangled like a carrot in front of the slave's nose.

Although these family tombs were inclusive, but somewhat vague, in their view of future members of the community of death, the *dominus* or *patronus* was selective in determining who would share his monument with him. 'Dasumius' certainly had a preference for his own freedmen: 'I request of [...] my heirs, [of you in particular, my dearest daughter...not to] allow anyone after me to be buried in that place, except those whom I myself manumitted...or those whom you wish in future of your own freedmen.' It was also not uncommon for the tomb-owner to bar some of his dependants from the tomb, naming them specifically in his will and in the titular inscription that was a lasting record of it. The reasons given for the rejection of certain freedmen and freedwomen from the burial community are usually vague, although a freedman's 'ungrateful and offensive behaviour' (*CIL* VI 11027; *ILS* 8285) or a freedwoman's 'disloyalty towards her patron' (*CIL* VI13732; *ILS* 8115) might be given as justification. These accusations are based on the legal definition of ingratitude: a lack of respect by a freedman (*obsequium*) for his patron. This might involve a freedman's refusal 'to look after the management of his master's property or to act as his children's guardian' (*Digest* 37.14.19; Gardner 1998, 75).

Freedmen perpetuate the patron's memory

Whilst, on the one hand, ex-slaves could benefit by the patron's provision of a place for them in the family tomb, a frequent benefit for the patron, on the other, was that his freedmen and freedwomen might erect a tomb (perhaps as part of a condition for their manumission) for him when he died. The will of 'Dasumius', for example, contains the condition that his funerary monument was to be completed within a certain time after his death by his freedmen, and it also determined how much they were to spend on it. Such wishes were compelling, especially for the heir or the person(s) designated, and they represented a moral obligation within the legal relationship (Meyer 1990, 77–78). In this way, the *patronus* had a proper burial and an appropriate commemorative monument. Relations between patrons and freedmen in funerary practice, therefore, reflect both the responsibilities of the patron relative to his freedmen's rights and property (*bona*) and the system of *operae* which the freedman was obliged to perform for his former owner (Watson 1975, 108–110; Garnsey 1981; Mouritsen 2001). The epitaph of Publius Varius Ampelus and Varia Ennuchis at Portus discussed above also illustrates the custom of *liberti* honouring their patrons by building them a commemorative monument. They built their tomb, as the titular inscription tells us, not only for themselves and their dependants, but also their *patrona* Varia Servanda.

Elsewhere, in Pompeii, the freedman Publius Vesonius Phileros, erected a grand funerary monument outside the Porta Nocera around the mid-first century AD for his *patrona* Vesonia, himself and his friend (D'Ambrosio and De Caro 1983, Tomb 23OS) (Fig. 8.4). Vesonia not only was thereby given a prestigious and conspicuous built tomb, with her own statue preserving her appearance, but she was also able to rely on a grateful freedman, his family and his household who will have continued to pay their respects dutifully and perform obsequies in her memory. Recent excavations have demonstrated just how frequented this precinct was as the focus of funerary rites and commemorative performances for the dead (Lepetz and Van Andringa, 2006, 2008 and 2010). Occasionally epitaphs contain very specific instructions that access to the tomb must be ensured to the freedmen and freedwomen of the deceased, even to the point that the heir was to let them have the key to the tomb 'so that they may sacrifice as often as is necessary (*CIL* VI 12133; *ILS* 8365). Such rituals of remembrance – sacrificing, pouring libations, commemorative meals – were essential acts performed repeatedly and regularly in honour of the dead (Graham 2005a, 2005b).

Gratitude and duty towards the patron is also apparent in the text of an epitaph with high quality portraits of the freeborn Lucius Antistius Sarculo and his freedwoman wife Antistia Plutia from Rome (*CIL* VI 2170; *ILS* 5010; Zanker 1975, 296, fig. 34; Walker 1995, 80, fig. 57) (Fig. 8.5). The epitaph reveals that their two freedmen paid for this monument out of their own money in the late first century BC to perpetuate the memory of their patrons. As an added bonus and a reciprocal benefit, they, and three other named freedmen of Sarculo and Plutia, were allowed to share their patrons' tomb, as a second, lengthier inscription tells us (*CIL* VI 2171). Freedmen were also often required to care for and see to the upkeep of the patron's tomb long after his death. Trimalchio's (fictional) declared intention to put one of his freedmen in charge of his burial place to protect it (Petronius, *Sat.* 71) is reflected in actual practice. Sextus Iulius Aquila, a Gallo-Roman aristocrat from Langres in Gaul, for example, left a will in the second century AD specifying the details of his monument and determining that his freedmen, both those freed while he was alive and those who were provided for in the will, were to tend his monument and observe his birthdays in perpetuity with commemorative rituals (*CIL* XIII 5708; *ILS* 8379; Hatt 1951, 66–69; Lavagne 1987, 162–163).

Owning slaves, particularly if there were vast numbers of them, was an indication of wealth and status in Roman society. But substantial prestige and status in society could also be gained by freeing slaves and thereby increasing one's entourage of loyal clients. Commemorative inscriptions that reflected a lengthy client list of freedmen contributed significantly to the reputation of a *patronus* and reflected on his magnanimity in releasing slaves. Epitaphs survive that list numerous *liberti*, all of them, of course, taking the family name of the patron and perpetuating it for generations. Cicero (*Tusc.* 1.31) includes 'the propagation of the name' as a means of caring for the future. The elder Pliny (*HN* 2.154) mentioned monumental inscriptions as 'giving a longer life to men's name and

Fig. 8.4 Tomb of the freedman P. Vesonius Phileros built for himself, his patroness and his friend in the Porta Nocera cemetery at Pompeii. Photo: M. Carroll.

Fig. 8.5 Portraits and epitaph of L. Antistius Sarculo and Antistia Plutia, commemorated by their freedmen. Photo: British Museum.

memory', and the more times that name would be adopted by one's dependants and appear in public inscriptions the greater the prestige. For Pliny the Younger (*Ep.* 9.19.3), 'everyone who has done some…memorable deed should be…praised if he wishes to ensure the immortality he has earned and…seeks to perpetuate the undying glory of his name'. Although manumitting slaves was not necessarily an act of historical importance or a great deed of social relevance to all, as an act of *humanitas* it was certainly viewed by those it immediately affected as a memorable deed. The master's desire to have his actions publicised and remembered are understandable in the competitive climate of Roman society.

In particular in and around Rome, funerary inscriptions can list very large numbers of individuals freed by a generous patron, casting light on the wealth of the family to have owned so many slaves and to be able to free so many (and replace them with new slaves). It is not uncommon to find a dozen or more names of freedmen and freedwomen in one inscription. Such lists of names may represent a burial club or *collegium*, formed by the joint efforts of all *liberti* who had worked for the same master, in which case they took their burial and commemoration into their own hands, rather than relying on their patron to provide for them. A couple of examples here will suffice to illustrate the importance of perpetuating the name of the patron. The *liberti* Marcus Aurelius Asclepiades, Aurelia Salvia, and Marcus Aurelius Eucratus list sixteen other Aurelii in their titular inscription in Rome who had the right to be buried with them (*CIL* VI 38076). Even more impressive is the inscription commissioned by the freedmen of the Lucius Appuleius family in Salerno to commemorate well over sixty individuals, all with the family name of Appuleius (*CIL* X 557). The desire of the *patronus* for a lasting name would certainly be given some fulfillment here. Although such inscriptions send immediate signals about wealth and prosperity and the maintenance of a substantial *familia* and circle of dependants, they still, however, might be giving us only part of the picture. They tell us nothing about the total number of other slaves not named here that the owner might have freed in the course of his life because we have insufficient evidence about the slave-holdings of any individual (Gardner 1992, 348).

Freed slaves could act as the property heirs of the patron, but they were also heirs to his name. This factor was perhaps particularly important if there were no children to inherit the estate of the patron and keep the (adopted) blood-line and the name alive. In an epitaph from Margum in Moesia Superior, Lucius Valerius Seranus, a legionary veteran, says: 'A husband I was not, but I freed slaves' (*CIL* III 1653, Suppl. 8143). These freed slaves, ten in all, were his heirs and they set up the monument to their unmarried and childless patron whose name they all took as their own and passed on to subsequent generations.

Anonymous but visibly effective freedmen in Roman Gaul

The manumission of slaves clearly was viewed as a sign of the owner's generosity and worth being publicly displayed. This could be conveyed by including the names of the freed slaves in the text of the epitaph, as we have seen. There is, however, a unique group of funerary monuments in Gaul which does not always refer explicitly in the text to *manumissio testamento*, but which nevertheless provides some indication of how many slaves the owner set free and how the magnanimity of the patron was expressed in this part of the empire.

This assemblage of funerary monuments from Nîmes, Narbonne and Lyon includes altars, *stelae* and mausolea; on all of them there are carved or incised depictions of caps of liberty somewhere on the face of the memorial (Carroll 2006, 238–239). It is certain that the carved *pilei* on the Gallic gravestones are symbols representing freedmen and freedwomen. The number of *pilei* will have informed the viewer how many slaves the owner had freed. These *pilei* are often arranged in rows, ranging in number from one to thirteen, the average number being four (Fig. 8.6). On the funerary altar commemorating Sextus Granius Boudo in Nîmes, the number of *pilei* corresponds directly to the number of freedmen named in the inscription, three caps are depicted and three freedmen are named, (Sextus Granius) Homullus, (Sextus Granius) Iaphys, and (Sextus Granius) Alchimedo (*CIL* XII 3603). But the names and the *pilei* do not always correspond in number. One freedman may be named as the commemorator,

Fig. 8.6 Funerary altar of T. Boduacius Karus and his wife Gaia from Nîmes depicting three stylised caps of freedom on the base. Photo: M. Carroll, courtesy of the Musée Archéologique de Nîmes.

and yet four caps of liberty are represented (*CIL* XII.3760; Fig. 8.7), or the unspecified heirs (*heredes*) are said to be responsible for the monument and there are five *pilei* in total. Attia Philendis in Nîmes, for example, received a funerary altar in the second century AD from her freedmen and freedwomen who were her designated heirs; no personal names are stated, but six *pilei* are depicted at the bottom, so that it can be assumed that she had liberated six former slaves (*ILGN* 442). If only depictions of caps survive in fragmentary monuments, we cannot tell whether freedmen were mentioned in the accompanying, but now lost, inscription (Fig. 8.8).

Perhaps only those who paid for the stone will have had their names recorded in the text. If we remember the funerary monument with portrait busts of Lucius Antistius Sarculo and Antistia Plutia from Rome, only those two freedmen who provided the funds for the monument of their patrons are named; the other freedmen who shared the tomb are listed in a separate inscription, and there is no mention of any financial contribution on their part. The inclusion of *T P I* (*testamento poni iussit*), 'erection ordered by the will', at the end of the epitaph of Lucius Severius Severinus, an aedile of the second century AD in Nîmes, may be a reference to the testamentary obligation on the part of the three freedmen depicted as three *pilei* to set up a memorial to their patron (*CIL* XII.3273; Carroll 2006, 238, fig. 72). Perhaps the *dominus* had attached a condition to the emancipation of his slaves, the condition being that the *liberti* were obliged to set up a memorial to him. Perhaps cost also played a role, as it would have been cheaper to carve a series of *pilei* than to have a letter-cutter inscribe a series of names. If these six freedmen and freedwomen were obliged to erect a monument to their patron according to the will, they had fulfilled this obligation, whether or not they include their own names.

It is also possible that the anonymous caps of liberty refer to the number of freedmen, (and their families), who were to share the patron's tomb. Like the rather anonymous provision in Italian epitaphs of space provided in the tomb for the freedmen, freedwomen and their offspring (*libertis libertabusque posterisque eorum*, see fig. 8.3), these *pilei* might express the intention of the former owner to open up his burial community to other members of the *familia*.

In the end, however, it may be that the *pilei* were simply a visual indicator of the number of slaves generously freed than a list of the actual names and identities of the lucky ones. It is not uncommon on Gallic funerary monuments to find objects carved to convey symbolically a message, particularly in those regions along the Rhône river. Here, for example, the *ascia*, a tool used in building, is often depicted as a variant to what sometimes is written out in words: *sub ascia dedicavit*, 'dedicated while under the hammer' (see Carroll 2006, fig. 9). The *ascia* may reflect a rite of dedication to render the tomb inviolable and place it under divine protection or to signify the exclusivity of the tomb for the person(s) named in the epitaph (Hatt 1951, 85–107; De Visscher 1963, 285). The liberty caps carved on Gallic gravestones functioned much the same way that a series of names on funerary inscriptions in Italy and elsewhere did: they

Fig. 8.7 Funerary altar of C. Nemonius Plocamus set up by his freedman in Nîmes and showing four stylised caps of freedom on the bottom. Photo: M. Carroll, courtesy of the Musée Archéologique de Nîmes.

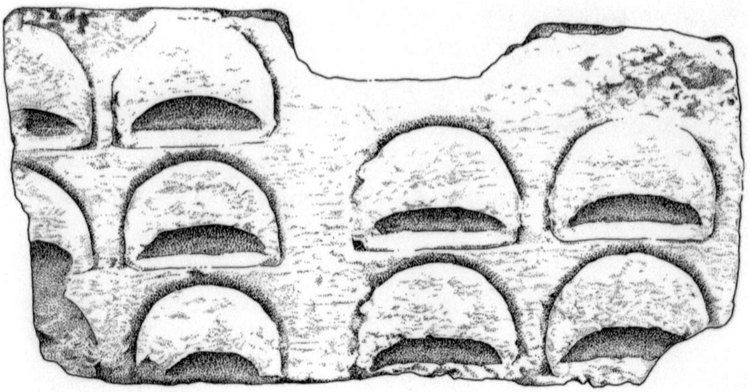

Fig. 8.8 Fragmentary stone block from a mausoleum in Narbonne depicting rows of caps of freedom. Drawing: J. Willmott.

conveyed information about the wealth, status and magnanimity of the patron, and they gave viewers an inkling of the number of manumitted slaves who bore the family name of the former owner for succeeding generations. Lists of names of freedmen or rows of *pilei* of freedmen communicated to the viewer that good deeds had been performed and accomplishments achieved, something, with Cicero (*Rab. Post.* 16–17), that was worthy to be 'handed on as a memorial to succeeding generations'.

Conclusions

Augustan legislature in the late first century BC limited the number of slaves that could be freed on the death of their master, forcing the owner to be selective in his choices. This law was designed to hinder the wealthy Roman from making his funeral a public spectacle with the aid of the slaves he had manumitted, especially those freed by testament at his death. The conspicuous participation of newly liberated slaves in the funeral procession of their patron was to be curbed and the public self-promotion of the liberators as good and magnanimous men displaying *humanitas* limited. Displays of mourning, gratitude and general lamentations nonetheless continued in this context in the first and second centuries AD, for a dead man's clients and *liberti* would be an important part of the funeral procession as mourners and pallbearers. For the non-elite, and particularly for freedmen who themselves had liberated slaves and who had no illustrious ancestors portraits to parade in the cortège or who could expect no high-ranking dignitaries at their funeral, the desire was strong to liberate slaves and thereby construct a well-attended, theatrical send-off.

Testamentary manumission is occasionally recorded in funerary epitaphs of freedmen, this most important change in status thereby being advertised in a permanent medium on public display. Surviving wills drawn up by slave-owners also survive as transcripts written in stone and they clearly demonstrate the power of the master to determine the fate of individuals, whether to free them or to deny liberty to them, and to subject their dependants, once freed, to certain conditions such as maintenance of the patron's tomb.

Both patrons and freedmen are well represented in funerary commemoration. The owners of slaves and those freed by them were concerned to have a proper memorial as a reflection of their status and dignity, and they used funerary monuments as a public form of self-representation, appearing either as liberal and generous patrons or as worthy and deserving freedmen. The wills and funerary inscriptions of slave-owners often specify that their freedmen and freedwomen had the right and privilege of inclusion in the burial community of the *patronus*, an advantage for the freedman being a decent burial and a vehicle with which to perpetuate his memory and display his new social status. Likewise, a frequent benefit of manumission for the patron was that his freedmen and freedwomen might choose to or were obliged to erect a tomb for him when he died. The patron could also rely on a grateful freedman and his household to pay their respects dutifully and perform obsequies in his memory. Furthermore, freed slaves took the family name of the patron as their own, passing it on to subsequent generations and fulfilling the desire of the *patronus* for a lasting name. Relations between patrons and freedmen in funerary practice, therefore, reflect both the responsibilities of the patron in regard to his freedmen's rights and property and the duties which the freedman was obliged to fulfill for his former owner.

Bibliography

Baldassare, I., Braqantini, I., Morselli, C. and Taglietti, F. (1996) *Necropoli di Porto. Isola Sacra.* Rome, Libreria dallo Stato.

Bodel, J. (2000) Death on display. Looking at Roman Funerals. In B. Bergmann and C. Kondoleon (eds) *The Art of the Ancient Spectacle*, 258–281. New Haven, Yale University Press.

Bradley, K. R. (1984) *Slaves and Masters in the Roman Empire. A Study in Social Control.* Brussels, Latomus.

Buckland, W. W. (1970) *The Roman Law of Slavery: The Conditions of the Slave in Private Law from Augustus to Justinian.* Cambridge, Cambridge University Press (reprinted from 1908).

Buckland, W. W. (1975) *A Text-Book of Roman Law from Augustus to Justinian* (Third Edition). Cambridge, Cambridge University Press.

Carroll, M. (2006) *Spirits of the Dead. Roman Funerary Commemoration in Western Europe.* Oxford, Oxford University Press.

Champlin, E. (1991) *Final Judgements: Duty and Emotion in Roman Wills, 200 BC–AD 250.* Berkeley, University of California Press.

Crawford, M. H. (1974) Roman Republican Coinage. Cambridge, Cambridge University Press.

D'Ambra, E. (2006) Imitations of life: style, theme and a sculptural collectiion in the Isola Sacra Necropolis, Ostia. In E. D'Ambra and G. Métraux (eds) *The Art of Citizens, Soldiers and Freedmen in the Roman World.* British Archaeological Reports International Series 1526, 73–90. Oxford, Archaeopress.

D'Ambrosio, A. and De Caro, S. (1983). *Un Impegno per Pompei. Fotopiano e Documentazione della Necropoli di Porta Nocera.* Milan, Touring Club.

De Visscher, F. (1963) *Le Droit des Tombeaux Romains.* Milan, Giuffre Editore.

Dexheimer, D. (2000) Portrait figures on sepulchral altars of Roman liberti: Evidence of Romanization or assimilation of attributes characterizing higher social strata? In J. Pearce, M. Millett and M. Struck (eds) *Burial, Society and Context in the Roman World*, 78–94. Oxford, Oxbow Books.

Dropsie, M. A. (1996) *The Roman Law of Testaments, Codicils and Gifts in the Event of Death.* Littleton, Fred B. Rothman and Co. (reprinted from T. & J. W. Johnson and Co., Philadelphia 1892).

Fabre, G. (1981) *Libertus: Recherches sur les rapports patron-affranchi à la fin de la république romaine.* Paris, Boccard.

Flower, H. I. (1996) *Ancestor Masks and Aristocratic Power in Roman Culture.* Oxford, Oxford University Press.

Flower, H (2006) *The Art of Forgetting. Disgrace and Oblivion in Roman Political Culture.* Chapel Hill, University of North Carolina Press.

Gardner, J. F. (1991) The purpose of the Lex Fufia Caninia. *Echos du Monde Classique/Classical Views* 35, 21–39

Gardner, J. F. (1992) Roman will-making. Review of E. Champlin, Final Judgements: Duty and Eomtion in Roman Wills, 200 BC–AD 250. *The Classical Review* 42.2, 347–349.

Gardner, J. F. (1998) *Family and* Familia *in Roman Law and Life.* Oxford, Oxford University Press.

Gardner, J. F. and Wiedemann, T. (1991) *The Roman Household: A Sourcebook.* London, Routledge.

Garnsey, P. (1981) Independent freedmen and the economy of Roman Italy under the Principate. *Klio* 63, 359–371.

George, M. (2006) Social identity and the dignity of work in freedmen's reliefs. In E. D'Ambra and G. Métraux (eds) *The Art of Citizens, Soldiers and Freedmen in the Roman World.* British Archaeological Reports International Series 1526, 19–30. Oxford, Archaeopress.

Gordon, A. E. (1983) *Illustrated Introduction to Latin Epigraphy.* Berkeley, University of California Press.

Graham, E-J. (2005a) The quick and the dead in the extra-urban landscape: the Roman cemetery at Ostia/Portus as a lived environment. In J. Bruhn, B. Croxford and D. Grigoropoulos (eds) *TRAC. Proceedings of the Theoretical Roman Archaeology Conference,* 133–143. Oxford, Oxbow Books.

Graham, E-J. 2005b Dining al fresco with the living and the dead in Roman Italy. In M. Carroll, D. Hadley and H. Willmott (eds) *Consuming Passions: Dining from Antiquity to the Eighteenth Century,* 49–65. Stroud, Tempus.

Giuliano, A. (1968) *Documenti per servire allo studio del monumento degli Haterii.* Memorie della Accademia Nazionale dei Lincei 13, 449–482.

Hatt, J. J. (1951) *La Tombe Gallo-Romaine.* Paris, Presses Universitaires de France.

Hesberg, H. Von (1992) *Römische Grabbauten.* Darmstadt, Wissenschaftliche Buchgesellschaft.

Horsley, R. A. (1998) The slave systems of Classical Antiquity and their reluctant recognition by modern scholars. In A. D. Callahan, R. A. Horsley and A. Smith (eds) *Slavery in Text and Interpretation = Semeia* 83/84, 19–66.

Hope, V. M. (1997) A roof over the dead: communal tombs and family structure. In R. Laurence and A. Wallace-Hadrill (eds) *Domestic Space in the Roman World. Pompeii and Beyond,* 69–88. Portsmouth, Journal of Roman Archaeology.

Hope, V. M. (2001) *Constructing Identity: The Roman Funerary Monuments of Aquileia, Mainz and Nîmes.* British Archaeological Reports, International Series 960. Oxford.

Kaser, M. (1980) Roman Private Law. Durban, Butterworths.

Kleiner, D. E. E. (1977) *Roman Group Portraiture: The Funerary Reliefs of the Late Republic and Early Empire.* New York, Garland Publishing.

Koortbojian, M. (1996) *In commemorationem mortuorum*: text and image along the 'streets of the tombs'. In J. Elsner (ed.) *Art and Text in Roman Culture,* 210–233. Cambridge, Cambridge University Press.

Koortbojian, M. (2006) The Freedman's voice: the funerary monument of Aurelius Hermia and Aurelia Philematio. In E. D'Ambra and G. Métraux (eds) *The Art of Citizens, Soldiers and Freedmen in the Roman World.* British Archaeological Reports, International Series 1526, 91–99. Oxford, Archaeopress.

Lavagne, H. (1987) Le tombeau, mémoire du mort. In Hinard, F. (ed.) *La mort, les morts et l'au-delà dans le monde romain. Actes du Colloque de Caen 1985*, 159–166. Caen, Université de Caen.

Leach, E. W. (2006) Freedmen and immortality in the tomb of the Haterii. In E. D'Ambra and G. Métraux (eds) *The Art of Citizens, Soldiers and Freedmen in the Roman World*. British Archaeological Reports, International Series 1526, 1–18. Oxford, Archaeopress.

Lepetz, S. and Van Andringa, W. *et al.* (2006) Pour une archéologie de la mort à l'époque romaine : fouille de la nécropole de Porta Nocera à Pompéi. *Académie des Inscriptions et Belles-Lettres : Comptes-Rendus*, avril-juin, 1131–1161.

Lepetz, S. and Van Andringa, W. *et al.* (2008) I riti e la morte a Pompei: nuove ricerche archeologiche nella necropoli di Porta Nocera. In M-P. Guidobaldi and P. G. Guzzo (eds), *Nuove ricerche archeologiche nell'area vesuviana (scavi 2003–2006), Convegno Internazionale organizzato dalla Soprintendenza archeologica di Pompei, Rome, 2007*, 377–387. Rome, "L'Erma" di Bretschneider.

Lepetz, S. and Van Andringa, W. (2010) *Publius Vesonius Phileros vivos monumentum fecit*: Investigations in a sector of the Porta Nocera cemetery in Roman Pompeii. In M. Carroll and J. Rempel (eds) *Living through the Dead. Burial and Commemoration in the Classical World*,.110–133. Oxford, Oxbow Books.

Meyer, E. A. (1990) Explaining the epigraphic habit in the Roman Empire: the evidence of epitaphs. *Journal of Roman Studies* 90, 74–96.

Mielsch, H. and Von Hesberg, H. (1995) *Die heidnische Nekropole unter St. Peter in Rom. Die Mausoleen E-I und Z-PSI*. Rome, "L'Erma" di Bretschneider.

Mouritsen, H. (2001) Roman freedmen and the urban economy: Pompeii in the first century AD. In F. Senatore (ed.) *Pompei tra Sorrento e Sarno*, 1–27. Rome, Editore Bardi.

Noy, D. (2000) *Foreigners at Rome. Citizens and Strangers*. London, Gerald Duckworth & Co.

Patterson, O. (1982) *Slavery and Social Death: A Comparative Study*. Cambridge, Mass., Harvard University Press.

Petersen, L. H. (2006) *The Freedman in Roman Art and Art History*. Cambridge, Cambridge University Press.

Purcell, N. (1987) Tomb and Suburb. In H. von Hesberg and P. Zanker (eds) *Römische Gräberstraßen. Selbstdarstellung – Status – Standard*, 25–42. Munich, Verlag der Bayerischen Akademie der Wissenschaften.

Scheidel, W. (1997) Quantifying the sources of slaves in the early Roman Empire. Journal of Roman Studies 87, 156–169.

Sinn, F. and Freyberger, K. S. (1996) *Die Grabdenkmäler. Die Ausstattung des Hateriergrabes* (Vatikanische Museen, Museo Gregoriano Profano ex Lateranense, Vol. I.2). Mainz, Von Zabern.

Sydenham, E. A. (1952) *The Coinage of the Roman Republic*. London, Spink and Son Ltd.

Toynbee, J. M. C. (1971) *Death and Burial in the Roman World*. Baltimore, Johns Hopkins University Press.

Treggiari, S. (1969) Roman Freedmen During the Late Republic. Oxford, Clarendon Press.

Walker, S. (1995) *Greek and Roman Portraits*. London, British Museum Press.

Watson, A. (1967) *The Law of Persons in the Later Roman Republic*. Oxford, Clarendon Press.

Watson, A. (1975) *Rome of the XII Tables. Persons and Property*. Princeton, Princeton University Press.

Weaver, P. R. C. (1991) Children of freedmen (and freedwomen). In B. Rawson (ed.) *Marriage, Divorce and Children in Ancient Rome*, 166–190. Oxford, Oxford University Press.

Wiedemann, T. (1981) *Greek and Roman Slavery*. London, Routledge.
Wiedemann, T. (1985) The regularity of manumission at Rome. *Classical Quarterly* 35, 162–175.
Zanker, P. (1975) Grabreliefs römischer Freigelassener. *Jahrbuch des Deutschen Archäologischen Instituts* 90, 267–315.
Zanker, P. (1992) Bürgerliche Selbstdarstellung am Grab im römischen Kaiserreich. In H.-J. Schalles, H. von Hesberg and P. Zanker (eds) *Die römische Stadt im 2. Jahrhundert n. Chr.*, 339–358. Cologne, Rheinland Verlag.

9

Poetic Monuments: Grief and Consolation in Statius *Silvae* 3.3

Jean-Michel Hulls

Silvae 3.3 is a poem written early in AD 93 for the wealthy equestrian patron of both Statius and Martial, Claudius Etruscus, to commemorate the death of his father. The father was an imperial freedman manumitted under Tiberius, who served under Caligula, Claudius, Nero and Vespasian, and it was Vespasian who admitted him to the equestrian order. Claudius Etruscus' father rose to the post of procurator *a rationibus*, married into a consular family, and became extremely wealthy. The father, whose name is not attested, continued to serve the Flavian emperors and was banished by Domitian in about AD 83 to Campania before being allowed to return in 90 or 91 and dying probably at the end of AD 92 (for a more extensive reconstruction of the father's life, see Martial 6.83; 7.40; Statius, *Silv.* 3.3 with Weaver 1965; 1972, 284–94; Evans 1978; Nauta 2002, 230–1. On Claudius Etruscus himself, see also Martial 6.42; Statius, *Silv.* 1.5; White 1975, 275–9). *Silvae* 3.3 is normally described as a *consolatio*, but this paper will show that this title is misleading or perhaps that this is a category that is worth reassessing and redefining;[1] Statius' poem undoubtedly taps into the complex tradition of consolation, but resists easy categorisation within that tradition and, indeed, ultimately fails to provide a genuine sense of *consolatio* for its addressee. Ultimately, Statius leaves Claudius Etruscus to find his own, unsatisfactory consolation. Central to Statius' play on the theme of consolation is the relationship of different consolatory utterances within the poem and the implicit opposition between physical monuments of remembrance and displays of grief on the one hand, and Statius' poetic text as a more nuanced and long-lasting expression of grief and consolation on the other. The poem displays competing forms of memorialisation, funereal and poetic, and is underpinned by an analysis and critique of differing modes of mourning and the impact of the contemporary political climate upon them.

The nature of familial and quasi-familial relationships within the poem and in particular Claudius' relationships with his father and other family members are presented in a way that suggests disunity. Looming over this uncomfortable portrait of family life lies a further set of relationships between Etrusci and their imperial patrons. Statius' poem depicts a conflict between imperial and familial concerns, public and private life, which centres on the virtues of *pietas* and *clementia* in Domitianic Rome. The wider political impact of the poem runs in parallel to the themes of consolation, and the evaluation of responses to exile and death.

We will confine ourselves to exploring Statius' monumentalisation of consolation and his presentation of family themes within this context. We will only have the space for a brief exploration of the consolatory traditions with which Statius' poem interacts, and comparison with other, perhaps more conventional, *consolationes* in the *Silvae* (especially 2.6) and some of the consolatory literature of Seneca. Furthermore, this paper will invite further exploration of the often extraordinary encomium of Claudius' father and his life as an imperial civil servant and in particular his relationship with the emperor Domitian. These passages provide us with the means to construct the funeral and the *consolatio* as a clash of ideologies and as a locus where the poet explores the political impact of grief and consolation. Statius' intertwining of political and consolatory themes provides a further, crucial layer to a deeply complex poem, but sadly we will only have the opportunity to scratch at the surface of some of these issues here.

Our poem can be divided into three main sections. The opening forty-two lines develop the theme of *pietas* as the defining feature of the funerary rites and of Etruscus' grief; the long central section, lines 43–171, consists of an encomium which depicts the father's public and private life and includes a more brief *laudatio* of Etruscus' mother (111–37); finally the concluding lines of the poem (172–216) report Etruscus' lamentations for his father and give further details of the funerary rites.

In general terms, Statius incorporates many common themes from funerary and consolatory literature (the most important work on consolation literature in general remains Kassel 1958. On *consolatio* in Statius' *Silvae*, see Hardie 1983, 103–18; Markus 2004, 105–35, esp. 127–32, although neither discusses 3.3 directly. For detailed analysis of rhetorical and funerary themes in 3.3, see the introduction and commentary in Laguna-Mariscal 1992, 241–303). All Roman consolations seem to have had a similar basic form; they often begin with encouragement to lamentation (the obvious exception being philosophical approaches, especially the Stoic doctrine of *apatheia* and its rejection of any emotional response) which was followed by a command to cease grieving, usually involving some sort of peremptory reproach. However, the category of 'consolatory poetry' or 'consolatory literature' is extremely difficult to define in abstract or formal terms, not least because so much of what survives of consolatory writing seems to deviate from a hypothetical norm rather than exemplifying that norm itself. Although there is a consistent theme of offering consolation to a bereaved party, *consolationes* frequently have other and more complex agendas; the way in which people mourn and remember the dead becomes closely intertwined with a variety of public roles and duties. Whilst we will suggest that much of the nature and content of *Silvae* 3.3 is aberrant in some sense, the poem fits into this broader picture of written consolation rather well.

Indeed, Statius' poem sits comfortably in a variety of consolatory traditions; it belongs to the Greek *epicedion* tradition which began in Hellenistic Greece and flourished in

Greek writings in the imperial period and the Second Sophistic. This increased interest in consolation in the Hellenistic world was mirrored in philosophical texts both Greek and Roman and the philosophical approach to consolation effectively provides a separate strand of influence on Statius' work (we will consider Seneca's importance very briefly later on). Finally, the Romans themselves had a separate tradition of mourning and consolation; the *laudatio funebris* ('eulogy') was largely independent of Greek rhetorical models and the *nenia* ('funeral lament') seems to have fulfilled similar functions to Greek *threnoi* ('lament'). Roman *consolationes* were most commonly either written as letters and/or in verse, especially elegiac verse, and perhaps the most extensive verse example is the *Consolatio ad Liviam.*

All these areas of consolation clearly overlap (and I should say that my separation of these categories is highly artificial) and Statius' poem does, I suggest, show influence from all three. Moreover, modern scholars have used all three traditions as the basis for their analysis of Statius' consolatory poems. Hardie is especially concerned with Greek prose models such as Aelius Aristides, Markus uses the *consolatio ad Liviam* as a primary model in an article that focuses more on Statius' *Thebaid* than the *Silvae*, while Laguna-Mariscal principally uses the rhetorical treatises of Menander Rhetor and pseudo-Dionysius to categorise different elements and sections of 3.3. All three approaches are valid, of course, yet all three also close off the richness of the traditions that a poet like Statius was willing to explore and, in their desire to create a normalised understanding of what constitutes a Statian *consolatio*, avoid investigating the extent to which the poet is prepared to buck the trends he found in those traditions.

The titles of Statius' *Silvae* were probably not the author's own, and may well have been added by a near contemporary (see Coleman 1988, xxviii-xxii), but whoever added the later title *CONSOLATIO AD CLAUDIUM ETRUSCUM* ('Consolation addressed to Claudius Etruscus')[2] to *Silvae* 3.3 was doing so on Statius' own recommendation. The prose preface to the third book of Statius' *Silvae* is explicit about the kind of poem we should expect (*merebatur et Claudi Etrusci mei pietas aliquod ex studiis nostris <u>solacium</u>, cum <u>lugeret</u> <u>veris</u> (quod iam rarissimum est) <u>lacrimis</u> senem patrem*, 3 *praef.* 15–17, 'the filial devotion of my friend Claudius Etruscus deserved some solace from my pen as he mourned his father with unfeigned tears – something very unusual nowadays'). Etruscus needed real consolation to stop the genuine tears that he shed for his father – a display of grief that is *rarissimum* in Domitianic Rome. It is usually assumed that Statius is here making a political point – in Domitian's Rome, where dissimulation and doublespeak rule (see Bartsch 1994, *passim*; Hershkowitz 1998, 242–74), such frank displays of emotion are remarkable.

Yet I would suggest rather that Statius introduces here a further dimension to Etruscus' display of grief, contrasting it with the traditional approach to public displays of grief by important Roman men, where the aristocratic Roman male would not show any overt emotion in public. There is only a hint of castigation here, but a reader alert to the traditions of Roman consolation, such as the famous use of Republican *exempla* in the exchange of letters between Cicero and Sulpicius Rufus for example (*ad Fam.* 4.5, 4.6), or the list of great Roman statesmen adduced by Seneca in his consolation of Polybius (Seneca, *ad Poly.* 14.4–16.3), would be aware that it was a golden rule that the aristocratic Roman male did not show grief in public. Seneca invites Polybius to play the great general, and hide his grief for the sake of his surviving brothers (*ad Poly.* 5.4–5). Claudius Etruscus' display is, by contrast, very visible indeed (*cf.* Seneca, *ad Poly.* 17.2, *nam et non sentire mala sua non est hominis et non ferre non est viri*, 'for it is not human not to feel misfortunes, and it is not manly not to bear them'.[3] On consolation in Cicero's letters, see Kassel 1958, 89–103; Hutchinson 1998, 49–77; Wilcox 2005a, 237–55. On the theme of public grief in Cicero's letters, see Wilcox 2005b, esp. 268–70). We should be cautious in ascribing criticism of Etruscus, however, as Statius' other (ostensibly) consolatory poems contain similar exhortations to mourn openly. Nonetheless, Etruscus' approach to grief does look like something of a different order.

Silvae 3.3 opens with an invocation to the goddess *Pietas* to come to the funeral of Etruscus' father (3.3.1–7). Here Statius plays herald, inviting not public mourners, but a goddess to the funeral (in blending Pietas with Astraea, Statius is perhaps thinking of the depiction of Pietas in his *Thebaid* 11. 457–96, where she flees the horror of Polynices' and Eteocles' mutual fratricide. It takes a great display of filial *pietas* to bring her back to earth); *Pietas* is invited to look upon a mild funeral and see the son's pious tears:

> huc vittata comam niveoque insignis amictu
> ...
> mitibus exsequiis ades et lugentibus Etrusci
> cerne pios fletus laudataque lumina terge

> Come hither with fillets on your hair ... come to a gentle funeral and behold the pious tears of sorrowing Etruscus, praise his eyes and wipe them. (*Silv.* 3.3.3, 6–7)

The opening of the poem gives Etruscus' grief a further public dimension; the gods are also invited to look upon this display of emotion; Pietas dressed as priestess may even imply that she takes over from Claudius Etruscus in performing sacrifices at the funeral (there appears to be an implicit contrast with the divine Domitian as embodiment of *clementia*). Following the opening invocation to Pietas, Etruscus is extolled as a paragon of filial devotion, while Statius' exhortation *lumina terge* suggests even a consolatory role for *Pietas* herself. Yet what follows exceeds even the expectations created in these lines; Etruscus' lamentation is truly extraordinary:

> nam quis inexpleto rumpentem pectora questu
> complexumque rogos incumbentemque favillis
> aspiciens non aut primaevae funera plangi
> coniugis aut nati modo pubescentia credat
> ora rapi flammis? pater est qui fletur.

> For who that saw him bursting his breast with insatiable lament and embracing the pyre and bending over the ashes but would think his mourning was for a young wife or that the flames were devouring the face of a son just growing to manhood? It is a father he weeps for. (*Silv.* 3.3.8–12)

Few who were unaware of the circumstances would believe that Etruscus could be weeping for his father. His grief is, frankly, extreme. Statius draws in a familiar *topos* of consolatory literature, that of premature death, in an unusual way (on premature death, see Kassel 1958, 80–2). Normally, excessive grief would be expected in a parent who has lost a young child.[4] Etruscus' grief is noteworthy because it would be more appropriately (or plausibly?) prompted by the death of a young wife or adolescent son.

Unrestrained weeping was an entirely regular element in portrayals of grief and in and of itself, Etruscus' grief need not be read as being excessive (see Horace *C.* 1.24.1 with Nisbet & Hubbard 1970, *ad loc.* and see also Euphorion 21 Powell; *cons. Liv.* 7–8, 317–18; Ovid, *Rem.* 127–8; Statius, *Silv.* 2.1.14–35; 2.6.1–2; 5.5.59–65 for further examples of encouragement to lamentation). Statius clearly rejects a strictly Stoic approach to lamentation which would seek to restrain Etruscus from weeping altogether (For the range of possible responses, see Kassel 1958, *passim*).[5]

Yet the public context (both at the funeral and then in Statius' poem) of the son's grief *is* surprising; there is a sense that Etruscus takes his grieving to a higher level; this a funeral where only the pure and chaste may attend (3.3.12–17, esp. *insontes castosque voco*, 'I summon the innocent, the pure'), and he resents the long and successful life his father has had as too short by far (*celeres genitoris filius annos | (mira fides!) nigrasque putat properasse Sorores*, 3.3.20–1, 'A son thinks his father's years too swift (wonderful but true!), thinks the dark sisters went too fast!'). There is something a little unnatural about this display and we see a clear reversal of the pattern that is established, for example, in Polybius' famous description of the aristocratic funeral (Polybius 6.53–4, see also Brooke, this volume), where the surviving son's speech moves not only mourners, but the Roman public as a whole to sympathy for the loss. Etruscus' behaviour has clearer parallels with the funerals of Augustan elegy (*e.g.* Tibullus 1.1.61–8, Propertius 1.17, 19 and esp. 2.13), but the twist is that he behaves in the way the elegists would *like* their *puellae* to behave at their funeral (see *e.g.* Papanghelis 1987, 64; Lyne 1998, esp. 527–30, 536–8; and esp. Houghton, this volume). Statius may even be pushing the notion that this excessive grief is dangerous, or at least unsettling, because it transgresses gender boundaries.

Statius' description of Etruscus rings particularly true with another depiction of extreme grief in the letters of the Younger Pliny. There we see Regulus (*Ep.* 4.2 and 4.7) grieving unrestrainedly for his son, slaughtering the many animals the son kept around his pyre (*Ep.* 4.2.3), commissioning countless statues of the boy (*Ep.* 4.2.5, 4.7.1) and having a memoir of his son read in public throughout Italy (*Ep.* 4.7.2). Pliny does not hold back in his criticism (*luget insane*, *Ep.* 4.2.3, 'he mourns with wild extravagance') of what he sees as 'not grief, but a parade of grief' (*non dolor erat ille, sed ostentatio doloris*, *Ep.* 4.2.4) and of Regulus finding consolation in his irritation of the city (*quod vexat, solacium putat*, *Ep.* 4.2.6, 'he finds consolation in the nuisance he makes of himself').[6] Pliny's letters place Etruscus' emotional response to his father's death in a particularly harsh light.

The funeral for Etruscus' father is one where grief is focused solely in the son and outsiders are forced to take on his role in the obsequies (Pietas as sacrificant, Statius as orator). Statius describes the father's shade descending into Hades (3.3.22–30) and then exclaims:

> macte pio gemitu! <u>dabimus</u> <u>solacia</u> dignis
> luctibus Aoniasque tuo sacrabimus ultro
> inferias, Etrusce, seni. tu largus Eoa
> germina, tu messes Ciliciumque Arabumque superbas
> merge rogis; ferat ignis opes heredis et alto
> aggere missuri nitido pia nubila caelo
> stipentur census: nos non arsura <u>feremus</u>
> munera, venturosque tuus durabit in annos
> me monstrante dolor. neque enim mihi flere parentem
> ignotum; similis gemui proiectus ad ignem.
> <u>ille</u> mihi tua damna <u>dies</u> compescere cantu
> suadet: et ipse tuli quos nunc tibi confero questus.

> Hail to your pious groans! I shall give consolation to your worthy lament, Etruscus, and unasked consecrate Aonian offerings to your aged parent. Lavishly plunge Eastern gums into the flames, the proud harvests of Cilicia and Arabia. Let the fire bear your inheritance and wealth be piled on the tall mound to waft pious clouds to the wide sky. I shall bear gifts that do not burn and your grief shall endure through years to come as I portray it. For I too know what it is to weep for a father, like you I have groaned prostrate at the pyre. That day moves me to assuage your loss by song. I myself have borne the plaints I now offer to you. (*Silv.* 3.3.31–42)

Statius commands a sacrifice not for the father, but to honour Etruscus' pious mourning. He himself promises *solacia* to accompany funeral rites; this is to be an everlasting, poetic monument. The first thirty lines have merely been a prelude and celebration of Etruscus' piety and not his father's life (note the future tenses, *dabimus, feremus*). Statius promises that his *consolatio* will come on the same day as the funeral (*ille dies*, 41), but this promise is not entirely fulfilled. Indeed, Statius gives the lie to his own promise in his desire to construct a poetic gift that will perpetuate Claudius' suffering, not relieve it (*tuus durabit...dolor*, 38–9).

The funeral rites will be as extreme as the grief of Etruscus; it will be lavish (*largus*) and burn all the incense of the East (*messes...superbas*). This is to be a funeral on an epic scale;[7] Etruscus will destroy the fortune his father had left him (*ferat ignis opes heredis*) to create pious clouds of smoke to be carried heavenward (*pia nubile*).[8] The extent of this ostentatious display reflects grief on an epic scale. Thus the opening 42 lines build a very clear picture: Etruscus is so destructive that he comes to resemble one of Statius' epic heroes; he is displaying almost superhuman levels of grief and as such is a hugely impressive example of *pietas* (yet this self-indulgent, introverted example is implicitly a negative version of Domitianic largesse and *clementia*, see below).

We might now expect that the extended encomium of Etruscus' father (3.3.43–171) and the account of his rise from imperial freedman to Flavian *eques* might constitute the epic *solacia* that Etruscus so clearly requires to end his grief. [9] Yet the concluding section of the poem suggests that Etruscus has still not been consoled. Indeed, it is the *pietas* of Etruscus that demands such a song:

> hic maesti pietas me poscit Etrusci
> qualia nec Siculae modulantur carmina rupes
> nec fati iam certus olor saevique marita
> Tereos. heu quantis lassantem bracchia vidi
> planctibus et prono fusum super oscula vultu!
> vix famuli comitesque tenent, vix arduus ignis
> summovet. haud aliter gemuit per Sunia Theseus
> litora quem falsis deceperat Aegea velis.

> Now the day is ending and the inexorable thread runs out. Here sad Etruscus' piety asks of me such a song as the rocks of Sicily do not modulate, nor the swan now sure of his fate, nor the bride of savage Tereus. Alas! with what blows of lamentation did I see him wearying his arms, spread out with face prone to kiss! Not otherwise by Sunium's shore did Theseus mourn for Aegeus whom his false sails had deceived. (*Silv.* 3.3.173–80)

Etruscus' *pietas* continues to be the driving force of his grief and the long biographical section of Statius' poem (on which more in a moment) has not proved to be sufficient consolation for his patron. The *exempla* suggest that quasi-epic song is still required. The list of *exempla* – the Sirens, dying swan, Philomela and Procne, and Aegeus and Theseus – may seem a little peculiar in the circumstances, but the Sirens and Philomela are both standard examples of grief. Three examples of grief in *Silvae* 3.3 are repeated in Statius' lament for his father at *Silvae* 5.3.80–5 while the Sirens and Philomela as *exempla* of grief are also paired by Seneca (*HO* 189–93; *cf. Silv*. 2.4.21). Statius' choices here are also motivated by a desire to link this moment back to the equally dangerous mourning of *Thebaid* 12.474–80. Statius has, thus far, failed to produce the more-than-epic consolation that Etruscus' more-than-epic grief demands. Seemingly it is left for Etruscus to provide his own consolation by giving his own speech to his father's shade over the funeral pyre (3.3.182–204).

Etruscus' speech is effectively a *consolatio* within a *consolatio*, and follows the familiar rhetorical pattern of lamentation (182–94) and consolation (195–204). The lamentation compares the recent ending of his father's exile, made possible by Etruscus' supplications before Domitian, to the impossibility of similarly persuading the Fates or the gods of the Underworld. Etruscus regrets, in another list of epic *exempla*, that he could not be another Aeneas rescuing Anchises from Troy, or Scipio rescuing his father from the Carthaginians, or imitate the *pietas temeraria* ('rash piety') of Lausus.[10] The epic resonance of this poetic narrative reaches its climax here. Claudius Etruscus cannot display epic *virtus* on the field of battle, so he must instead display epic *pietas* by the funeral pyre. Careful readers of Roman epic will prick up their ears at this – Claudius should know that, in epic poetry, excessive grief is rarely a healthy option (see below on the intertextual allusion to Dido's suicide). Finally, he complains that he cannot match Alcestis, who died of grief, or Orpheus, who persuaded the Underworld gods to let Eurydice return. We have come full circle here. Where, earlier on in the poem, we might have thought that Claudius would be grieving for a wife or child (3.3.10–12) and in doing so imitated the behaviour of the idealised *puella* by the funeral pyre of the elegist, now Etruscus himself can only explain his grief by drawing on erotic *exempla*. *Pietas* is conflated with elegiac *mollitia* (it is a comparison on which Seneca also draws, *ad Poly.* 6.2, *quid autem tam humile ac muliebre est quam consumendum se dolori committere?*, 'Yet what is so base and so womanish as to give oneself over to be utterly consumed by sorrow?').

Etruscus' consolation will come in the 'deification' of his father, who will become the *lar* ('household god') of Etruscus' own family. Etruscus' *pietas* is transformed into acute religious observance; it is monumentalised, both by his own construction of a *tumulus* and by the poem that is dedicated upon it. The father will effectively continue to rule his clan as guardian and master (*custos dominusque*),[11] sacrifices will be made and expensive idols will be crafted. Yet as Etruscus finishes his speech we do not see the consolation that we expected. Instead it appears that it is the father who is consoled by Etruscus' promises (the father's shade, like *Pietas*, remains until after the funeral rites are completed):

> talia dicentem genitor dulcedine laeta
> audit, et immites lente descendit ad umbras
> verbaque dilectae fert narraturus Etruscae.

> So he spoke, and sweet were his words to the happy father's ear. Slowly he descended to the pitiless shades, there to tell them to his beloved Etrusca. (*Silv.* 3.3.205–7)

The father can take comfort in the assurances of his son, but there is no indication that Etruscus himself has taken any consolation whatsoever, either from his own speech or from Statius' earlier encomium of his father or the surrounding panegyric narrative. Statius himself concludes by consoling *the father* that his monumental tomb will always be well maintained whilst the son is alive (3.3.208–14). The poem ends with the assertion that Statius' own poem has become more than a sacrificial dedication at the father's altar (picking up *macte*, 31) despite the fact that Etruscus himself had earned these verses by the example of his grieving (*exemplo meritus*, 3.3.215, 'earned by his example'), Statius' poem has become the sepulchral monument itself (*sepulchro*, 3.3.216, 'to this sepulchre', see Laguna-Mariscal 1992, *ad loc.*). The poem ends in a strange position; this is a *consolatio* where two attempts at consolation fail to console the addressee and the only (vaguely) consoled party is the dead man for whom Statius' patron grieves.

I think this issue needs to be addressed from two directions; I leave the content of the central encomium of Etruscus' father for the moment. The other part of the answer to this problem lies in the nature of the family that Statius depicts and this suggests that an unsolicited poem (note *ultro*, 32) was never meant to console at all. Rather it questions the singular value of the *pietas* that Etruscus displays and exposes it as a value that excludes other, more praiseworthy, virtues. We noted already that Etruscus' grief is presented from the outset as extreme, even immoderate. His father's descent into the Underworld increases the potential for our discomfort:

> exsultent placidi Lethaea ad flumina manes,
> Elysiae gaudete domus, date serta per aras,
> festaque pallentes hilaret altaria lucos.
> felix heu, nimium felix plorataque nato
> umbra venit. longe Furiarum sibila, longe
> tergeminus custos, penitus via longa patescat
> manibus egregiis. eat horrendumque silentis
> accedat domini solium gratesque supremas
> perferat et totidem iuveni roget anxius annos.

> Let ghosts benign exult by Lethe's stream; Elysian dwelling, rejoice. Strew garlands on the altars, let festal offerings cheer the dim groves. Happy, oh too happy, comes the shade, mourned by a son. Far be the hisses of the Furies, far the threefold warden; the long road lies open for choice spirits. Let him go and approach the dread throne of the silent lord. Let him bring last thanks and anxiously ask as many years for his son.
> (*Silv.* 3.3.22–30)

At first the picture of Elysium rejoicing seems benign, but the performance of religious rites in the Underworld (*date serta...lucos*, 3.3.23–4) suggests an alternative set of rituals to the ones performed by the son. Moreover, the depiction of the father's shade as *felix heu nimium felix* recalls Virgil's Dido speaking just before she commits suicide:

> felix, heu nimium felix, si litora tantum
> numquam Dardaniae tetigissent nostra carinae!"
> dixit, et, os impressa toro, "moriemur inultae,
> sed moriamur" ait. "sic, sic iuvat ire sub umbras:
> hauriat hunc oculis ignem crudelis ab alto
> Dardanus, et nostrae secum ferat omina mortis."

> 'So fulfilled, fulfilled to excess if only Dardanian
> Vessels had never, oh never, touched in the shores of my country.'
> This said, she pressed her face to the covers: 'We'll die without vengeance,
> But let us die! This is it, this the path that I choose to the dead world.
> This is the fire that, far out to sea, the cruel Dardanian's
> Eyes must absorb. He must carry with him these omens of our death.'
> Such were her words.[12] (*Aen.* 4.657–62)

Where Dido would have been happy had Trojan ships never come to Carthage, Etruscus' father is happy to reach the Underworld and leave behind his mourning son (for another unsettling reworking of this phrase, see *Silvae* 5.5.59, *o nimium felix, nimium*, with Gibson 2006a, *ad loc.*). Oddly, despite the promise of *Elysiae gaudete domus* (24), the father's shade does not go to Elysium directly but instead goes to appeal to Pluto and beg for a long life for his son (he is also seen at the end of the poem observing his own funeral rites, perhaps undermining the narrative logic of this poem even further). As Etruscus will hope to do later in the poem, the father now plays Orpheus, but instead of begging the Underworld gods for release (*immitem potuit Styga vincere supplex* | *Thracius*, 193–4, 'could the suppliant Thracian vanquish pitiless Styx?'), he anxiously begs for Etruscus not to be allowed in for some time. The poem subtly creates a sense of tension between father and son, which can also be seen in Etruscus' own speech. Typical *consolationes* include a command to cease mourning that carries a sense of admonishment. A prime example is Statius' consolation of Flavius Ursus on the death of his slave boy:

> quid caram crucias tam saevis luctibus umbram?
> eximius licet ille animi meritusque doleri,
> solvisti. subit ille pios carpitque quietem
> Elysiam clarosque illic fortasse parentes
> invenit, aut illi per amoena silentia Lethes
> forsan Avernales alludunt undique mixtae
> Naides, obliquoque notat Proserpina vultu.

> Why do you torture the dear shade with such savage mourning? Matchless though he was and worthy to be grieved for: you have paid. He joins the blessed, enjoys Elysium's peace, perchance finds illustrious parents there. Or in the pleasant silence of Lethe perhaps Nymphs of Avernus mingle from all sides and play with him, and Proserpina marks him with sidelong glance. (*Silv.* 2.6.96–102)

Here Statius condemns his addressee for torturing the dear shade with savage mourning and hopes that Ursus' favourite slave may find illustrious parents in Elysium. There is a strong sense that mourning can be commendable, but that it also needs to find an appropriate limit (see *e.g.* Seneca, *ad Poly.* 6.1–2). Flavius Ursus *is* mourning for a child (albeit a favourite slave boy) and the implication of the ending of *Silvae* 2.6 is that he does stop mourning.[13] There is also an important difference in the language of piety here: those who display *pietas* are in Elysium, not performing the funeral rites. The funeral in 3.3 appears to invert our expectations; Claudius is the embodiment of *pietas* and his father apes the living Orpheus and begs for his son's exclusion from the Underworld. In *Silvae* 2.6, while grief was warranted, Ursus has paid his dues and is consoled by Statius' rhetorically powerful utterance. In our poem, it is Etruscus who makes the most aggressive speech:

> cur nos, fidissime, linquis
> Fortuna redeunte, pater? modo numina magni

praesidis atque breves superum placavimus iras
nec frueris, tantique orbatus muneris usu
ad manes, ingrate, fugis.

'Why do you leave us, truest one, when Fortune is coming back? We have just appeased the godhead of our great ruler and the brief anger of the High Ones, and you profit not; robbed of the benefit of so great a boon, you flee to the Underworld, ingrate! (*Silv.* 3.3.182–6)

The key moment of consolatory writing – the command to cease weeping – is (mis)appropriated and redirected by the poem's addressee as an admonishment to his dead father. There is surely a certain irony that Etruscus' regret, that his father has not profited from the placation of the emperor's anger, is mentioned in such angry terms (*ad manes, ingrate, fugis*). Etruscus attacks his father as ungrateful and emphasises the separation between father and son. This discordant note is a constant theme in Statius' portrayal of the Etrusci.[14] Etruscus himself often seems the absolute opposite of his father in character and behaviour. His excessive display of emotion is in marked contrast to the sober, almost Stoic life of his hard working father (*hinc tibi rara quies animoque exclusa voluptas | exiguaeque dapes et numquam laesa profundo | cura mero*, 3.3.106–8, 'hence rest was rare for you, pleasure excluded from your thoughts, meagre your repasts, your care never dulled by deep draughts of wine'). Moreover, the astonishing expenditure on the funeral (33–9) and the luxury of the shrine constructed for the father (198–202, 211–13) suggest that Etruscus will destroy his inheritance in displaying his *pietas* (35), a further hint that the physical monument is not to be the lasting one. The father is characterised by his frugality, both in his professional control of state finances (86–105, esp. 98, *vigil idem animique sagacis*, 'watchful was that same and shrewd') and in his unselfish provision of a fortune for his children:

quam dives in usus
natorum totoque volens excedere censu
testis adhuc largi nitor indesuetus Etrusci,
cui tua non humiles dedit indulgentia mores

How rich he was for his sons' behoof, how ready to step away from his entire fortune, the unchanging elegance of lavish Etruscus still stands witness; 'twas your love that gave him his high style. (*Silv.* 3.3.147–50)

The *indulgentia* shown by father to son has led to Etruscus becoming a big spender of his father's hard earned fortune. The picture of singular indulgence is emphasised by the contrast between Etruscus and his brother:

hunc siquidem amplexu semper revocante tenebas
blandus et imperio numquam pater; huius honori
pronior ipse etiam gaudebat cedere frater.

For you held him in an embrace that ever called him back, a father in affection, never in authority. Even his brother too was glad to give him precedence, more eager for his advancement than for his own. (*Silv.* 3.3.151–3)

Etruscus' father was no authority figure, a nature that seems implicitly linked to Etruscus' own unrestrained largesse and grief. Statius' patron dominates the family picture. The brother has no place in the funeral that Statius describes and, like the father, remains unnamed and is characterised only by his passivity towards his brother (compare the similar phrases at *Silv.* 1.4.70 and 5.2.75. Contrast Seneca, *ad Poly.* 4.1–6.3, where the brothers of Polybius clearly participate in the funeral). Similarly, the central digression on Etruscus' mother (111–37), who may have died in childbirth (as 124–6, *si longa dies, si cernere vultus | natorum viridesque genas tibi iusta dedissent stamina* suggests, 'if length of days and just threads had vouchsafed you to see your children's faces'), is most notable for the extravagant funeral that she did not receive because Etruscus was not yet old enough to mourn (135–7, a further reflection of the father's frugality). Mother and sons have never even seen each other – Etrusca is only accessible to Statius and, one must assume, to Claudius Etruscus, through the portrait that attests to her beauty (112–14), a portrait that seemingly would be found at the family shrine. There is something a little disturbing in the way in which Etruscus constructs family relationships through monuments.

Yet her relationship is a love affair with the father alone; Etrusca receives extravagant funeral rites, but these are provided by the *Amores* (126–34; for the floral simile, *cf.* Homer, *Il.* 8.306–7; Catullus, 11.22; Virgil, *Aen.* 9.435–7; Ovid, *Am.* 3.7.65–6; *Met.* 10.190–4). Here again, Statius picks up the hint at a second 'funeral' for Etruscus in the Underworld (3.3.23–4) and anticipates Claudius' desire to supersede his mother by becoming an Orpheus or an Alcestis for his father (192–4), a desire that will be thwarted (207). Here, the dynamics of erotic poetry appear in what we might read as 'their proper place'. Meanwhile, the other male members of the Etrusci seem entirely inert compared to the flamboyant, super-pious Claudius, while mother-son relations are entirely absent. The picture here makes for a pointed contrast to Statius' own family in *Silvae* 3.5 (esp. 50–71). Despite being his wife's second husband and being step-father to her marriageable daughter and despite the potential stresses of moving from Rome to Naples, Statius presents a carefully crafted picture of family unity. I think it no coincidence that Statius concludes this poem by berating himself for questioning that family unity in language reminiscent of Etruscus' speech in 3.3:

> sed <u>ingratus</u> qui plura adnecto tuisque
> moribus indubito: <u>venies</u>, carissima coniunx,
> <u>praevenies</u>que etiam. Sine me tibi ductor aquarum
> Thybris et armiferi sordebunt tecta Quirini.

> But ingrate that I am, adding this, that, and the other, doubting your character. You *will* come, dear wife, you will even go ahead. Without me you will reck little of Tiber, prince of waters, or the dwellings of arm-bearing Quirinus. (*Silv.* 3.5.109–112)

Statius' construction of unsettling family dynamics in this consolatory poem suggests a strong similarity in theme and content with Seneca's *Consolatio ad Marciam*. The work was written in about AD 40, ostensibly to console Marcia on the death of her son three years earlier. The bulk of the consolation is a more generalised examination of how parents mourn for their children, but this is framed and contextualised by an extensive panegyric of her dead father Cremutius Cordus, who committed suicide some fifteen years earlier. Such is the extent to which Cremutius Cordus dominates the treatise that Rudich (1997, 24), observes: 'Marcia herself becomes a pale shadow, and her son Metilius, on whose death it was supposed to be written, is reduced to a non-person.' Similar deconstruction of family is at work in Seneca's *Consolatio ad Polybium*, a work written whilst Seneca was in exile on Corsica in AD 43 or 44 and addressed to the powerful freedman *a studiis* (and probably *a libellis*) of Claudius to console him over the death of a younger brother. Again, the brother barely figures in the treatise, to the extent that he is not even named. Seneca's own grief at life in exile is mentioned before Polybius' brother (2.1) and Seneca concentrates on flattering freedman and emperor. It seems more likely that the consolation was written to secure a release for Seneca from his sentence of exile. Consolation is a literary form that has the potential to override family ties and favour political themes.[15]

Etruscus meanwhile can now idolise both parents by gazing at their statues. The sense of family duty implicit in *pietas* is recast as religious observance. His *pietas* has such a singular nature that it becomes a disconcerting 'virtue' that crushes family unity. His father's shade seems almost pleased to be separated from his son, and the family's history is one of fracture and separation. Statius' poem plays up Etruscus' overbearing nature and the sharp contrast between father and son. Yet the joke is on Statius' patron; the real loss for his father was separation from Claudius' mother, not from his son.[16]

It is a sense of separation that informs the central bulk of Statius poem that is taken up by the encomium of Etruscus' father (3.3.43–171), in which we find the second half of our 'answer' to the problem of Etruscus' grief. Statius' depicts a life of astonishing social transformation and financial and political success. Fundamental to this portrayal is opposition of career and lineage. Etruscus' father, a slave from Smyrna, has no lineage of his own. Instead, he became *the* example of how to be successful in imperial Rome:

> non tibi clara quidem, senior placidissime, gentis
>   linea nec proavis demissum stemma, sed ingens
> supplevit fortuna genus culpamque parentum
>   occuluuit nec enim dominos de plebe tulisti,
> sed quibus occasus pariter famulantur et ortus.
>   nec pudor iste tibi

> Gentlest of greybeards, no lustre of lineage was yours, no pedigree handed down from forbears, but a splendid career supplied the place of family, veiling your parents' shortcomings. For the masters you served were no common folk; east and west alike are in thrall to them. No shame to you in that. (*Silv.* 3.3.43–8)

Etruscus' father and his career illustrate the massive changes in social structures that accompanied the shift from Republic to principate. When all the world is a slave (*famulantur*, 47), it makes good sense to serve those at the top of the pile. Distinction comes by close association, not through good birth and famous ancestors. Statius follows the introduction to his praise of Claudius' father with an astonishing passage that elucidates his idea of how the universe works on a principle of obedience:

quid enim terrisque poloque
parendi sine lege manet? vice cuncta reguntur
alternisque premunt. propriis sub regibus omnis
terra; premit felix regum diademata Roma;
hanc ducibus frenare datum; mox crescit in illos
imperium superis. sed habent et numina legem:
servit et astrorum velox chorus et vaga servit
luna, nec iniussae totiens redit orbita luci.
et (modo si fas est aequare iacentia summis)
pertulit et saevi Tirynthius horrida regis
pacta, nec erubuit famulantis fistula Phoebi.

For what in earth or heaven stays outside the law of obedience? All things are subject, and rule in their turn. All earth is under particular kings. The crowns of kings are pressed down by fortunate Rome. Rome's governance is given to her leaders. Over them again rises the dominion of the High Ones. But even deities have their law. Serves the swift choir of stars, serves the wandering moon, nor uncommanded does the light return so often on its course, and (if only it be lawful to compare the lowly with the highest) the Tirynthian bore the harsh covenant of a cruel king and Phoebus' flute did not blush when he obeyed a master. (*Silv.* 3.3.48–58)

In an era where aristocratic Romans were still desperately trying to improve their reputations and garner *virtus* and *gloria*, Statius' depiction of universal order through neat hierarchy and mute compliance runs almost directly against the system of competitive display that Rome's senatorial and equestrian classes had inherited from the Republican period. Statius' political view is starkly pragmatic, of course, and tailored to the needs of Domitian's Rome in AD 93, suffering as the emperor became increasingly censorious of the upper classes in particular and as his brutal reign of terror reached its climax (see Griffin 2000, 60–9). The pay-off is for those freedmen like Etruscus' father, who acted as career civil servants under successive regimes and whose very lack of lineage meant that they could not threaten imperial prestige with their own successes. Etruscus' father can, under Statius' system, become the equal of Hercules or Apollo (3.3.57–8; see *e.g.* Habinek 2000; Mayer 2001, 1–12. The Apollo comparison is one that Statius himself uses in *Silvae* 4.2.56, see Newlands 2002, 260–83).

The father's birth in Smyrna anticipates his future fortune. He is thus (like Statius) a civilised Greek, not a barbarian (3.3.59) and Statius' allusion to him bathing in the waters of the gold-bearing river Hermus (3.3.61) may not simply be a reference to his future role at the imperial treasury (so Vollmer 1898, *ad loc.*), but may also hint that his success will be based on gathering wealth, not reputation. We may instinctively look down upon the materialistic instincts of the *nouveaux riches*, but it was certainly a safer strategy than searching for acclamation.

Statius then charts the father's career under the Julio-Claudians. Etruscus' father was freed under Tiberius (66–9), then survived under Caligula, travelling with him to Germany (69–75). He was promoted by Claudius who then passed him onto Nero (76–8; note how Statius depicts the emperor Claudius, from whom Vespasian and his sons derived a great deal of their legitimacy as rulers, as the best of the four whilst almost entirely ignoring Nero. See Weaver 1965, 148; Griffin 2000, 11–25). In a world where *lex parendi* is the dominant principle, and where emperors are revered as deities (note the emphasis on Claudius' divinity, 3.3.77), Etruscus' father exceeds the gods in his ability to obey divine rule:

> quis superos metuens pariter tot templa, tot aras
> promeruisse datur? summi Iovis aliger Arcas
> nuntius; imbrifera potitur Thaumantide Iuno;
> stat celer obsequio iussa ad Neptunia Triton:
> tu totiens mutata ducum iuga rite tulisti
> integer, inque omni felix tua cumba profundo.

> Who that fears the gods is said to have served equally so many temples, so many altars? The winged Arcadian is the messenger of highest Jove, Juno is mistress of the rain-bearing daughter of Thaumas; prompt to obey, stands Triton at Neptune's orders. You duly bore the yoke of leaders, so often changed, without mishap, your boat was fortunate on every sea. (*Silv.* 3.3.79–84)

The nature of the father's success must have peculiar importance for the son. The measure of the father's *pietas* is such that he becomes the equivalent of Mercury, Iris and Triton all rolled into one. His healthy religiosity not only stands him in good stead for the future, but also lies in stark contrast to that of his son, obsessed with his father alone. Statius provides us with an evocative description of the father's responsibilities at the imperial exchequer (*Silv.* 3.3.85–110). The responsibilities of the procurator *a rationibus* themselves assume epic proportions, and the catalogue of exotic locations (Spain, Dalmatia, Africa, the Nile, Eastern seas, Sparta, Massylia, India, 3.3.89–95), exotic produce (not just Spanish gold, but also jewels, wheat and other foodstuffs, pearls, crystal, exotic wood, ivory), the catalogue of winds (3.3.96) and the theme of countless riches (*hibernos citius numeraveris imbres | silvarumque comas*, 3.3.97–8, 'sooner would you number winter's rains or the leaves of the forest') all lend this passage a distinctively epic air (as the clichés pile up, we get a sense of the real world being more epic than epic. This is a familiar theme in the *Silvae*, compare 1.6; 4.2; Newlands 2002, 227–83; Hulls 2007).

Yet Etruscus' father transcends epic countlessness in his enumerations, as he itemises and finances military expenditure, corn doles, aqueducts, harbours, roads, imperial buildings and controls the imperial mint itself (98–105; for *propugnacula ...| aequoris* (3.3.101–2) as harbours, see Shackleton Bailey 2003, *ad loc. Quod domini celsis niteat laquearibus aurum* (3.3.103, 'the gold that shines in our lord's lofty ceilings') is a reference to Domitian's palace on the Palatine, see Laguna-Mariscal 1992, *ad loc*; Darwall-Smith 1996; Hulls 2007, 198–9). Etruscus' father effectively becomes a ruler in his own right; he controls every aspect of the Roman empire and is responsible, on his own, for the military exploits, construction of infrastructure and architectural feats from which emperors themselves derived much of their prestige. In keeping with this paradoxical ruler status, made possible by Statius' unusual universal order, is the sense that Etruscus' father displays many of the stock characteristics of the good ruler. He is watchful and wise (*vigil idem animique sagacis*, 3.3.98), rarely rests and never allows the pursuit of pleasures, especially food and wine, to interrupt his work.[17] The father displays not only the characteristics of a Stoic, but also those of a good emperor (*cf.* the description of the emperor Claudius in a consolatory context, Seneca, *ad Poly.* 7.2).

Etruscus' father did gain prestige through marriage into a consular family (111–37). His wife provided the lineage that the freedman lacked. Yet this suggestion that the father married his way into respectability is somewhat undercut. Statius seems to finesse the chronology of the marriage, which, given where it lies in Statius' encomium, presumably took place under Claudius' or Nero's reign. Yet the brother-in-law gets most praise for an exploit which did not happen until Domitian's reign. What is more, it is likely that the campaign in which the brother-in-law fought did not take place until Etruscus' father had been in exile for two years.

The date of the brother-in-law's consulship is also uncertain. Claudius Etruscus' father may have married into a family that was considerably less aristocratic than is suggested by Statius and one which, like Etruscus himself, gained its status under the Flavians. Statius certainly plays up the standing of the new in-laws; Etrusca's brother was not only a consul but also commanded Domitian's army in the campaign against the Dacians in AD 85 (more epic language, 3.3.115–18). Yet even the consular brother-in-law obeys Statius' rule of obedience. There can be no doubt that the great triumph (*magno triumpho*, 118) was celebrated by Domitian alone. The key epithet for the unnamed brother-in-law is *fidus* (116); he is, for all his aristocratic standing, as much an imperial servant as a freedman like Etruscus' father. The picture of an orderly hierarchy of rulers is continued in the scene of Vespasian raising Etruscus' father to equestrian rank (3.3.138–45):

> illum et qui nutu superas nunc temperat arces,
> progeniem claram terris partitus et astris,
> laetus Idymaei donavit honore triumphi
> dignatusque loco victricis et ordine pompae
> non vetuit, tenuesque nihil minuere parentes.

He that now governs heaven's heights with his nod and has divided his progeny between earth and stars gladly granted him the honour of the Idumaean triumph, deeming him

> worthy of a place in the order of the victory procession and not gainsaying. His humble parentage was no detraction. (*Silv*. 3.3.138–42)

Vespasian is referred to obliquely, as ruler of heaven (*nutu* effectively identifies the deified Vespasian with Jupiter). Domitian is thus only a ruler on earth, still subordinate to his father. Claudius' father maintains his own status as quasi-ruler, even being allowed to participate in the Jewish triumph of AD 81. The combination of financial power, status acquired through marriage and participation in triumph serve to make Claudius' father appear a ruler in his own right.

This exceptional success continued for sixteen years until Domitian banished Etruscus' father to exile in Campania in about AD 83. Domitian allowed him to return in 90 or 91 before he died, probably at the end of AD 92 (3.3.154–71). Here our poem takes a surprising turn, the long encomium of Etruscus' father becoming a frame for a brief panegyric of Domitian and his *clementia*. The exploration of imperial ideology is pointed and highlights some of the miscalculations in Etruscus' own behaviour:

> quas tibi devoti iuvenes pro patre renato,
> summe ducum, grates, aut quae pia vota rependunt!

> Highest of leaders, what thanks do the young men, devoted to you as they are, give for the father reborn! (*Silv.* 3.3.154–5)

Statius hints at a moment when Etruscus' *pietas* was directed in a more appropriate manner; the sons (*iuvenes* presumably indicates Etruscus' nameless brother) supplicate the emperor in order to gain a pardon for their father and do so in the manner of worshippers at a shrine. Statius explores the reasons for the father's exile (he posits old age and exhaustion due to his heavy workload) and the shock of the punishment (for the theory that Etruscus' father was exiled for opposition to Domitian's coinage reforms in AD 82, see Carradice 1979). He also attributes his return from exile to the efforts of Claudius and praises Domitian for his mercy (3.3.154–67).

Claudius *does* get to play Orpheus here, recalling his father not from the Underworld, but from exile in Campania. Indeed, Statius praises Domitian for his *clementia* in allowing the return of Etruscus' father and the redemption of his house (*maerentemque foves inclinatosque penates | erigis*, 166–7, 'soothing his grief and raising up the fallen house'); the suggestion is that the emperor can reintegrate Etruscus' household in a way that Etruscus himself cannot. Moreover, the act of exiling his freedman servant becomes itself an act of integration into the imperial household; Etruscus' father is a guest of the emperor, not an exile (*hospes, non exsul erat*, 3.3.164).[18] Etruscus' behaviour at the funeral is, by contrast, a metaphorical exile; he is alienated from family, society and, by implication, from the emperor (for the notion of exile as a metaphor for social displacement, see Whitmarsh 2001, 137–8; Williams 2006, esp. 148). Domitian becomes the true consoler of *Silvae* 3.3, both by meting out a mild sentence on Etruscus' father, and ultimately by recalling him to Rome.

The theme of status aggrandisement continues here. If Etruscus' father can be elevated to the status of world ruler, then Domitian becomes Jupiter.[19] The epithet *summe ducum* has singularly Jupiter-esque connotations (*cf.* Martial, 6.83.2), while the mildness of his sentence, banishment only as far as Campania, deploys the imagery of emperor as Jupiter: Etruscus' father anticipates a lightning bolt from the emperor, but is spared and Domitian only deploys thunder and a gentle storm (*Silv.* 3.3.158–60; *cf.* Martial 6.83.3–6; for the conventional identification of Jupiter and Domitian, see Sauter 1934, 54–78; Liebeschuetz 1979, 173–4; Fears 1981, 78–80. Dio 67.1 shows Domitian attack with the speed and violence of a thunderbolt). Yet for the hapless father, this display of mercy has important implications; this is the same *clementia* Domitian shows towards defeated enemies in war:

> nec longa moratus
> Romuleum reseras iterum, Germanice, limen
> maerentemque foves inclinatosque penates
> erigis. haud mirum, ductor placidissime, quando
> haec est quae victis parcentia foedera Cattis
> quaeque suum Dacis donat clementia montem,
> quae modo Marcomanos post horrida bella vagosque
> Sauromatas Latio non est dignata triumpho.

> And after no long delay, Germanicus, you once again unbar the gates of Romulus, soothing his grief and raising up the fallen house. No wonder, most merciful of rulers! For this is the clemency that grants mild terms to the vanquished Chatti and their mountain to the Dacians, that lately after rough warfare did not deem the Marcomani and the nomad Sarmatians worthy of a Latian triumph. (*Silv.* 3.3.164–71)

Domitian's *clementia* is exercised towards foreign peoples after they have been conquered in battle (the historical reality of these conflicts was rather different from the way in which they are depicted here: see Mattern 1999, 92–3; Griffin 2000, 64–5 and n.314). His exploits are cleverly played up; fighting against the Marcomani and Sarmatians is described as *horrida bella*, a phrase that evokes its uses in the *Aeneid* during the Sibyl's prophecy of Book 6 and the second proem at the beginning of Book 7 (*cf.* the Sibyl's prophecy, *bella, horrida bella*, at *Aen.* 6.86, 'warfare, hideous warfare'; the second proem, *dicam horrida bella*, *Aen.* 7.41, 'I'll speak about hideous warfare').[20]

Yet Statius subtly undercuts the allusion to Virgilian epic; Domitian's *horrida bella* are not even worthy of a triumph (*non est dignata triumpho*).[21] By partaking in such a heroic, epic, culture-defining conflict, Domitian is almost demeaning himself. He is superior to such warfare, which has been delegated to Claudius' uncle (115–17), while Claudius' father can revel in triumphs (140–1) and Claudius himself can only dream of playing the epic hero (188–94).

The description of Domitian as *ductor placidissime* (Shackleton Bailey 2003, *ad loc.* tellingly translates *ductor placidissime* as 'most merciful of rulers') in such a military context is almost paradoxical, evoking images of the mild and frightening expression of Domitian on his equestrian statue (*iuvat ora tueri | mixta notis, bellum placidamque gerentia pacem*, *Silv.* 1.1.15–16 'on whose face it is pleasant to gaze, where marks are mingled; war it bears and gentle peace'; Statius at *Silv.* 4.2 observes the facial paradox from the opposite direction, marvelling at Domitian's warlike appearance in a non-military context. *cf.* Hulls 2007). Yet this description also taps into the comparison between emperor and Jupiter; Domitian is an earthly Jupiter (*cf.* 3.3.156–64), a calm and indulgent conqueror, overthrowing foreign peoples and dispensing justice amongst them (note the description of Domitian as an earthly Jupiter at *Silv.* 3.4.17–19, *misisti Latio placido quem fronte ministrum| Iuppiter Ausonius pariter Romanaque Iuno | aspiciunt*, 'you sent to Latium a servant whom Ausonian Jupiter and Roman Juno alike regard with kindly love').[22] Domitian does not grant his *clementia* to citizens but to barbarians (note the arbitrary and autocratic qualities of *parcentia* and *donat* chiming in with the doctrine of *lex parendi*; in Domitian's Rome, *all* are conquered subjects). The association of this sort of imperial posture with the exile of Etruscus' father, who, as Statius told us, was most certainly *not* a barbarian, is powerfully effective. The procurator *a rationibus* is put very firmly in his place – he can play the ruler, but when a divine emperor dispenses justice, he is no different to the lowest foreigner.

Statius's incorporation of ideological and political discourse in a poem of consolation takes a clear cue from Seneca's consolatory writing. While Seneca's *Consolatio ad Marciam* plays the game of consoling Marcia, it seems to have more depth of political feeling. The work also celebrates the life of a Stoic suicide and opposition hero to such an extent that Cremutius Cordus comes to resemble a Stoic Jupiter, observing the entire universe:

> iuuabat unius me saeculi facta componere in parte ultima mundi et inter paucissimos gesta: tot saecula, tot aetatium contextum, seriem, quidquid annorum est, licet uisere; licet surrectura, licet ruitura regna prospicere et magnarum urbium lapsus et maris nouos cursus. nam si tibi potest solacio esse desideri tui commune fatum, nihil quo stat loco stabit, omnia sternet abducetque secum uetustas.

> It was once my delight to compile the history of what took place in a single epoch in the most distant region of the universe and among the merest handful of people. Now I may have the view of countless centuries, the succession and train of countless ages, the whole array of years: I may behold the rise and fall of future kingdoms, the downfall of great cities, and new invasions of the sea. For if common fate can be a solace for your yearning, know that nothing will abide where it is now placed, that time will lay all things low and take all things with it. (Seneca, *ad Marc.* 26.5–6)

Seneca uses the theme of consolation to make a political and ideological point, using the heroisation of a famous opponent of tyranny as an *exemplum* for negotiating the appropriate position of a Roman aristocrat in Julio-Claudian society (the *Consolatio ad Helviam* exhibits a similar pragmatic political aim in its promotion of Seneca's image as a Stoic sage). If such themes strike a chord with the politically minded reader of *Silvae* 3.3, then Seneca's *Consolatio ad Polybium* seems an even more apposite comparand.

The emperor Claudius assumes Cremutius Cordus' role as supreme moral arbiter, a quasi-Jupiter (*cf. nam quamdiu numen tuum intueberis, ad Poly.* 8.1, 'for as long as your divinity is before your eyes') and Polybius becomes, as Etruscus' father will, a miniature universal ruler:

> magna seruitus est magna fortuna. non licet tibi quicquam arbitrio tuo facere: audienda sunt tot hominum milia, tot disponendi libelli; tantus rerum ex orbe toto coeuntium congestus, ut possit per ordinem suum principis maximi animo subici, exigendus est.

> A great fortune is a great slavery; you may not do anything according to your wish. You must give audience to countless thousands of men, countless petitions must be disposed of; so great is the pile of business, accumulated from every part of the world, that must be carefully weighed in order that it may be brought to the attention of a most illustrious prince in the proper order. (Seneca, *ad Poly.* 6.5)

Furthermore, Seneca's invocation of Claudius is remarkably similar to Statius' description of Domitian, including a lengthy glorification of the emperor's virtues, and a eulogy of his planned military victories and *clementia*:

> hic Germaniam pacet, Britanniam aperiat, et paternos triumphos ducat et nouos; quorum me quoque spectatorem futurum, quae ex uirtutibus eius primum optinet locum, promittit clementia.

> May he bring peace to Germany, open up Britain, and celebrate again both his father's triumphs and new ones! And his mercy, which in the list of his virtues holds the chief place, raises the hope that of these I also shall not fail to be a spectator.
> (Seneca, *ad Poly.* 13.2)

Moreover, that Seneca was only exiled and not executed is a direct result of the emperor Claudius' *clementia* and his desire to argue Seneca's case in the Senate (*deprecatus est pro me senatum et vitam mihi non tantum dedit sed etiam petit*, 13.2, 'he besought the Senate on my behalf, and not only gave me my life, but even begged it'). The Senecan analogue to the image of Domitian thundering rather then wielding a lightning bolt is the image of Claudius' preventing Seneca from falling into the abyss (*impulsum a fortuna et cadentem sustinuit et in praeceps euntem leniter divinae manus usus moderatione deposuit*, 13.2, 'but when I had been smitten by Fortune and was falling, he checked my fall, and, using the mitigating power of his divine hand, he let me down gently'; Seneca's imagery suggests Stoic suicide, *cf.* Seneca, *Ep.* 58.34–5). If Seneca's praise of the emperor seems irrelevant to the process of consolation, then the point is this. Polybius is encouraged not to follow the Stoic doctrine of philosophical contemplation of the *summum bonum* (addressing Domitian as *summe ducum* becomes a little suggestive), but rather physically to contemplate his master (*intueberis*, 8.1; *cf. Silv.* 4.2.16), in whose presence he cannot experience grief (*ad Poly.* 8.1–2); Claudius becomes a living embodiment of virtue, and that virtue is *clementia*. To quote Rudich (1997, 35): 'the emphasis lies above all on the celebration of clemency, the noblest virtue, which elevates the entire argument, while making it complimentary to the emperor and expedient to the author.' This picture has implications for Claudius Etruscus; Statius' poem acts as an implicit encouragement to reject the pseudo-exilic isolation of his grief and integrate himself in the imperial society of Domitian. Neither death nor exile are suitable topics for consolation, but Etruscus' behaviour is.

Yet what is surprising about the complex, hierarchical portrayal of emperors and their subjects in *Silvae* 3.3 is the similarity between Etruscus' father and the man who exiles him. In particular, the father displays the mildness that is characteristic of the merciful ruler, Domitian most of all. The funeral rites are *mitibus exsequiis* (3.3.6, 'gentle funeral') and characterised as *pios* (3.3.7 'pious') which, given the excessive nature of Etruscus' display, seems to suggest the father's mild nature; Statius' encomium begins by addressing the father as *senior placidissime* (3.3.43, 'gentlest of greybeards'); he is later referred to as *senior, mitissime patrum* (3.3.208, 'gentlest of fathers').

Etruscus' father reflects his emperor's virtues more accurately than does his son. The contrast between father and son therefore runs to ideological levels. Etruscus' father is as much representative of a different virtue, that of *clementia*, as his son is of *pietas*.[23] Throughout the poem the father is referred to as *mitissimus* and *placidissimus*, epithets that are highly suggestive of the link between mildness and *clementia* normally to be found in the person of an absolute ruler. This imagery seems especially potent in a poem that refers to Domitian as *ductor placidissime* (167) as he displays *clementia* (169) by bringing the father back (*cf.* also Claudius, perhaps ironically, calling his father *fidissime*, 3.3.182. The connection between mildness, *clementia* and imperial power goes back to Seneca, *Clem.* 1.9.1). The father-son relationship mimics that between emperor and subject, and indeed the poem implies a specific comparison with the relationship between the father and Domitian.

Thus Etruscus' father assumes a quasi-imperial status in Statius' presentation and this is also visible in the description of his becoming the procurator *a rationibus* under Vespasian (3.3.85–105).[24] He is the representative of a *piam domum* (85, 'a loyal house') despite at this stage of Statius' biographical account not yet being married nor having respectable lineage (43–4); one gets the impression that this is *pietas* as it should be, directed towards the emperor, not exhibited in a highly introverted familial context. Moreover, Etruscus over-estimates the value of *pietas* as a virtue in comparison to obedience to the natural order of authority and the *clementia* a ruler displays to his subjects (or a father to his son?). That Etruscus' *pietas* is a destructive virtue becomes a starting point for Statius to deconstruct the traditional value-system of the Roman élite. The society where men of good family competitively acquired *virtus, pietas* and *gloria* has been consigned to the dustbin of history. Now a natural hierarchy oblivious to ancestry and desirous of wealth is imposed by divine rulers. The consolation of Etruscus has been hijacked by Statius in order to make an important political and ideological point.

The strategy of integrating themes from Senecan consolatory writing into his poetic project allows him to explore some of the ideological moves that have to be made to survive in Domitian's Rome. Both Seneca and Statius write consolations where emperor is elevated to the status of supreme deity, and imperial freedman to the status of universal ruler. Exile is treated as a subject which reflects the mildness and virtues of the emperor. Furthermore, the singular virtue embodied in the figure of the emperor is *clementia*; contemplation of the imperial person is (explicitly in Seneca, implicitly in Statius) the highest good. Claudius Etruscus should, therefore, reject *pietas* as his defining virtue. He will not find consolation in extreme grief, in the building of tombs, or even in the reading of Statius' commemorative poem, but in contemplation of Domitian.

Silvae 3.3 fails in its stated mission, to console Claudius Etruscus. It does so because of his excessive and misdirected sense of *pietas*, which recasts the consolatory nature of the poem. Instead the encomium of Etruscus' father presents the late procurator as a quasi-emperor whose own virtues mimic the emperor's *clementia*. The funeral and the poem which commemorates it become a battleground where conflicting family values are staged and deconstructed. The nature of mourning and in particular the way in which an individual is remembered through mourning become in Statius' hands a battleground where games of considerable political significance are fought. Much more remains to be said on this poem, but we have at least taken some steps forward in reading Statius' unusual consolation.

Notes

1 David Scourfield's paper 'The Genre(s) of Consolation' at a colloquium *Acts of Consolation: Approaches to Grief and Mourning from Crantor to Al-Kindi*, London 2007 proved enormously helpful for my own thoughts about categorising *consolatio*. Scourfield posits a narrower 'genre' of consolation and would probably exclude *Silvae* 3.3 from such a genre.

2 All translations of Statius are taken from Shackleton Bailey (2003).

3 All translations of Seneca are from Basore (1935).

4 Cicero grieving for Tullia is a classic example; *cf.* also Seneca's Marcia, *ad Marc.* 1.6–7; Scourfield in his lecture noted that consolation is normally *only* given (there are rare exceptions) after the death of a spouse or a child. Statius clearly plays on this very precise set of expectations in these lines.

5 Manning 1974 has a good general summary of the philosophical traditions. Menander Rhetor provides a catalogue of standard rhetorical approaches to grief in the *Paramuthetikos* ('consolatory address' 413.5–414.30), *Epitaphios* ('funeral oration' 418.5–422.4) and *Monodia* ('monody' 434.10–437.4), see the edition and commentary by Russell & Wilson 1981, *ad loc.*

6 Translations of Pliny's *Letters* are taken from Radice (1969).

7 *Aonias inferias* recalls the description of the *Thebaid* as *Aonia arma*, 'Aonian arms', the gemination of - *que* in line 34 is a typically epic device; these details add resonance to the choice of hexameter, not elegiac couplets, as the metre.

8 Is it ironic that Etruscus will burn his inheritance for pious heaven-bound smoke when *Pietas* has descended for the funeral? Etruscus' funeral apes the extravagant Saturnalian celebrations depicted in *Silvae* 1.6, another poem with epic pretensions, see Newlands 2002, 227–59.

9 I note in passing that Menander Rhetor 437.1–4 suggests that the *monodia* be no more than 150 lines in length as those grieving cannot stand anything longer: 'This speech should not exceed 150 lines in length. Mourners do not tolerate long delays or lengthy speeches at times of misfortune and unhappiness'.

10 The inclusion of Scipio in an otherwise 'mythological' list is arresting, but Scipio is, after all, the hero of Silius' epic *Punica*. Statius may also be thinking of Seneca, *Ad Marc.* 25 where Cremutius Cordus is depicted joining the *coetus sacer* ('sacred company') of Scipios and Catos in Elysium. In this consolatory context, Etruscus' 'rescue' would therefore be to take his father *away* from the Scipios in the Underworld!

11 One wonders if this might echo the notorious epithet for Domitian, *dominus et deus*, 'master and god', especially as that emperor had built a temple to Jupiter Custos, see Fears 1981, 78. On the epithet, see Suetonius, *Dom.* 13.1–2; Dio Chrysostom 45.1; Dio 67.4.7; 67.13.3–4; Aurelius Victor, *de Caes.* 11.2; *Epit. De Caes.* 11.6; Eutropius 7.23; Orosius 7.10. See Scott 1936, 102–12 for uses of the title in Martial and Statius. *cf.* Vessey 1983, 217; Jones 1996, 108–9.

12 Translations of Virgil's *Aeneid* taken from Ahl (2007).

13 There is a certain amount of play on social status and family connections in *Silvae* 2.6, and I would be very reluctant to read that poem as portraying a *normal* funeral and consolatory moment, *cf.* Esteve-Forriol 1962, 84–7. Yet the behaviour of Ursus does comply much more strongly with accepted standards; this is part of Statius' joke of course – he mourns a slave as one would a son. For similar social inequalities in consolation, see Bernstein 2005, on *Silvae* 2.1; Newlands forthcoming, *ad loc.*

14 It is worth noting, however, that subversion and parody are not uncommon themes in *consolationes*. The consolation addressed to Atedius Melior on the death of his parrot, *Silvae* 2.4, is a classic example of a subversive consolation. Moreover, the parrot in that poem is a perfect example of a subservient courtier, a role which the Etrusci and Statius himself must play in their relationship with the emperor. See Newlands 2004; James 2006.

15 It is also worth noting that Cicero never mentions Tullia by name when writing of his grief for her and, at least when writing to Sulpicius Rufus, views his grief through 'political' themes.

16 Etruscus may have been in exile with his father, *cf.* the hint at Martial 6.83.8, with *comiti* suggesting the formula *comes exilii*, although the suggestion that Etruscus may have gained his father's return by petitioning Domitian indicates that he remained in Rome. If so, the exile might have been something of a blessing!

17 The portrayal of the dedicated imperial freedman is closely modelled on Seneca's portrayal of Polybius, *ad Poly.* 6.4–5. The depiction of frugality versus gluttony is reminiscent of Vespasian in contrast to Vitellius, see Griffin 2000, 11–25. The elder Etruscus has a close comparand in that archetype of imperial servants, the Elder Pliny, see Pliny, *Ep.* 3.5.7–17.

18 This is rather different from the philosophical point of view, very much in vogue in Statius' time, that exile was a paradoxical form of empowerment, see Whitmarsh 2001, 149; Williams 2006, 149–57. Here the power is with the emperor, but submission does not, for the exile, involve dismissal from society.

19 Martial 6.83, also concerned with the exile of Etruscus' father and Domitian's mercy, makes similar ideological moves. Etruscus' father as guest reverses the pattern established by Ovid when begging for a closer and thus milder place of exile and invoking Augustus' *clementia* at the same time, *mitius exilium...quantaque in Augusto clementia*, Ovid, *Trist.* 4.4.51, 53, 'a milder place of exile ... such is Augustus' mercy'.

20 The phrase occurs three times in the *Thebaid*, 4.601; 6.457; 6.864, see Lovatt 2005, 29, 204–5, 270. Laguna Mariscal 1992, *ad Silv.* 3.3.167b–171 notes parallels with Ovid and the tradition of the *basilikos logos*, but also important is Statius' willingness to depict Domitian's foreign conquests

as epic deeds. The 'epicising' of Domitian's *clementia* is an important theme for Statius; *cf.* Gibson 2006b.

21 Domitian celebrated at least two and perhaps four triumphs including a double triumph over the Chatti and Dacians in AD 89; see Statius, *Silv.* 4.2.66–7; Suetonius, *Dom.* 6.1, 13.3; Griffin 2000, 63. Although Domitian's 'conquests' were scorned by later writers, triumphal processions clearly remained among the most important and most jealously guarded imperial privileges in the imperial period, *cf.* Mattern 1999, 167–8.

22 The description of Jupiter as *placidus* is unusual, although *cf.* Propertius, 2.16.47–8. The adjective *placidissime* clearly conveys similar, if not synonymous notions as the adjective *serenus*, which often describes Jupiter wielding power, and by analogy to Jupiter describes the power of an absolute ruler. *Serenus* and associated imagery is used by Lucan to describe Julius Caesar's *clementia*, by Seneca to describe Nero's power in the *de Clementia*, and by Martial and Statius to describe Domitian; see Leigh 1997, 56–67.

23 *Cf.* Seneca's construction of Cremutius Cordus and the emperor Claudius as embodiments of *clementia* in the *ad Marciam* and *ad Polybium* respectively, Rudich 1997, 22–36. Yet Etruscus' father follows the role of the freedman Polybius, who acquires clemency through association with Claudius, *ad Poly.* 6.5, esp. *ad misericordiam mitissimi Caesaris pervenire cupientem*, 'and desire to obtain mercy from Caesar's clemency'.

24 Laguna Mariscal 1992, *ad loc.* has even read the encomiastic section of the poem as partaking in the rhetorical tradition of the *basilikos logos*, comparing in particular with Menander Rhetor 368.1–377.30, and the description of the wealth that the father handles as beyond counting is certainly an element in that tradition. *Cf.* Menander Rhetor 368.21–369.2, although as Menander himself admits, indefinite examples are common to all epideictic subjects, 369.2–5. My personal feeling is that Laguna overstates the case somewhat and that the excessive praise that Statius employs need not be the exclusive province of the emperor.

Bibliography

Ahl, F. (2007) (ed.) *The Aeneid / Virgil.* Oxford, Oxford University Press.

Bartsch, S. (1994) *Actors in the Audience: Theatricality and Doublespeak from Nero to Hadrian.* Cambridge MA, Harvard University Press.

Basore, J. W. (ed.) (1935) *Seneca – Moral Essays.* 3 vols. Cambridge, Mass, Harvard University Press.

Bernstein, N. (2005) Mourning the *puer delicatus*: status inconsistency and the ethical value of fostering in Statius, *Silvae* 2.1. *American Journal of Philology* 126.2, 257–80.

Carradice, I. A. (1979) The banishment of the father of Claudius Etruscus: numismatic evidence. *Liverpool Classical Monthly* 4.5, 101–3.

Coleman, K. (ed.) (1988) *Statius Silvae IV.* Oxford, Oxford University Press.

Darwall-Smith, R. H. (1996) *Emperors and Architecture: A Study of Flavian Rome.* Brussels, Latomus.

Esteve-Forriol, J. (1962) *Die Trauer-und Trostgedichte in der römischen Literatur.* Munich diss.

Evans, J. K. (1978) The role of *suffragium* in imperial political decision-making: a Flavian example. *Historia* 27, 102–28.

Fears, J. R. (1981) The cult of Jupiter and Roman imperial ideology. *Aufstieg und Niedergang der römischen Welt* 2.17.1, 3–141.

Gibson, B. J. (ed.) (2006a) *Statius Silvae 5.* Oxford, Oxford Univeristy Press.

Gibson, B. J. (2006b) The *Silvae* and epic. In Nauta *et al.* 2006, 163–84.

Griffin, M. (2000) The Flavians. In *Cambridge Ancient History*[2] vol. 11, 1–83.
Habinek, T. (2000) Seneca's renown: *gloria, claritudo* and the replication of the Roman elite. *Classical Antiquity* 19.2, 264–303.
Hardie, A. (1983) *Statius and the Silvae: Poets, Patrons and Epideixis in the Graeco-Roman World.* Liverpool, Francis Cairns.
Hershkowitz, D. (1998) *Valerius Flaccus' Argonautica: Abbreivated Voyages in Silver Latin Epic.* Oxford, Oxford University Press.
Hulls, J-M. (2007) Lowering one's standards – on Statius *Silvae* 4.2.43. *Classical Quarterly* 57.1, 198–206.
Hutchinson, G. O. (1998) *Cicero's Correspondance – A Literary Study.* Oxford, Oxford University Press.
James, P. (2006) Two poetic and parodic parrots in Latin literature. In J. Courtney and P. James (eds), *The Role of the Parrot in Selected Texts from Ovid to Jean Rhys,* 1–32. Lampeter, New York, Queenston, Edwin Mellen Press.
Jones, B. W. (1996) *Suetonius – Domitian.* Bristol, Bristol Classical Press.
Kassel, R. (1958) *Untersuchungen zur griechischen und römischen Konsolationsliteratur.* Munich, C. H. Beck.
Laguna Mariscal, G. (ed.) (1992) *Estacio, Silvas III. Introducción, edición crítica, traducción y comentario.* Madrid-Seville, Universidad de Sevilla.
Leigh, M. (1997) *Lucan: Spectacle and Engagement.* Oxford, Oxford University Press.
Liebeschuetz, J. H. W. G. (1979) *Continuity and Change in Roman Religion.* Oxford, Oxford University Press.
Lovatt, H. (2005) *Statius and Epic Games.* Cambridge, Cambridge University Press.
Lyne, R. O. A. M. (1998) Propertius and Tibullus: early exchanges. *Classical Quarterly* 48.2, 519–44.
Manning, C. E. (1974) The Consolatory tradition and Seneca's attitude to the emotions. *Greece and Rome* 21.1, 74–84.
Markus, D. D. (2004) Grim pleasures: Statius' poetic consolations. *Arethusa* 37.1, 105–35.
Mattern, S. P. (1999) *Rome and the Enemy.* Berkeley, University of California Press.
Mayer, R. (ed.) (2001) *Tacitus – Dialogus de Oratoribus.* Cambridge, Cambridge University Press.
Nauta, R. R. (2002) *Poetry for Patrons.* Leiden, Brill.
Nauta, R. R., van Dam, H-J., and Smolenaars, J. J. L. (eds) (2006) *Flavian Poetry.* Leiden, Brill.
Newlands, C. E. (2002) *Statius' Silvae and the Poetics of Empire.* Cambridge, Cambridge University Press.
Newlands, C. E. (2004) Animal Claquers: *Silvae* 2.4 and 2.5. In W. W. Batstone and G. Tissol (eds) *Defining Genre and Gender in Latin Literature,* 285–95. New York, Peter Lang.
Newlands, C. E. (ed.) (forthcoming) *Statius Silvae Book 2.* Cambridge, Cambridge University Press.
Nisbet, R. G. M. and Hubbard, M. (eds) (1970) *A Commentary of Horace Odes Book 1.* Oxford, Oxford University Press.
Papanghelis, T. D. (1987) *Propertius: A Hellenistic Poet on Love and Death.* Cambridge, Cambridge University Press.
Radice, B. (1969) (ed.) *Pliny – The Letters and Panegyricus.* 2 vols. Cambridge, Mass, Harvard University Press.
Rudich, V. (1997) *Dissidence and Literature under Nero: The Price of Rhetoricization.* New York and London, Routledge Press.

Russell, D. A. and N. G. Wilson (eds) (1981) *Menander Rhetor*. Oxford, Oxford University Press.

Sauter, F. (1934) *Der römische Kaiserkult bei Martial und Statius*. Stuttgart and Berlin, Tübinger Beiträger 21.

Scott, K. (1936) *The Imperial Cult under the Flavians*. Berlin and Stuttgart, W. Kohlhammer.

Shackleton Bailey, D. R. (ed.) (2003) *Statius*. 3 vols. Cambridge, MA, Harvard University Press.

Vessey, D. W. T. C. (1983) *Mediis discumbere in astris*. Statius *Silvae* 4.2. *l'Antiquité Classique* 52: 206–20.

Vollmer, F. (ed.) (1898) *P. Papinii Statii Silvarum Libri*. Leipzig, Teubner.

Volk, K. and Williams, G. (eds) (2006) *New Developments in Seneca Studies. Columbia Studies in the Classical Tradition. Leiden, Brill.*

Weaver, P. R. C. (1965) The father of Claudius Etruscus. Statius *Silvae* 3.3. *Classical Quarterly* 15, 145–54.

Weaver, P. R. C. (1972) *Familia Caesaris. A Social Study of the Emperor's Freedmen and Slaves.* Cambridge, Cambridge University Press.

White, P. (1975) The friends of Martial, Statius, and Pliny, and the dispersal of patronage *Harvard Studies in Classical Philology* 79, 265–300.

Whitmarsh, T. (2001) *Greek Literature and the Roman Empire: the Politics of Imitation*. Oxford, Oxford University Press.

Wilcox, A. (2005a) Sympathetic rivals: consolation in Cicero's Letters. *American Journal of Philology* 126.2, 237–55.

Wilcox, A. (2005b) Paternal grief and the public eye: Cicero *ad Familiares* 4.6. *Phoenix* 59.3–4, 267–87.

Williams, G. (2006) States of exile, states of mind: paradox and reversal in Seneca's *Consolatio ad Helviam Matrem*. In Volk and Williams 2006, 147–74.

10

Remembering to Mourn: Personal Mementos of the Dead in Ancient Rome

Valerie M. Hope

These verses your patron, with never-ending tears, gives you.
As a gift to you who are lost, from your patron from whose heart you will never be taken.
These are welcome gifts to be given to those who are lost.
After you no woman can seem good,
And living without you he beholds his own end.
In gold he carries your name everywhere on his arm
In so far as he can retain it – Potestas, matched with gold.
However, as much as my praise may have power,
You shall live as long as possible through my verses.
In your place I hold an image of you as a comfort,
Which I revere and offer many garlands to,
And when I come to you it will keep me company and follow.
But I am unhappy for to whom can I consign so sacred a duty?
If however there is someone to whom I can entrust so much,
I shall perhaps be happy in this even though I have lost you.
(*CIL* VI 37965 = *CLE* 1988, lines 35–49. Translation based on Horsfall 1985)

Introduction

In recent years much has been written about the role and function of public monuments in ancient Rome, how the history of Rome was inscribed into the fabric of the city, how to live in Rome or to stroll through its streets was an experience or a journey which interwove present and past (*e.g.* Zanker 1988; Edwards 1996; Favro 1996; Cooley 2000). Tombs and funerary monuments, mainly located at the edge of Roman settlements, also fit into this general pattern since they urged the viewer, whether a considered visitor or casual passer-by, to remember the dead inhabitants. Tombs reminded the living that they too would die while simultaneously promoting the names, faces, identities, successes and sometimes even the failures of the dead. Death was final, but a funerary monument, however basic, spoke through its words, pictures and location to posterity. Inevitably funerary monuments – any monument – created an edited impression of the dead. Tombs often constructed an identity which homed in on certain aspects that mattered to the commemorated or commemorators such as a public or familial role. Furthermore certain types of monument and décor were preferred by certain social groups, and indeed the very act of funerary commemoration itself appealed more to some than to others (see, *e.g.* Zanker 1975; Kleiner 1977; Kleiner 1987; MacMullen 1982; von Hesberg 1992; Mouritsen 2005). The Roman cemetery then played an integral role in promoting memories of the past, memories that could be carefully edited and selected.

To focus in on the public role of cemeteries in memory promotion, however, is to risk overlooking the more private and emotional dimensions to remembering the dead. A funerary monument through its public, exterior elements could speak to all-comers, but it could also hold a more personal significance to those who loved, and those who actually knew the dead. The tomb could be a place of pilgrimage and reverence, a home or shrine for the dead, which kept not just their name alive, but also fulfilled the emotional needs of the survivors to both mourn and remember.

In this chapter I wish to make some tentative investigations into this more personal world of memory promotion, and focus primarily not on tombs, but on objects which intertwined the names and images of the dead with the domestic and everyday settings of the living. However, the initial entry point does originate from a Roman cemetery, in the form of the epitaph to Allia Potestas (*CIL* VI 37965 = *CLE* 1988; Fig 10.1). In many ways this inscription epitomises the public aspects of memory promotion and identity construction for both the deceased and the bereaved. The epitaph, at least as far as we can tell, was for general consumption, probably attached to a tomb or monument façade with the potential to be read by all and sundry. The words of the epitaph were carefully chosen, or more accurately poetically composed, to capture certain aspects of Allia's character, looks and life. Allia Potestas' identity for posterity was created and projected through the epitaph, which the author ruefully noted would keep her alive as long as it survived (line 43). This epitaph has long intrigued scholars, because of some unusual aspects to its content, especially the physical description of Allia and the reference to her two lovers, but the epitaph also provides an unusual insight into the world of memory and mourning occupied by the bereaved, a world not just centred on publicly inscribed and decorated monuments. The memory of Allia Potestas was tied to more portable items – specifically a bracelet (lines 40–41) and a portrait (line 44) – and these references open up questions and issues about the role of personal mementos, keepsakes and heirlooms in both promoting memory and assuaging grief which have been little explored in the Roman context, and which can be related to recent social-historical and archaeological explorations of the role of material culture in both memory and mourning (*e.g.* Gell 1998; Hallam and Hockey 2001; Jones 2007). The epitaph of Allia Potestas suggests that the tomb, and visiting the tomb, was undoubtedly important, but the presence of the dead was also to be found in more domestic, personal contexts.

Allia Potestas

The epitaph of Allia Potestas was found on the Via Pinciana, Rome, in 1912. The marble panel (67×59×2.5 cm) has nail holes in each of its corners suggesting that originally it was attached to a tomb or monument façade (Fig 10.1). The invocation to the *manes* (DIS MANIB(us)) and the name of Allia Potestas, are written in large capital letters (8 cm), followed by a 50 line poem divided into two columns written in regular small

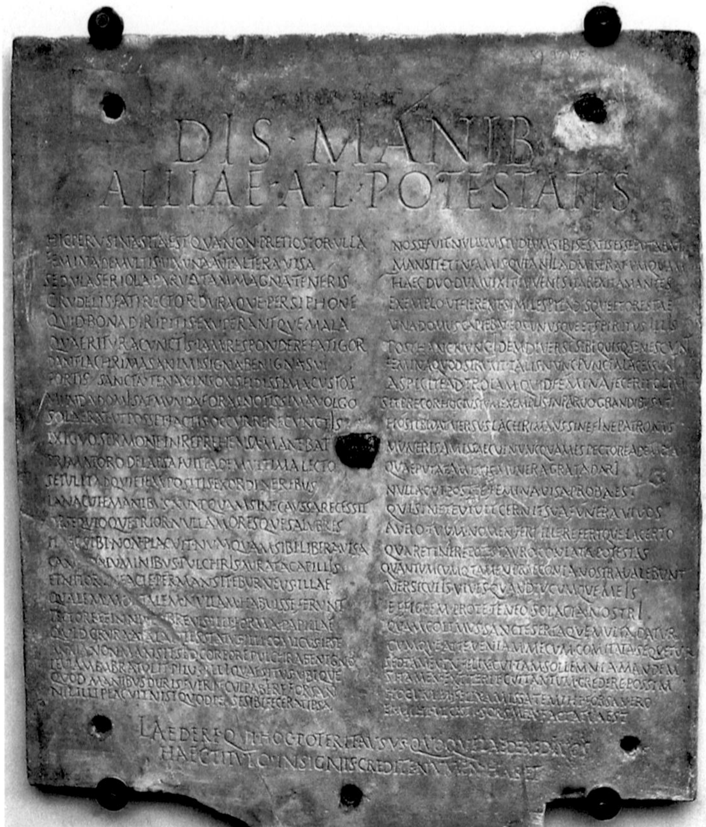

Fig. 10.1 Epitaph of Allia Potestas (CIL VI 37965), Rome. Photo: P. Perkins.

characters. At the bottom, in slightly larger letters, is a two line warning for would-be tomb violators. The date of the inscription is debated, it could be as early as the first century AD, although some have placed it as late as the fourth century AD; the second century AD is perhaps the most probable date.[1]

Allia Potestas is identified as the freedwoman of Aulus. The poem begins by noting that she came from Perugia, and the unfairness (blamed on the Fates and Persephone) that such a great woman is now contained in such a small urn. The poem is then broadly divided into three sections. The first focuses on Allia's virtues, describing her as an exemplary Roman *matrona*, she was 'courageous, chaste, frugal, honest, and a trustworthy guardian' (line 9). Allia was also clean and tidy, extremely hardworking and never neglected her wool-work. The second section is more unusual since it details Allia's physical appearance and beauty with semi-erotic descriptions of her body, including her pale complexion, golden hair, small nipples, smooth limbs and legs like Atalanta. This section continues to note that Allia lived harmoniously with two lovers. Finally, the author (and possibly one of the aforementioned lovers) laments her death and notes how he mourns and remembers her. The final lines claim that anyone who damages the tomb will offend the gods, especially since Allia herself has power (for discussion, commentaries and translations see Fant and Lefkowitz 1982, 137; Gordon 1983, 145–7; Horsfall 1985; Baldwin 1987, 68–76; Friggeri 2001, 168–9).

It is the third section of the poem (lines 35–49; quoted at the beginning of the chapter) that is of most interest here. In this Allia's commemorator laments her death and his own loss. The patron paints a poignant image of his suffering, his never-ending tears and a life that without her is hardly worth living. But live it he must, and an aspect of his strategy for carrying on, is to keep Allia with him. The funerary urn may contain her physical remains, to be entombed, marked and visited in the cemetery, but the name and image of Allia Potestas are not just tied to the tomb; they, through objects, can accompany the patron, and potentially stay with him at all times.

Portraits

The patron of Allia Potestas notes that he owns an image of her (line 44, *effigiem*), and that this has become an object of reverence, frequently adorned with garlands. What form this image or portrait of the dead woman took, or in what material it was rendered, is not clear from the epitaph. The patron implies that the image will accompany him to the grave, and the use of the word 'hold' (*teneo*) may suggest that it was small and light enough to be moved. A portrait bust or statuette seems most probable since this would have been relatively portable and easily decorated.

We cannot tell whether the image so dear to Allia's patron had been fashioned before or after her death. The focus on the one image, and fears for its ultimate fate, may suggest that it was a one off, and that Allia's portrait was not replicated elsewhere, such as at her tomb. The importance of portrait images on and in tombs has often been noted, and in particular how such portraits appealed to certain social groups in Rome especially freed-slaves, of which Allia was one (Zanker 1975; Kleiner 1977; Kleiner 1987; Kockel 1993; Mouritsen 2005; see also Hackworth Petersen 2006). But the image described here seems more private than public, although as often in the Roman world absolute distinctions between public and private may be somewhat misleading. The image of Allia, at least in this stage of its use, seems primarily domestic. The portrait has taken on a special status, it symbolises Allia's former self, her looks and beauty, but it is also a token of mourning. The image has become a personal treasure to the patron, maybe even his most valued possession, something that he displays and respects, an object with which he interacts, and which aids both his memory and his mourning.

In the Roman world portraits of the dead could take varied forms and be found in varied contexts. Statues, busts, paintings and even ring intaglios could depict and memorialise the dead. In general, however, we know more about the public and display role of portraits, how they played a part in promoting the identity of the living and the dead (and their associated family), than their role as more personal or intimate reminders. The study of Roman portraiture, especially statuary, is bound to that of public identity especially for the elite. Portraits were commissioned of the living, whether statues, busts or on coins, primarily as display and honorific items. Once the subject was dead such portraits might retain their significance, and for elite families ancestral images were a traditional way of promoting power and prestige. The *imagines*, or masks displayed at funerals, were an elite distinction, objects for public parade at funeral processions, but also for semi-public display in the home (Flower 1996; Noy, this volume). Picture galleries of famous relatives and connections, alive and dead, may have been a characteristic of many an aristocratic household (Pliny, *NH* 34.17; 35.4–5), whether as statues, statuettes, portrait busts or shield portraits (a *clipeata imago*).[2] At the Villa Aspri at Grottaferrata ten bases for statues survive and the inscriptions suggest a gallery of family members, the images dedicated by grateful clients and presumably representing living (at the time of commission) rather than dead subjects (Stewart 2003, 85–86, 259). A portrait may have taken on a new or different significance once its subject was dead, but in general such images were for display (public or semi-public) and designed to impress, and were thus less about individualising memory and more about promoting the values and identities to which the living survivors subscribed.

For the non elite portraiture was associated primarily with the dead and the funerary context. Portraits in relief and in the round, and some painted on tomb interiors were a common aspect of tomb decoration. Tombs, and varied funerary markers such as stelae, urns, altars and sarcophagi, could be constructed prior to death and hence the portrait subject may have been alive when the initial image was commissioned. Note, for example, the freed-slave Trimalchio's discussions with a stonemason about the portraits and images which were to adorn his tomb (Petronius, *Sat* 71). Part of preparing for death was imagining oneself dead and the image to be left behind (*cf.* Llewellyn 1991,

17–18), although this must have often created a disjunction between the living, ageing person and the unchanging image. In cases where portraits had not been previously commissioned, a mask could be made at death which would be used in the production of post-mortem portraits (Noy, this volume). However examples of such masks are rare and the contexts in which such portraits would have been subsequently displayed or used is often unclear. The specialness which the commemorator of Allia Potestas associates with her image may suggest that, whether made pre or post death, this was a unique image, and that for many people, beyond the elite, any images of the dead would be rare and thus highly treasured. We can compare early post-mortem photographs of the nineteenth century, which might be the only photograph or 'portrait' of the deceased ever taken and represented a last attempt by the survivors (often of modest means and backgrounds) to create a memento of the departed that kept death at bay. In these photographs the deceased was often artfully arranged with eyes open, sometimes with living family members, even embracing or holding the dead body, creating an image that reinforced family ties (Burns 2002; for photographs as material memory objects see Edwards 1999; Batchen 2004).

> People with limited means and the very poor feel that they must do all that is possible for the dead to make up for the deprivations suffered while alive.....when death comes their relatives are inconsolable at the thought of laying dear ones away without something besides a mental picture to remind them of the loved forms now to be laid to rest.
> Memorial Photographer, New York 1896 (quoted in Burns 2002).

Roman funerary portraiture was often retrospective, with little open acknowledgement of death and decay, and or any 'life' beyond the grave, instead idealising the dead, presenting them in the prime of life, well and healthy, sometimes engaged in work or leisure pursuits, sometimes with other family members (alive or dead) or occasionally in the guise of a god or hero. A few surviving images do depict deathbed scenes (Noy, this volume; Fig 1.1), and the deaths of heroes or mythical characters could also be used as allegories for the death of the commemorated person, but then the dead are seen most often as elegant sleeping and peaceful characters at the centre of the tableau (for example the sleeping Endymion, see Koortbojian 1995). A few images also acknowledge prior family deaths and simultaneously (and of particular relevance here) suggest the role of portraits in maintaining contact between the living and the dead. Some so-called *kline* monuments depicted a reclining figure clasping a portrait bust, showing the individual as it were embracing the dead and celebrating connections, and a sense of devotion, that lasted to the grave (D'Ambra 1995, 673). The 'Testamentum Relief' (Noy, this volume; Fig 1.2) portrays a man (presumably deceased) reclining, with a seated female figure (his mourning wife or mother) at his side, and with a shield portrait bust behind (probably his father). Together the figures unite the living and the dead, the recently deceased and the more distant dead and make claims for familial continuity and ties of affection (D'Ambra 1995). But the juxtaposition of the portraits also suggests the active role that images played in remembering the dead, which may not have been confined to the tomb, and that this family could afford to commission portraiture and display it within their house (D'Ambra 2002, 230). The shield portrait may evoke the home where the image of the father had continued to watch over his family, just as the image of Allia Potestas remained with the living even if ultimately it was destined to lie with the patron in the tomb.

In the main funerary or tomb portraiture was aimed at a public audience, it was largely an exterior and visible statement that commemorated the dead in a suitable fashion. The images often froze time and arrested any sense of bodily decay. Such portraits projected an image of the deceased and often at least by association, if not in accompanying images as well, of the wider family and the values and social standing to which they aspired. Funerary monuments sought to engage the living; the portraits of the dead which adorned them were static and unchanging, but gave the dead a visual presence complemented by an audible one, if we imagine the epitaph speaking on behalf of the dead (*cf.* Tarn Steiner 2001, 151–156; and for the voice and presentation of the dead in epitaphs see Erasmo 2008, 159–76). Put simply most portraits on funerary monuments were public statements, not personal mementos. However some funerary images were of a more private aspect – placed in the interior of a tomb or enclosure, accessible and visible only to a few who had reason to visit the tomb (see, *e.g.* Anderson and Nista 1988). This serves perhaps to underline that however public a portrait might be, and artful and considered in its design, to the bereaved it may have retained a more personal and powerful aspect. It may have been the only image that they had of the dead person, and helped to imbue the tomb or burial space with a shrine like quality. This could be particularly the case if images of the dead placed at the tomb were given divine qualities and attributes. An ex-slave of the early second century AD built a tomb to his wife and son, and in the epitaph noted that the garden was to contain statues of the dead Claudia Semne in the form of the goddesses Spes, Fortuna and Venus (*CIL* VI 15593, 15594; Wrede 1971). The commemorator was creating a gallery at the tomb which gave the chosen goddesses Claudia Semne's face. Similarly the poet Statius claimed that at Priscilla's tomb she was 'made anew' in bronze and clay as Ceres and Ariadne (Statius, *Silv.* 5.1, 232–3). Such images were not just about commemorating the dead in a publicly acceptable fashion, but were also tied to how the bereaved expressed the extent of their grief and loss. As one set of parents put it in commemorating their son, 'when we gaze upon your features, you will give solace' (*CIL* VIII 19606 = *CLE* 1607). An image could still be personal, or have personal resonance, even when placed in public or semi-public view.

Portraits of the dead, that is specifically commissioned portraits of dead rather than living subjects, were not exclusively confined to the tomb. Admittedly for most surviving portraits, especially statues and busts, it is hard to reconstruct their original context, their precise use or the exact time of their commission. In short we do not know whether the portrait subject was alive or dead, or whether the portrait was on public or private display, placed in a tomb, home, or public building or space. However literary texts do provide some insights into how the bereaved interacted with portraits and the role of the latter as emblems of both memory and mourning. The poet Statius, for example, noted that although he never personally met her the portrait (*imago*) of the dead Etrusca preserved her beauty; a beauty which was also seen in the faces of her children (*Silv.* 3.3, 112–14). Statius did not reveal where the portrait of Etrusca was displayed, but evoked the connections and sense of continuity between the living and the dead and the place of images in this. Seneca the Younger, in the *Consolation to Marcia* provided some significant insights into the role that portraits could play in the grieving process, how the bereaved could react both positively and negatively to images of dead loved-ones. Admittedly Seneca was focusing on dead public figures, pre-mortem images of whom would have been commonplace and something that readily confronted the bereaved. According to Seneca, at the death of her son Marcellus, Octavia, sister to the emperor Augustus, was so overcome by her grief that she did not wish to have any portraits of her darling son (*ad Marc.* 2.4: *Nullam habere imaginem filii carissimi voluit*) or have anyone mention his name in her hearing. Image and name had become painful reminders of all that Octavia had lost. The bereft mother could not be consoled. By contrast the empress Livia at the loss of her son, Drusus the Elder, spoke of him often, encouraged others to do so and had him pictured everywhere in private and in public places (*ad Marc.* 3.2: *ubique illum sibi privatim publiceque repraesentare*). For Livia name and image were a comfort and a consolation. A small carved gem may celebrate the role of images in the continued relationship between mother and son. The 'Marlborough Turquoise' now held in Boston has been interpreted as a depiction of Livia, in the nurturing guise of Venus, gazing at a portrait bust of the Elder Drusus (Bartman 1999, 83, Figs. 68 and 69).

Marcellus, Drusus, Octavia and Livia were all powerful public figures and Seneca was setting up literary and philosophical oppositions, about the pursuit of power, but above all about behaviour that defined both good and bad mourning in public figures. However all this at the very least suggests that portraits, which could be placed in both private and public contexts, had powerful associations as reminders to the bereaved. Portraits were not just about constructing acceptable public identities for the dead and the living, instead portraits and images of the dead could be a way of mediating and coping with grief as much as memorialising the dead. Pliny the Younger noted that, 'we seek consolation in sorrow in the busts (*imagines*) of our dead we set up in our homes; still more then should we find it in the statues standing in public places' (Pliny, *Ep.* 2.7).

The poignancy of such images, and their placement in relatively private contexts is suggested by another anecdote involving Livia and her husband, the emperor Augustus. The couple were said to have kept an image of a favourite dead grandson, in the guise of Cupid, in their bedroom which Augustus would kiss fondly whenever he entered (Suetonius, *Gaius* 7). The image idealised the child, preserved his physical likeness, and was the object of ritual. Augustus interacted with the image in a habitual fashion; it was not simply a passive display object. Statius has the son of Claudius Etruscus proclaim that he will keep his father's spirit alive in the home, bring offerings to and worship his image, and preserve his likeness in marble, wax, ivory and gold (Statius, *Silv.* 3.3, 195–204; *cf.* Statius, *Silv.* 2.7, 124–31).The Greek novelist Apuleius in his account of the grief of the young widow, Charite, noted how she had images of her dead husband made in the guise of the god Liber which she would worship (*Met* 8.7). These examples all suggest a blurring of distinctions between the human and divine, and that imbuing the dead with divine attributes may have more readily facilitated and justified ritual acts and perhaps elevated and justified grief (compare Claudia Semne above). The commemorator of Allia Potestas also imbued her image with a certain potency, although there was no explicit reference to the statue being akin to a divinity. The image of Allia Potestas was a focus of reverence, concern and anxiety, as well as admiration, and was regularly touched and adorned. Portraits could evoke physical and habitual reactions in the living; in the eyes and hands of the beholder they ceased to be inanimate objects (*cf.* Gell 1998, 17–22; Jones 2007, 22). Portraits could be moved, decorated, anointed and garlanded.[3] The most striking example of the animation of images of the dead was through the *imagines*, masks that could be worn by actors, bringing the dead back to life, but the epitaph of Allia Potestas suggests that even in more private, and non-elite contexts, portraits and people interacted.[4] Allia's portrait was not just something to be gazed upon but was a tactile object (see Stewart 1999 on the importance of touch). Portraits could in some ways make the dead person present, especially by appealing to the senses of the living, for example sight, touch and even smell (from flowers, incense *etc.*). It is also worth noting that the portrait of Allia Potestas cannot be divorced from the description of her great beauty, a central and distinctive feature of the epitaph overall. The image of Allia was also prized because it preserved that beauty, the portrait must be as aesthetically pleasing as Allia was herself: it was an art object held in a masculine gaze (*cf.* Bronfen 1992, 71).

The desire to interact with images of the dead, however, sometimes took on negative, even sinister overtones, symbolising the inability of the bereaved to let go of the dead. Pliny the Younger in his diatribe against the excessive mourning of his rival Regulus lists the excessive construction of images of Regulus' dead son, 'in wax, bronze, silver, gold, ivory and marble', as a negative trait (Pliny, *Ep.* 4.7). For Pliny this is just a show of false grief, but once more it suggests the importance of such images to the bereaved and how they were intimately connected to both remembering the physical likeness of the dead and evoking their continued presence. Could this become obsessive? The possibility is suggested, albeit in an earlier Greek context, by the Euripides' character Admetus, who in the *Alcestis*, promises his dying wife that he will put a likeness of her in his bed, so that he can embrace and caress it, 'so that I will seem to hold my dear wife in my arms even though I am not holding her' (348–54). Ovid has Laodicea make a wax image of her absent husband which she embraces and speaks to (Ovid,

Heroides 13, 151–158). Seneca the Younger in criticising the grief of the emperor Caligula (Gaius) at the loss of his sister Drusilla, notes how he shut himself away, neglected his personal appearance and built numerous temples and shrines, presumably containing cult images of the dead woman, in her memory (Seneca, *Polyb.* 17, 4–6). We can also note Nero's alleged behaviour after the death of his wife Poppaea, finding a reincarnation of Poppaea, a living portrait, in a eunuch who had similar facial features, and even wearing Poppaea's mask himself in some theatrical productions (Cassius Dio 62.28, 2–3; 63.9, 5; 63.12, 3–13).[5] A fascination or love of such images of the dead was often a sign of weakness; rather than alleviating grief the images made it worse, and increased the longing for what was absent. By contrast Tacitus at the death of his father-in-law recommended that the bereaved remember Agricola's mind, actions and words rather than the features of his face and body; such things would be everlasting whereas images fade and decay (Tacitus, *Agri.* 46; *cf.* Tacitus, *Ann.* 4.38; Cassius Dio 52.35). Real memory should be in the mind and heart, contained in mental rather than physical images (Koortbojian 2005). Portraits and images were all very well, and were appropriate reminders for some, but for the intellectual male elite such physical objects had limitations and in the hands of the intellectually or morally inferior could even be perceived as dangerous.

The bereaved could react to and use images of the dead in a variety of ways. The images themselves might be large or small, public or private or cover a full range of possibilities. For some people portraits were primarily about projecting the public values, role and identity of the deceased and the family. For others portraits were intimate and personal reminders of the facial features of their lost one – perhaps the only physical record and then a record produced after death. Portraits could have a positive affect on the bereaved, being a source of pride and triggering fond memories tinged with only a little sadness. For others portraits were potent, almost active reminders of the continuing presence of the dead. For others still images of the dead were too painful, a symbol of all that had been lost which could not be readily or easily confronted. When related to the bereaved, and the expression of grief, images and portraits could form part of an assessment of good and bad mourning, especially in philosophical dialogues. How someone reacted to portraits was part of how they were coping with their grief. There was a 'bittersweet' quality to interacting with an image of the dead which could be trivialised by some as over-sentimental (*cf.* Hallam and Hockey 2001, 19). But whether viewed negatively or positively portraits served to link the living and the dead, and were not just passive display objects, since they could be touched, kissed, decorated and revered, thus through habit and the senses giving the dead a presence among the living. Portraits of the dead undoubtedly present an ironic dichotomy; on the one hand making the dead, or at least their appearance, seemingly immortal, while simultaneously marking absence and thus making death ever present (*cf.* Bronfen 1992, 111). The significance of portraits as memory objects treasured by the bereaved may also shift and change with the passing of time and ultimately the death of the mourner.

The image of Allia Potestas would have had its own life-history, placed initially in the home of the bereaved, then in the tomb of the latter (if his wishes were ever fulfilled) or perhaps it was destined to become an art-object divorced from other aspects of her identity and that of her patron.

Jewellery and heirlooms

The commemorator of Allia Potestas also mentions what would seem to be a gold bracelet inscribed with her name (line 40: *auro tuum nomen fert ille refertque lacerto*; note Horsfall suggests a ring rather than a bracelet, Horsfall 1985, 270). Once more the exact details of the design and nature of this object are not specified. The commemorator stresses how the bracelet is with him in all his travels, and he plays with a pun on the name of the deceased – claiming to derive *potestas* (power) from the wearing of this item (line 41). The commemorator seems to derive strength, comfort and almost companionship from the bracelet. This is not just a display item; the gold band maybe visible to others and advertise that the commemorator can afford to wear such adornments (Stout 1994), but it is also something with which he interacts on a personal and intimate level. If inscribed on the inside of the bracelet, the name of Allia Potestas would not even be visible to others, 'remembrance jewellery presents….a hidden intimate network, from which other viewers are excluded. Mourning jewels are exhibited secrets' (Holm 2004, 140). The bracelet affected the appearance of the commemorator's body and represented an embodied and ritualised act of remembrance, the full significance of which may have only been understood by the commemorator himself.

Mourning could and can alter the human body; the sense of loss is registered through the living body, its dress and adornment (Llewellyn 1991, 93; Hallam and Hockey 2001, 69). In ancient Rome mourners would have had a distinctive appearance, wearing dark clothing, soiling their hair with ashes, tearing their cheeks, and generally having a dishevelled and distressed look (for references see Hope 2009, 73 with note 10). Those in mourning were not supposed to wear jewellery, and other adornments, and purple and white clothing (Paulus, *Sent.* 1.21. 2–5; see also Cicero, *de leg* 2.23.59). The bereaved were thus easy to identify, with their external appearance symbolising internal suffering (real or assumed), by the reversal of usual expectations and norms, at least, that is, well-to-do and elite norms (dark clothing, unadorned dress, grubby and dishevelled demeanour and dramatic noisy gestures, opposed to pale clothing, jewellery, cleanliness, tidy demeanour and unassuming behaviour). How long people were supposed to appear and behave like this was regulated according to who had died and the relationship between the deceased and the bereaved, with no mourning supposed to last more than ten months (Plutarch, *Num.* 12, Paulus, *Sent.* 1.21.13). However mourning regulations were aimed more at women, especially widows, than at men. A strong male character, especially with a public role to fulfil, would be expected to set aside public mourning and get back to work. Grief, or at least its continued public expression, was womanly (Cicero, *Fam.* 9.20.3; Seneca, *ad Marc.* 2.3.4; Plutarch, *Cons. Ad Uxor.* 4). The bracelet or bangle worn by the commemorator of Allia Potestas may seem to transgress the legal statement of no jewellery for those in mourning, but in this case the mourner was a man, no doubt with obligations to fulfil, who despite genuine grief was not expected to express this overtly through his dress and demeanour much beyond the funeral. For the commemorator of Allia Potestas the bracelet may have been then a relatively subtle way of marking his grief and memorialising the dead.

Mourning and memorial jewellery is found in many other cultures and we may think particularly of that employed in the Victorian era which could encompass everything from simple sombre black jet jewellery to items fashioned from the hair of the deceased, or lockets and brooches which were adorned with portraits of the dead. There is a need to distinguish, however, between different functions associated with these items. Some jewellery, especially that produced in the seventeenth and early eighteenth centuries, performed the role primarily of a *memento mori*, reminding the owner and wearer that they too would die rather than commemorating a specific dead person.[6] Later pieces had a more overt memorial function, often being given as gifts, sometimes even specified in the will, to act as souvenirs and mini memorials. We can note, for example, that Samuel Pepys left instructions in his will for 128 rings, totalling over £100 in value, and falling into three price bands, to be distributed at his death (Llewellyn 1991, 86). Victorian mourning jewellery was often more individualised and personalised, viewed as unique products created to commemorate specific individuals, which were to be treasured and worn only by those who were intimately connected to the dead (*e.g.* hair jewellery, see Pointon 1999; Holm 2004). There could then be differences and shifts between, but also merging purposes, in jewellery worn as a memory object and jewellery worn as a symbol of grief and loss, that is between remembering the dead person and remembering the mourning (Holm 2004). In addition we can note that jewellery, originally owned by the dead or already personalised through portraiture or inscription may have taken on a new significance or role on the death of the owner or donor.

How the bracelet worn by the patron of Allia Potestas should be classified is unclear. The epitaph does not specify whether the bracelet had once belonged to Allia Potestas or was specifically commissioned by the patron after her death. What we can say is that for the bereaved patron the bracelet was a way of carrying the dead, and sense of mourning, with him. This was an individual piece and for the wearer the bracelet was a 'personalised and miniaturised' form of memory (Hallam and Hockey 2001, 141).

There is little other evidence for specifically commissioned mourning jewellery from the Roman world. Perhaps the closest to commissioned pieces are intaglios some of which may have been fashioned with images of the dead. The example of Livia gazing at a bust of the Elder Drusus, mentioned above, is the most notable example.[7] However this piece is unusual and we cannot be certain who commissioned it or the contexts in which it would have been used, worn or displayed. In general images of the dead were probably not the norm for intaglios. We could also hypothesise that some names inscribed onto rings and bracelets may have been intended to evoke the name of dead loved-ones. These may have sought to keep the name of the dead alive, drawing on the mystical power of naming. Naming the dead was an important part of funeral ritual; the name of the dead person was called out at the moment of death (*conclamatio*), and again as the funeral pyre was lit; and names were regarded as the essential aspect of epitaphs (Cicero, *Sen.*7.21; Ausonius, *Parentalia* 1–18). However names found inscribed on jewellery, are more readily interpreted as ownership or manufacturers' labels. Jewellery, whether inscribed or not, could, however, be commissioned for specific commemorative purposes. Suetonius tells of how the emperor Nero had a snake skin set into a golden bracelet which he would wear on his right arm. This was primarily a talisman or lucky charm since the snake was thought to have saved his life, however, Nero also associated the item with his mother, who had urged him to preserve the skin. At Arippina's death Nero threw away the bracelet because it reminded him too vividly of his mother (Suetonius, *Nero* 6). This underlines that jewellery could have personal associations for the wearer even if these were not readily visible to the casual observer.

Jewellery, as precious objects, may have become imbued with resonant associations, and might take on a new significance in the hands of a new owner. Jewellery and other precious items were generally expected to be handed down across the generations. The large scale destruction of property at death and disposal of valuables on the funeral pyre or in the grave was generally frowned upon (see in particular *Digest* (Ulpian) 11.7.14.5; and, *e.g.* Pliny, *Ep.* 4.2, Lucian, *Luct.* 14). Precious items, including jewellery and gold and silver plate, could become heirlooms, passed down across the generations.[8] But how an individual recipient reacted to these items is difficult to gauge. In the will of Dasumius, for example, the testator specified certain items which were to be left to members of the household including tableware, a large gold dish or plate and some statues or images of unspecified subject (*CIL* VI 10229; Gardner and Wiedemann 1991, 133–39). Would the recipients have treasured these items and viewed them as reminders of a beloved dead master, or were they primarily interested in the intrinsic value, preserving them as something that could be sold or melted down if the need arose? It is difficult to trace personal associations because these were linked to individual memories both of the object (its role and use) and of the dead person (or familial associations). Suetonius once more includes a telling anecdote about the emperor Vespasian, a man who had no ancestral portraits on display in his house, but treasured a small silver cup that had belonged to his paternal grandmother who had raised him. Vespasian would drink from this cup on festival days, 'so dear was her memory to him' (Suetonius, *Vesp.* 2). This item was precious to the emperor, and had a value which went far beyond its intrinsic value. For Vespasian the cup was a prized possession, but its worth was linked to his own personal memories, the full significance of which could not be passed onto another. A family heirloom could eventually become little more than another trinket.

Personal items, and not just precious items, can take on the significance of mementos for the bereaved. A mundane item may become a 'powerful register of loss' (Hallam and Hockey 2001, 213). It has been noted that sorting through the belongings of the deceased, deciding what has personal significance and what does not, can be viewed as an essential act of the bereaved; a process to be confronted, almost savoured by some, and one avoided by others. Intimate items such as clothing may become emotionally powerful. Clothes worn at the point of death – items which had the last contact with the conscious body – may become a treasured item and a point of connection between the living and the dead (Hallam and Hockey 2001, 115, 118–20). The extent to which these or equivalent 'grieving processes' were experienced in the Roman context is difficult to judge. Many people would have had few belongings to be picked over by survivors, and for those with property strict inheritance laws and the employment of slaves to perform domestic duties may have created an emotional distance between some personal items and the bereaved. Wills made by women in which they specified the fate of their gold, jewels and toilet items, naming their daughters or other females who were to inherit these objects (*Digest* (Paul) 34.2.32.4; 34.2.8; (Scaevola) 34.2.40.2), do suggest that some items may have served as potent lasting reminders of women in particular. Some of these objects may have had intrinsic value, but they could also be highly resonant of the deceased evoking touch, sight and smell. Toilet items could include mirrors, jars, perfumed oils, bottles for perfumes, washing vessels and storage chests (*Digest* (Ulpian) 34.2.25.10) some of which may have been extremely evocative to the recipient. These items, were often associated with the body (its adornment, touch and smell) and thus would have created bodily connections and identifications between the recipient mourner and that of the deceased. The power of everyday objects to retain meaning and significance as great as that associated with the grave or tomb, should not be underestimated.

The bracelet inscribed with the name of Allia Potestas, habitually altered the body of her commemorator. This was a small, to many-an-observer, insignificant item, something worn in public, but which had personal and intimate connotations. Jewellery, and other domestic items, were imbued with their own history and associations which could affect the living and how they remembered the dead. There must have been differences in terms of the impact on mourners and observers between items which were deliberately manufactured as memory objects (*e.g.* post mortem portraits) and objects that because of personal associations came to act as memory objects (*e.g.* grandma's silver cup). It is difficult for us now to un-pack the role of and responses to different categories of items, but we can say that in general such material objects gave expression to mourning both private and public and integrated the dead with the everyday lives of the living. The commemorator of Allia Potestas, whether the portrait and bracelet were specifically commissioned after her death, or were objects that had existed before, had deliberately chosen to give these items special significance and thereby to place the past in his present, and use these objects to structure at least some aspects of his daily routine and existence.

Conclusion

The starting point to this chapter was the epitaph of Allia Potestas, and it could be argued that focusing on a few poetic lines is misleading, especially since the way in which the epitaph commemorates and characterises Allia Potestas is not quite the norm. Nevertheless the sections of the epitaph of interest here, especially when related to other evidence, suggest the role that objects could play in both memorialising the dead and facilitating mourning. This chapter represents only an initial foray into the role of objects, specifically portraits, jewellery and personal items, in these processes, but highlights the sensory, habitual and domestic aspects to remembering and mourning the Roman dead. Material objects have the potential to construct a sense of the absent person which resonates with the survivor and their present (Hallam and Hockey 2001, 85). Material objects are not just passive and inanimate since interaction between people and objects can evoke memory (Gell 1998; Jones 2007). Material objects also have their own 'life' or use trajectories, an 'artefact biography' (Hoskins 2006). Whether objects have actual 'agency' maybe debated (Hoskins 2006; Ingold 2007), but there can at least be a dynamic relationship between people and the things, items and objects with which they surround themselves.

Mourning and memory were characterised as gendered activities in the Roman world (see Šterbenc Erker this volume). To put it very simply great men were remembered and did not mourn (publicly at least); women were less deserving of memory and were expected to mourn. Inevitably such statements polarise the norms – gendered roles were not always attributed so neatly, and an interest in them was often the preserve of an intellectual minority. To simplify once more, women of distinguished birth, for example, could exhibit manly traits, and some men of high birth were weak and womanly (note how the emperor Gaius' mourning was characterised, see above). In many respects the epitaph of Allia Potestas enshrines traditional gender roles; Allia is a woman commemorated by a man, who highlights what is relevant and significant from his male gaze and perspective. Would Allia Potestas herself wished to have been remembered primarily for her thrift, beauty and her relationships? However in the context of the epitaph there is no denial of male grief, and the strategies the commemorator employs to confront and mediate that grief are not confined or defined by gender. The bracelet is particularly striking – an object which habitually alters his body – and evokes feminine mourning strategies involving jewellery and personal items. Legal texts and wills suggest that personal items such as a necklace, a jar of perfume or a mirror could be part of how women remembered each other, items that were singled out, because they had emotive, as well as, monetary value. Allia Potestas' commemorator suggests that how men remembered women could also be connected to such domestic items and bodily rituals.

The commemorator of Allia Potestas engaged in deliberate acts of memory making; the epitaph, the tomb, the image, the bracelet were considered choices in how Allia Potestas would be remembered. The actions of the commemorator gave Allia Potestas a life after death, and this new 'life' was not tied to a spiritual afterlife (although the epitaph does give some space to that possibility), but primarily a 'life', or at least a sense of continuity, grounded in the everyday actions of those that survived her. The commemorator placed the past in his present, integrating the memory of Allia into his on-going life. Remembering Allia meant daily practices that involved him interacting with certain objects (*cf.* Jones 2007, 22). The bracelet and portrait were visual and tactile, objects which triggered sensations that in turn triggered memory. Moreover these were not static mementos but objects which had a certain potency, and that evoked reactions and habits. For the commemorator there was a sensory and performative aspect to remembering the dead (*cf.* Graham this volume)

Remembering the dead was not solely or even primarily focused on the Roman cemetery. Memory was invested in other spaces, in material objects and habitual actions. Allia's commemorator did his remembering not just through accepted public funerary rituals, but through personally meaningful actions associated with the mundane aspects of his life. Specific objects were assigned specific memory meanings; these objects could be commissioned or created for that sole purpose, although other everyday objects could also be ascribed new meanings. Through these objects the dead were given a sense of physicality. It was this physicality that was significant to the commemorator of Allia. Remembering the name, appearance and conjuring up the physical presence of Allia Potestas was important, because it was part of how the commemorator mourned for her. The memory of what had been lost – the individual and all her qualities – explained and justified the grief of the commemorator. He wanted other people to know of and admire her beauty and qualities, but his memories of her were also personal and were what he was trying to recreate or preserve, and ultimately take with him to his own grave; he hoped the portrait would follow him there. The commemorator of Allia Potestas, and others too, through images and objects, tried to maintain links with and merge their living identities with that of the dead. Objects in particular created connections and a sense of identification between the body of the mourner and that of the deceased (Hallam and Hockey 2001, 13). For some ancient commentators these processes and actions could be problematic; memory was in general a positive thing, but for some mourners remembering the dead could literally take over their lives, become centred too much on physical objects, thus making them bad mourners who were not able to let go of the dead. There was a clear interconnectedness between memory and mourning, one could affect the other, and both could have a positive or a negative impact on the self-definition of the living.

Notes

1 For a summary of the arguments surrounding the dating of the inscription see Horsfall 1985, 252–53. Baldwin (1987, 68) plumps for a late date on 'philological grounds'; Friggeri (2001, 169) opts for the second century.

2 Note people could have galleries of images of famous writers and the like which might also be treated with great reverence, and act as a symbol of learning, education and status: Vitruvius 9, praef 16; Pliny, *Ep.* 4.28, 3.7.8; and see Beard and Henderson, 2001, 235; Stewart 2003, 256–59; Kondoleon 2006. The exiled Ovid's reference to people owning his portrait image suggests that this honour could be extended to the living (if absent) as well as the dead, Ovid, *Tr* 1.7.6. For the collectors' demand for images, statuettes, paintings, trinkets and souvenirs see Métraux 2006.

3 Compare the ritual acts associated with public statues. Statues of the gods could be washed, adorned, touched and carried in processions. Inscriptions recording foundations noted that statues of notable individuals should be garlanded and become the locus for annual ceremonies such as the distribution of gifts; see Tarn Steiner 2001, 105–113; Feiffer 2002; Stewart 2003, 148–54, 192–3, 263–4; Laird 2006.

4 The opposite of the honoured animation of the *imagines*, was the destruction of *imagines* and the toppling, beheading and dragging through the streets of statues, see Stewart 2003, 267–78. For *damnatio memoriae* see Varner 2001; 2004; Flower 2006.

5 Compare also the Pygmalion myth in Ovid, *Met 10.* 242–97. Note also that the veneration of images of people could be scorned, Lucian, *Philop.* 18–20; Pliny, *NH* 35.5.

6 *Memento mori* objects were displayed in the Roman world, particularly mosaics and tableware adorned with skeletons, which could juxtapose the pleasure of dining with the shortness of life, see Dunbabin 1986; Grotanelli 1995; Dunbabin 2003. Such a theme does not seem to have been a motif on or purpose for jewellery.

7 Another carved gem, the 'Vienna cameo', shows Livia as a priestess gazing at a bust of Augustus, whose radiate crown, suggests his post-death status as a god, Bartman 1999, 103, fig. 79. For portraits on gemstones see Vollenweider 1972. The difficulty lies in identifying the subjects of the portraits, but most were probably public figures with the ring intaglios being worn as a symbol of allegiance. That private individuals may have been so depicted and commemorated is suggested by a few intaglios, see, *e.g.* Henig 1994, cat no.221 and 222.

8 For gold and silver plate and the range of domestic items made from precious metals see Strong 1966.

Bibliography

Anderson, M. and Nista, L. (1988) *Roman Portraits in Context. Imperial and Private Likenesses from the Museo Nazionale Romano*. Rome, De Luca.

Baldwin, B. (1987) *An Anthology of Later Latin Literature*. Amsterdam, Gieben.

Bartman, E. (1999) *Portraits of Livia. Imaging the Imperial Woman in Augustan Rome*. Cambridge, Cambridge University Press.

Batchen, G. (2004) *Forget Me Not. Photography and Remembrance*. Princeton, Architectural Press.

Beard, M. and Henderson, J. (2001), *Classical Art. From Greece to Rome*. Oxford, Oxford University Press.

Bronfen, E. (1992) *Over her Dead Body. Death, Femininity and the Aesthetic*. Manchester, Manchester University Press.

Burns, S. (2002) *Sleeping Beauty II. Grief, Bereavement and the Family in Memorial Photography, American and European Traditions.* New York, Burns Archive Press.

Cooley, A. (2000) Inscribing history at Rome. In A. Cooley (ed.), *The Afterlife of Inscriptions. Reusing, Rediscovering, Reinventing and Revitalizing Ancient Inscriptions*, 7–20. London, Institute of Classical Studies.

D'Ambra, E. (1995) Mourning and the making of ancestors in the Testamentum Relief. *American Journal of Archaeology* 99, 667–681.

D'Ambra, E. (2002) Acquiring an ancestor: the importance of funerary statuary among the non-elite orders of Rome. In J. Munk Højte (ed.), *Images of Ancestors*, 223–246. Aarhus, Aarhus University Press.

Dunbabin, K. (1986) Sic erimus cuncti..... The skeleton in Graeco-Roman art. *Jahrbuch des Deutschen Archaologischen Instituts* 101, 185–255.

Dunbabin, K. (2003) *The Roman Banquet. Images of Conviviality.* Cambridge, Cambridge University Press.

Edwards, C. (1996), *Writing Rome. Textual Approaches to the City.* Cambridge, Cambridge University Press.

Edwards, E. (1999) Photographs as objects of memory. In M. Kwint, C. Breward, and J. Aynsley (eds), *Material Memories: Design and Evocation*, 221–36. Oxford, Berg.

Erasmo, M. (2008), *Reading Death in Ancient Rome.* Columbus, Ohio State University Press.

Fant, M. and Lefkowitz, M. (1982) *Women's Life in Greece and Rome.* Baltimore, John Hopkins University Press.

Favro, D. (1996) *The Urban Image of Augustan Rome.* Cambridge, Cambridge University Press.

Feiffer, J. (2002) Ancestral aspects of the Roman honorary statue. In J. Munk Højte (ed.), *Images of Ancestors*, 247–256. Aarhus, Aarhus University Press.

Flower, H. (1996) *Ancestor Masks and Aristocratic Power in Roman Culture.* Oxford, Oxford University Press.

Flower, H. (2006) *The Art of Forgetting. Disgrace and Oblivion in Roman Political Culture.* Chapel Hill, University of North Carolina Press.

Friggeri, R. (2001) *The Epigraphic Collection of the Museo Nazionale at the Baths of Diocletian.* Rome, Electa.

Gardner, J. F. and Wiedemann, T. (1991) *The Roman Household: A Sourcebook.* London, Routledge.

Gell, A. (1998) *Art and Agency: An Anthropological Theory.* Oxford, Clarendon Press.

Gordon, A. E. (1983) *An Illustrated Introduction to Latin Epigraphy.* Berkeley and London, University of California Press.

Grottanelli, C. (1995) Wine and death – East and West. In O. Murray and M. Tecuşan (eds.), *In Vino Veritas*, 62–87. Oxford, Alden Press.

Hackworth Petersen, L. (2006) *The Freedman in Roman Art and Art History.* Cambridge and New York, Cambridge University Press.

Hallam, E. and Hockey, J. (2001) *Death, Memory and Material Culture.* Oxford, Berg.

Henig, M. (1994) *Classical Gems. Ancient and Modern Intaglios and Cameos in the Fitzwilliam Museum, Cambridge.* Cambridge, Cambridge University Press.

Holm, C. (2004) Sentimental cuts: eighteenth century mourning jewellery with hair. *Eighteenth Century Studies* 38.1, 139–43.

Hope, V. M. (2009) *Roman Death. The Dying and the Dead in Ancient Rome.* London and New York, Continuum.

Horsfall, N. (1985) *CIL* VI 37965 = *CLE* 1988 (Epitaph of Allia Potestas): A commentary *Zeitschrift für Papyrologie und Epigraphik* 61, 251–73.

Hoskins, J. (2006) Agency, biography and objects. In Tilley *et al.* (eds), *Handbook of Material Culture*, 74–84. London, Sage Publications.

von Hesberg, H. (1992) *Römische Grabbauten*. Darmstadt, Wissenschaftliche Buchgesellschaft.

Ingold, T. (2007) Materials against materiality. *Archaeological Dialogues* 14 (1), 1–16.

Jones, A. (2007), *Memory and Material Culture*. Cambridge, Cambridge University Press.

Kleiner, D. E. E. (1977) *Roman Group Portraiture: The Funerary Reliefs of the Late Republic and Early Empire*. New York, Garland.

Kleiner, D. E. E. (1987) *Roman Imperial Funerary Altars with Portraits*. Rome, G. Bretschneider.

Kockel, V. (1993) *Porträtreliefs Stadtrömischer Grabbauten*. Mainz, Zabern.

Kondoleon, C. (2006) Provincial pretensions: salons of literati in Roman mosaics. In E. D'Ambra and G. Métraux (eds), *The Art of Citizens, Soldiers and Freedmen in the Roman World*, 59–72. British Archaeological Reports International Series 1526. Oxford, Archaeopress.

Koortbojian, M. (1995) *Myth, Meaning and Memory on Roman Sarcophagi*. Berkeley, University of California Press.

Koortbojian, M. (2005) Mimesis or phantasia? Two representational modes in Roman commemorative art. *Classical Antiquity* 24, 285–306.

Laird, M. (2006) Private memory and public interest: municipal identity in Imperial Italy. In E. D'Ambra and G. Métraux (eds), *The Art of Citizens, Soldiers and Freedmen in the Roman World*, 31–46. British Archaeological Reports International Series 1526. Oxford, Archaeopress.

Llewellyn, N. (1991), *The Art of Death. Visual Culture in the English Death Ritual c.1500–c.1800*. London, Reaktion Books.

MacMullen, R. (1982) The epigraphic habit. *American Journal of Philology* 103, 234–246.

Métraux, G. (2006) Consumers choices: the arts of the age of the late Roman 'mechanical' reproduction. In E. D'Ambra and G. Métraux (eds), *The Art of Citizens, Soldiers and Freedmen in the Roman World*, 135–52. British Archaeological Reports International Series 1526. Oxford, Archaeopress.

Mouritsen, H. (2005) Freedmen and Decurions: epitaphs and social history in Imperial Italy. *Journal of Roman Studies* 95, 38–63.

Pointon, M. (1999) Materializing mourning: hair, jewellery and the body. In M. Kwint, C. Breward, and J. Aynsley (eds), *Material Memories: Design and Evocation*, 39–58. Berg, Oxford.

Stewart, P. (2003), *Statues in Roman Society: Representation and Response*. Oxford, Oxford University Press.

Stewart, S. (1999) Prologue: From the museum of touch. In M. Kwint, C. Breward, and J. Aynsley (eds), *Material Memories: Design and Evocation*, 17–38. Oxford, Berg.

Stout, A. (1994) Jewellery as a symbol of status in the Roman Empire. In J. Sebesta and L. Bonfante (eds), *The World of Roman Costume*, 77–100. Wisconsin, University of Wisconsin Press.

Strong, D. E. (1966), *Greek and Roman Silver Plate*. London, Metheun & Co Ltd.

Tarn Steiner, D. (2001) *Images in Mind. Statues in Archaic and Classical Greek Literature and Thought*. Princeton and Oxford, Princeton University Press.

Varner, E. R. (2001) Punishment after death: mutilation of images and corpse abuse in ancient Rome. *Mortality* 6, 45–76.

Varner, E. R. (2004) *Mutilation and Transformation. Damnatio Memoriae and Roman Imperial Portraiture.* Leiden, Boston and Cologne, Brill.

Vollenweider, M-L (1972) *Die Porträtgemmen der römischeb Republik.* Mainz, Von Zabern.

Wrede, H. (1971) Das Mausoleum der *Claudia Semne* und die bürgerliche Plastik der Kaiserzeit. *Mitteilungen des Deutschen Archaeologischen Instituts Roemische Abteilung* 78, 125–66.

Zanker, P. (1975) Grabreliefs römischer Freigelassener *Jahrbuch des Deutschen Archäologischen Instituts* 90, 267–315.

Zanker, P. (1988) *The Power of Images in the Age of Augustus.* Translated by A. Shapiro. Michigan, University of Michigan Press.

Index